When Things Become Property

Max Planck Studies in Anthropology and Economy
Series editors:
Stephen Gudeman, University of Minnesota
Chris Hann, Max Planck Institute for Social Anthropology

Definitions of economy and society, and their proper relationship to each other, have been the perennial concerns of social philosophers. In the early decades of the twenty-first century these became and remain matters of urgent political debate. At the forefront of this series are the approaches to these connections by anthropologists, whose explorations of the local ideas and institutions underpinning social and economic relations illuminate large fields ignored in other disciplines.

When Things Become Property

Land Reform, Authority, and Value in Postsocialist Europe and Asia

THOMAS SIKOR, STEFAN DORONDEL,
JOHANNES STAHL AND PHUC XUAN TO

berghahn
NEW YORK · OXFORD
www.berghahnbooks.com

Published in 2017 by
Berghahn Books
www.berghahnbooks.com

© 2017 Thomas Sikor, Stefan Dorondel, Johannes Stahl and Phuc Xuan To

Library of Congress Cataloging-in-Publication Data

A C.I.P. cataloging record is available from the Library of Congress

British Library Cataloguing in Publication Data

A catalogue record for this book is available from the British Library

Printed on acid-free paper.

ISBN: 978-1-78533-451-1 hardback
ISBN: 978-1-78533-558-7 paperback
ISBN: 978-1-78533-452-8 ebook

To our families

Contents

Preface

This book develops a special perspective on political economy by examining the intersections of property with issues of authority and value in three postsocialist countries. Specifically, it recounts the life experiences, achievements and frustrations of rural people, and their responses to land reforms in Albania, Romania, and Vietnam. Our examination of the changes associated with land reforms in these countries reveals unique insights into more general dynamics of property, authority, and value.

One may wonder why the book compares two countries in Europe with a country in Asia. One may even question if such a comparison is possible, as the three countries have followed different historical and political trajectories, with therefore different implications for land relations. In general, such a broad comparison is unconventional for ethnographic studies. However, findings from our studies in the three countries reveal striking similarities in property dynamics. All three countries experienced similar processes of collectivization and decollectivization. These processes produced substantial changes in people's material and cultural lives and their relationships to land. In addition, we found that theoretical insights derived from one country were well applicable in the other countries. In fact, the work of Katherine Verdery on land reform in Romania inspired Thomas's earlier work on land reform in Vietnam.

Partly for these similarities, Thomas ventured to establish the Junior Research Group on Postsocialist Land Relations at Humboldt University, Berlin, in 2003. The group became the academic home for Stefan, Johannes and Phuc to pursue PhD studies under Thomas's supervision. The six empirical chapters in this book are based on their fieldwork in Romania (undertaken by Stefan), Albania (Johannes), and Vietnam (Phuc) conducted between 2003 and 2005. Our research in the three countries shared similar conceptual frameworks focused on property and employed an ethnographic approach. The similarities in our research in Albania, Romania, and Vietnam helped reduce challenges in comparing the three countries with diverse experiences. The empirical insights we gained from our research further allowed us to deepen our conceptual understanding of the interplay between property, authority, and value.

Writing this book has been a long journey for us, with up to three years of fieldwork plus ten years of writing. During this time, all four of us have been on the same ride, with Thomas at the helm, organizing our data and shaping up our key arguments. Stefan, Johannes and Phuc have contributed to the book in similar ways and they are listed as authors in alphabetic order by family names (Dorondel, Stahl, and To). Thomas's leadership and commitment have been decisive in bringing this writing project to fruition.

We would like to acknowledge the contributions of the institutions and people who supported us at various stages of our research and writing. All four of us would like to thank the people in Albania, Romania, and Vietnam, without whose hospitality, generosity, and support we could not have done the field research that forms the basis of this book. We would also like to thank Jeff Romm, Darla Monroe, and Daniel Müller for the long-standing fruitful exchange that has contributed valuable ideas to this book. We thank Chris Hann for his interest in our work, in particular the welcoming reception of our unconventional manuscript. Karl Zimmerer, Tatjana Thelen, and Peter Vandergeest provided comments on early drafts of chapters. Our thanks also go to our developmental editor, Denise Leto, who taught us to write academic texts in a manner that speaks to a wider audience. The Emmy Noether Programme of the German Research Foundation (Deutsche Forschungsgemeinschaft) provided generous financial support for the Research Group on Postsocialist Land Relations, which Humboldt University Berlin kindly hosted. At Berghahn Books, we would like to thank Duncan Runslem for handling all contractual procedures and administrative requirements. The entire manuscript greatly benefited from very constructive and detailed comments from two anonymous reviewers.

In addition, Thomas would like to thank Christian Lund for the inspiring exchange on property and authority, and Pauline Peters for her thoughts on property and value. He also wishes to thank the Department of Environmental Science, Policy and Management of the University of California at Berkeley for hosting him as a visiting fellow.

Stefan would like to thank James C. Scott and the 2005 cohort of the Yale Program in Agrarian Studies for supporting his work while he was a visiting scholar there. He is also grateful to Tatjana Thelen for her advice during, and after, this writing project, as well as for their long and fruitful theoretical debates.

Johannes gratefully acknowledges the funding from a S.V. Ciriacy-Wantrup Postdoctoral Fellowship at the University of California at Berkeley. He would like to thank Jeff Romm and Nancy Peluso who supported his work while he was at UC Berkeley.

Phuc would like to thank the German Educational Exchange Program (DAAD) for supporting the study in Vietnam, and Jesse Ribot and the late Franz von Benda-Beckmann for deepening his conceptual understanding of property. Different parts of the empirical chapters on Vietnam were compiled when Phuc was on a postdoctoral position at the Anthropology Department of the University of Toronto under the supervision of Tania Li. Phuc would like to thank the Australian National University (ANU) for hosting him. At ANU, his work benefitted greatly from useful exchanges with Sango Mahanty.

 # Acronyms

ACER — Albanian Center for Economic Research

CFPM/SNV — Communal Forests and Pastures Management Program and SNV Netherlands Development Organisation (Albania)

DFS — District Forest Service (Albania)

DGFP — Directorate General of Forests and Pastures (Albania)

FAO — Food and Agriculture Organization of the United Nations

GTZ — German Agency for Technical Cooperation

MARD — Ministry for Agriculture and Rural Development (Vietnam)

NGO — Non-governmental Organization

OECD — Organisation for Economic Co-operation and Development

SFEs — State Forest Enterprises

USAID — US Agency for International Development

Introduction

Turning Things into Property

Property reforms have conferred ownership titles and other legal certificates to many people throughout the world. Governments have initiated the reforms in the expectation that they would yield various kinds of benefits to the new owners, such as economic income and political empowerment. However, people have often found themselves embroiled in disparate economic, political, and cultural transformations that have prevented them from realizing such benefits. The varied and sometimes paradoxical ramifications of property reforms are shown in the following examples of land reforms in Romania, Vietnam, and Albania:

In Romania, George Ionescu, a police officer stationed in Dragomireşti, long benefited from the forest titles that Romanian state officials allocated to villagers there in the 1990s.[1] However, George did not benefit from these rights because he was among the recipients. He benefited because his status in law enforcement allowed him to profit from the woodcutters and traders who made money from the forest, sometimes illegally. He became one of the primary beneficiaries of forest wealth because traders paid him to overlook unlicensed wood transports. Sometimes, allegedly, the traders even paid him to accompany them on trips. Nevertheless, George was eventually caught and forced into early retirement.

In Vietnam, there are striking similarities. Duong Kim Binh was one of the primary beneficiaries of land allocation in Ho So. Yet, like George, he did not benefit because he received a land title from Vietnamese state officials. He instead profited from land allocation because of his past work as a local official, which provided him with experience and networks to capture profits generated in the thriving land market. In late 2003, Hanoi residents discovered Ho So as a site for weekend houses. In the beginning of 2004, Binh began brokering deals between urban buyers and villagers. He sometimes prodded fellow villagers to sell by colluding with his brother An, who was also a broker in Ho So. By the end of 2004, villagers had sold most of the suitable land and Binh had become rich in a matter of a year.

In Bagëtia, Albania, Maks Dulellari did not become rich in the process of land reform. Similar to what occurred in many other Albanian villages, a land commission set out to distribute the available agricultural land among the working population, giving each worker the same amount of land. Maks rejected the distribution because he wanted to get back his parents' land, which they had lost in the process of collectivization thirty years earlier. His family began cultivating the parents' land despite protests by a few villagers and the local government, Maks even carrying an old carbine to prove his determination. The occupation of land considered illegal and resistance against the official distribution got him into jail twelve times until the local government eventually backed down—facts that he proudly recalls. However, his actions, as important and significant as they were in village politics, were nonetheless of modest consequence in the context of the larger economic situation and the drastic deterioration of living standards in Albania. Most people, including his daughter, left the village in search of employment and a better life abroad, since agriculture no longer generated sufficient income.

This book addresses the life experiences, achievements, and frustrations of people like George, Binh and Maks. We explore their actions and reactions as they lived through major property reforms and we use the land reforms conducted by postsocialist governments for illustration.[2] We have a particular interest in people's claims on agricultural land and forestland, the recognition of their claims as legitimate property rights, and the benefits they derive from the rights. Our book is also about places such as Dragomireşti, Ho So, and Bagëtia, as they encountered radical state efforts to remake property relations over the past two and a half decades. We find significant variation amongst people and places. However, looking at villages from three countries with distinct histories and in different parts of the world, we also identify striking similarities in the nature of property dynamics that go beyond existing analyses of "privatization" (A. Schwartz 2006). We show that the economic, political, and cultural changes effected by property reforms mutually influenced each other and produced radical transformations of rural life. Taken together, they produced surprising open-endedness and indeterminacy of societal transformations.

Property was at the core of changes in livelihoods, politics, and cultures. Land titles symbolized some of the great promises made by governments and their international advisors to rural people. Rights to agricultural land and forestland were a primary concern for people in societies experiencing market liberalization, democratization, and urbanization. Property was a crucial factor underlying the radical nature of rural transformations, which left virtually no person or place in the same condition as they had been in twenty years earlier. Thus, property tells us much about changes in rural life, as the new landowners and a host of other actors reacted to new property laws. Changes in property relations were a central element of rural transformations in Albania, Romania, and Vietnam, as was true in many other postsocialist and postcolonial countries of Asia, Africa, Europe, and Latin America.

The Premises of Propertizing Projects and the Dynamics of Property

The book addresses the propertizing projects that are prevalent today.[3] Governments around the world have sought to refashion economies, politics, and environments through property reform. First among them, postsocialist governments have perhaps undertaken the most daring set of propertizing projects over the past two decades under the influence of their international advisors and donors. Postsocialist propertizing covers not only land and forest but also housing, industrial assets, the financial sector, and public utilities. It takes place throughout Central and Eastern Europe, Central Asia and East Asia as well as parts of Latin America and Africa, and is advocated by the leading international financial institutions, such as the World Bank and International Monetary Fund, as well as the European Union. These projects go far beyond privatization, in that they not only move publicly owned assets into private ownership but also encompass a much broader effort on the part of governments to assign rights and duties to private *and* public actors, the latter including various kinds of collective organizations, state agencies, and local and national collectivities.[4] Therefore, it is more effective to examine postsocialist property reforms not as instances of privatization but as propertizing projects.

Propertizing projects are also a frequent sight in the postcolonial world. On the advice of the World Bank and International Monetary Fund many governments in the Global South have embarked on significant property reforms in a variety of sectors, from public utilities to agriculture. These reforms often entail privatization, as in the case of Cochabamba, where the Bolivian government sold off the city's water services to transnational corporations (Perreault 2005).[5] However, in many instances they do not involve privatization. For example, international land reforms include significant efforts to recognize customary leaders' control over land or empower the representatives of indigenous groups to govern over so-called indigenous territories (Fitzpatrick 2005). Property reforms in forestry often occur via devolutions from national governments to village committees or user groups (Larson et al. 2010). The underlying drive is one of propertizing, not necessarily privatization.

Moving beyond the postsocialist and postcolonial contexts, almost all elements in the biophysical environment have become the target of propertizing projects. Governments assign statutory property rights and obligations to a multitude of "natural resources" and "ecosystem services" in national legislation or transnational agreements. They have long extended propertizing from the focus on tangible resources, such as land, forests, and water to more ephemeral phenomena such as ocean fisheries and air. Carbon has become the target of a new propertizing project of truly global dimensions, but there are also other frontiers of property-making, including cultural landscapes, food attributes, food crops, and genetic resources. The key idea in this broad trend has been intellectual property rights, legislated by governments and promoted in transnational agreements as a way to make intangible objects amenable to propertizing. In fact, there seems to be a constant drive to carve out new objects from nature to become targets for propertizing projects, as illustrated by efforts to patent rights to transgenic animals and the human genome (Mansfield 2008; Strang and Busse 2011).

A closer look at the myriad of propertizing projects reveals that national governments and their international advisors have expected them to serve various aims. It is difficult to read government officials' and advisors' statements without developing the impression that propertizing is expected to do wonders: serve as a foundation of economic growth and efficiency, create a basis for poverty alleviation, act as an important element in building democracy, contribute to the restoration of historical justice, establish a precondition for sustainable resource management, and so on. A particularly egregious expression of this unbeatable optimism is the Peruvian economist Hernando de Soto's assertion that the formalization of property rights was the single most effective strategy for poverty alleviation (de Soto 2000). States, the widely cited argument goes, just need to transfer titles to the poor for the assets already in their possession, thereby unlocking the poor's potential and making new objects available for small-scale accumulation. As illustrated by the simplicity and boldness of such expectations, propertizing has become a miracle tool to be employed for whatever aims governments or other agenda-setters deem desirable.[6]

The pervasiveness of propertizing rests on the premise that such projects allow states to allocate valuable objects to social actors. This premise relies on two critical assumptions: first, that the value of the objects is known and reasonably lasting;[7] and second, that the state is the sole institution designating and enforcing property rights according to a fixed set of procedures. Under such conditions, governments can grant property titles to the economically capable, the poor, the politically disadvantaged, the historically dispossessed or to a particular set of resource users, all with the reasonable expectation of achieving the desired outcome (e.g., economic efficiency, poverty alleviation, democracy, historical justice or sustainable resource management). However, this is only true if the objects' values are known and if a unitary state is in charge. Only then do propertizing projects allow governments and their international advisors to achieve the desired outcomes.

The two assumptions are essential. If the value of the objects was to change in the course of property reforms, then governments would no longer know what there was to distribute. Similarly, if the states mandated to conduct the reforms were to change in the process, then governments would no longer see the specific procedures applied for reform implementation. For example, governments could reasonably expect to rectify historical injustices, such as the dispossession of certain ethnic groups or collectivization of agricultural land, by giving land titles back to the historical landowners—but only if they can rely on state officials to follow the designated set of procedures and everyone to agree on the value of the affected land. If, on the other hand, state officials manipulated the implementation of national reform for their own purposes, or if people reconsidered their valuations of the affected land, then restitution to prior owners may not bring about historical justice.

In contrast to the premise underlying propertizing projects, we argue for a dynamic understanding of property. Property reforms do not take place within a static context. Instead, the dynamics of property are closely tied to broader changes in society, embedding property relations in a wider set of social relations and exposing them to wider economic, political, and cultural dynamics.[8] Moreover, property rights and duties relate to values that are not fixed but change as people make claims. Property, in other words, does not merely reflect value but is also a factor in creating, modifying, and taking away value. Similarly, claims and property rights affect the authority attributed to states, particular state actors, and sets of state procedures. Propertizing projects, therefore, are not about governments defining rights and duties with regards to objects of known value, they are actually subject to larger dynamics of property, value, *and* authority. The premise that governments can refashion economies, polities, and environments through property reforms does not hold up to reality.

In this book, we focus on land reforms because they offer unique insights to the dynamics of property. They are not only a classic example of the propertizing projects pervasive with governments, but they are also paramount on the international policy agenda today.[9] More importantly, they attest to the assumed omnipotence of the state; in other words, that states can implement policy at their liking (Sikor and Müller 2009). Governments around the world have long distributed land titles on the premise that they can allocate parcels of known value to smallholders, tenants, the landless, and so on, through land reform. Considering these expectations, the outcomes of land reform have often been disappointing. Nevertheless, a dynamic understanding of property suggests explanations for the apparent shortcomings of land reform, such as the failure to create or clarify property rights in many cases. A fuller appreciation of property dynamics also indicates the cause of certain outcomes generated by land reforms—for example, the tendency to foster land accumulation and dispossession.

We develop this argument by analyzing postsocialist land reforms. Postsocialist governments and their international advisors initiated the reforms with the expectation that they would lay the foundations for economic growth, democracy, and sustainable land use.[10] At least in part, these expectations materialized for some people and places. They also caused bitter disappointments for many other people and in many other places. The primary cause of the conflicting experience was not inappropriate policy design or implementation. Instead, we argue, the variation reflected the dynamic nature of property.

Postsocialist Property Dynamics

There are a significant number of writings on property in postsocialist settings, too many to be reviewed here comprehensively. We concentrate on the anthropological and geographical literature in this section, with some excursions into relevant work in political science and sociology. We are particularly interested in what the literature articulates about the connections between property, on the one hand, and changes in value and state, on the other. Attention to these connections suggests a powerful explanation for the frequently noted gap between the propertizing projects initiated by governments and actual property relations on the ground.

Property, we find in the literature, has been a battleground for competing claims made by a tremendous variety of social actors since the demise of socialism (e.g., Kaneff 1996, 1998; Verdery 1996, 2004). It is subject to ongoing negotiations over agricultural land, forests, houses, public buildings, machinery, and so on. These negotiations are a field of micropolitics and involve various kinds of social actors asserting rights to objects, such as in the case of agricultural land: villagers, urban residents, agricultural managers, and entrepreneurs, as well as village communities and ethnic groups. Parties to these negotiations are also various kinds of state officials, local power holders and other leaders seeking to regulate property matters, a matter we will return to later. The point we wish to make here is that, in many instances, the rights asserted by various social actors are in direct competition with each other. Struggles over agricultural land rights, for example, have pitted villagers against each other, villagers against local elites, rural against urban residents, old against young, and one ethnic group against another. Property relations, therefore, are politicized through power struggles permeating them.

The property relations resulting from these negotiations are often a far cry from the stipulations made in national law and reform regulations. The difference may come from the variation in whose claims are recognized to be legitimate. In Albania, for example, many villages restituted agricultural land to historical owners and their heirs, instead of distributing the land equally among the current agricultural workforce. Although the national land law ordered distribution, villagers restituted the land to historical owners with the conviction that it was the right thing to do (de Waal 2004). The difference may also take the expression of variation in the specific bundles of rights and obligations accorded to landowners. National law and local property relations may provide different answers to questions about what land owners can actually do with their land, what they cannot do, and what they ought to do. For example, agricultural producers have been observed to resist restrictions on land use practices and shed obligations of land stewardship laid out in environmental regulations. Their practices do not reflect ignorance but conscious efforts to negotiate the concrete rights and obligations attached to titles in an attempt to shore up the value that the land possesses for them (Sikor 2006). The landowners thus seek to untie the bundles of rights and obligations transferred to them as part of land reform, add additional rights, discard obligations and re-tie the bundle. This untying and retying takes place in agriculture, but even more so in relation to forests and protected areas, where villagers often oppose the obligations, duties, and restrictions imposed by environmental regulations on their land use practices.[11]

Postsocialist Struggles over Value

The literature demonstrates that this claim-making and negotiating takes place within wider struggles of value. On the one hand, people justify their claims on resources in reference to various kinds of social values, not limited to the notions of private ownership and capitalist individualism driving postsocialist propertizing projects (Hann 1993; Humphrey 1995; Kaneff 1995, 1996; Verdery 1998, 1999). Some assert the primacy of individual entitlement, such as the land rights accorded to them in national legislation. Others call for historical justice as the primary principle according to which land should be restituted to its owners prior to collectivization. And there are people who justify their claims on valuable objects in reference to kinship under the motto of, "I am the son, daughter, sister, brother of…," or diametrically opposed to this, the efficiency of the market, "I have paid for this." Alternatively, as Katherine Verdery reports, people may make claims on the basis of collective labor invested in the past. At her Romanian field site, villagers oppose the sale of a granary to a private entrepreneur even though he had made the highest bid in a public auction. The villagers argue that they built the granary together under socialist agriculture, and that this collective labor investment of the past still matters more than any monetary payment (Verdery 1999).

Negotiations over property thereby connect with people's identities and visions of a desirable future. The influence of identities and visions plays out in many ways. For example, a frequent observation during the initial years of land reform was that people attached surprisingly high significance to getting the land back that they or their parents owned prior to collectivization, and then went about working the land again. This significance, Chris Hann explains, had little to do with the material value of land, but largely reflected strong emotional attachments because property rights to land served as means for conserving family bonds (Hann 1993). Claims on land were closely tied to people's efforts to see themselves as members of a family or extended kinship group. Similarly, Katrina Schwartz finds that Latvians who reject proposed national parks do so less on material grounds than on their opposition to the vision of the cultural landscape underlying the proposals (K. Schwartz 2006). Their views of the landscape are firmly agrarian, as a productive landscape that is tightly connected with a broader discourse of Latvian identity as a "nation of farmers." Latvian park proponents, however, assert landscape visions stressing their function as habitats for biodiversity, alluding to a broader narrative of Latvia similar to Europe and European visions.[12]

On the other hand, even where people emphasize material over other kinds of social values, they rarely attribute a single economic value to particular objects. As Adrian Smith has shown, not even the economic forces unleashed by market liberalization gravitate into a single, uniform system of value (Smith 2000, 2002a, 2002b). As there are multiple systems of value at work, postsocialist countries witness "multiple geographies of economic practices" (Smith and Stenning 2006). Land and other assets become valorized in different ways, such as through the global commodity economy, national product markets, and local barter. These systems of value do not operate separately from each other, since people often engage with different economies simultaneously. A good illustration of this comes from the much noted rise of subsistence agriculture in Central and Eastern Europe (Bridger and Pine 1998; Smith 2002a; Meurs 2002; Pickles 2002). Many smallholders produce grains and vegetables to meet important dietary needs at home, or to prove good husbandry of their land. As important as the products are to them within their local systems of value, they do not possess significant value in the monetary economies. As a result, they experience a massive shortfall in monetary benefits, even though they continue working the land for other benefits. Given the opportunity, however, they would happily sell their products in the monetized economy or shift to producing other crops for sale.

These multiple systems of value do not operate to the equal advantage of everyone. A primary theme in the literature is that small landowners often find themselves in a disadvantaged position in relation to other actors, such as traders and the owners of agricultural machinery. Even though the landowners hold titles, they depend on access to complementary productive resources and markets to derive benefits from the titles (Verdery 1998, 1999, 2003; Zbierski-Salameh 1999; Giordano and Kostova 2002). Some have difficulty accessing necessary machinery, obtaining credit, and purchasing inputs. They encounter product markets controlled by a few buyers and urban speculators, such as the *akuli* (sharks) who have a hold over grain marketing in Bulgaria. Selling or leasing land is not a profitable option for many smallholders either, since they receive only meager payments. These observations do not deny that at least some small landowners do well in the new monetary economies. Some carve out profitable niches for themselves in local and regional product markets by shifting production to new crops and livestock (Sikor 2001a; Sikor and Pham 2005; Winkels 2008). Nevertheless, more often than not small landowners end up on the losing side.

Property and the "State" of the Postsocialist State

The literature shows that postsocialist negotiations are not only about the social values associated with property but also about the state as the ultimate enforcer of property rights and obligations. Negotiations over property involve various state officials at the local and central levels just as much as the social actors demanding ownership or use rights.[13] Legislators and central officials make laws and regulations to stipulate the procedures applicable to land affairs. Local officials staff the committees in charge of privatizing land and other assets, and implement the directives set down by central governments. Negotiations over property also raise questions about applicable state procedures and legitimate state practices (Harms 2009). Postsocialist property reforms, therefore, have as much to do with property as they do with the state.

Property reforms open up a space for local officials to maneuver, as Janet Sturgeon shows in her work in southern China (Sturgeon 2005). Various reform policies enacted by China's central government, such as land auctions, afford local cadres significant leverage on property rights. The local cadres exercise control over property to a greater extent than is afforded to them by law. The property dealings influence the position of the local government toward villagers, allowing the cadres to solidify their control over village affairs. They also help local governments to sustain relative autonomy from central directives and interventions. This struggle between central government and local officials is a dynamic also observed in many other postsocialist settings (Humphrey 1995; Kaneff 1996; Ho 2001; Lampland 2002; Verdery 2002; Kerkvliet 2005). Another, related dynamic originates from competition between different branches of a central or local government, such as forest departments and land administration agencies (Stark 1992; Sowerwine 2004; Sturgeon 2004).

In some circumstances, struggles over postsocialist property even challenge the state's monopoly over the definition and enforcement of property rights. For example, in some places, people justify their claims on valuable resources, not in reference to state law, but in regards to various forms of customary arrangements. The significance of custom as a definer and enforcer of property rights emerges strongly in Clarissa de Waal's research in Albania (de Waal 2004, 2005). De Waal recounts how many Albanians assert various kinds of customary rights to agricultural land and forests, restituting them to their historical owners in direct contradiction with state legislation. They also resolve land disputes on the basis of customary regulations. Customs thus offer justifications for claims on land and other resources, a phenomenon that has also been observed in the mountains of China and Vietnam, and the grasslands of Central Asia.[14]

More broadly, research on postsocialist negotiations over property demonstrates that people assert claims in reference not only to state laws and procedures but also to a variety of other institutions, including various forms of customs, transnational law, religious norms, rules enforced by powerful networks, and regulations governing the operations of international donors and non-governmental organizations.[15] States consequently encounter competition in their claim to hold the monopoly over the definition and enforcement of property rights. These contestations of control over property contribute to and simultaneously reflect what Katherine Verdery calls "parcelization of sovereignty" (Verdery 1996). The state is no longer the sole sovereign over people's affairs, if it ever was.

Research on postsocialist property dynamics, therefore, shows that property relations have been at the core of people's struggles to make sense of broader economic, political, and cultural changes. As governments propertize agricultural land and forests, in reaction people have not only questioned government definitions of legitimate claims but also negotiated the implicit definition of value and state. Moreover, the research shows, we suggest and seek to elaborate next, how propertizing projects and people's reactions to them are part of wider processes revalorizing productive activities and reconfiguring authority. Property relations reflect the influence of broader processes making and unmaking value and authority as much as property practices help constitute value and authority relations. We discuss this mutually recursive constitution of property, value, and authority in the following section, using observations from postsocialist Europe and Asia for illustration.

Concepts: Property, Value, and Authority

Before we begin our empirical inquiry, we will review a set of relevant concepts to guide us. It is useful to start with C.B. MacPherson's classic definition of a property right as being about "an enforceable claim to some use or benefit."[16] Property is about claims, this widely recognized definition states. In addition, two further elements are crucial. First, property requires some "use" or "benefit"—that is, it involves definitions of what is desirable to be used, or to derive benefits from. Objects must be considered useful or valuable, at least by some, to become worthy of rights and obligations. Second, claims become "enforceable" through sanctioning by institutions of authority. Claims turn into property rights only if recognized by a politico-legal institution with the authority to do so, such as the state. This definition of property gives a roadmap for our conceptual explorations. We begin with the concept of value, followed by a discussion of authority.

Value and Property

Value is integral to the idea of property, since at least some social actors must consider objects valuable to assert claims and demand rights to them. However, value is a problematic concept; it has been the subject of much debate in the social sciences.[17] For our purposes, we draw on David Graeber's work, in particular his argument for an integrated theory of value that captures both wider social norms and the worthiness attributed to a specific object (Graeber 2001). The benefit of such an integrated theory of value, Graeber shows, is that it helps to establish both qualitative and quantitative differences. Qualitative difference refers to "conceptions of what is ultimately good, proper, or desirable in human life"; in contrast, quantitative difference is about "the degree to which objects are desired" (ibid.). In other words, value is about different kinds of social values (wealth, happiness, etc.) and the particular benefit assigned to an object, including but not limited to its monetary value or price.

Therefore, we use value in two ways, as value regimes and the benefits attached to particular objects. Following Graeber, we articulate value regimes when we refer to imaginary totalities organized around different conceptions of value. Social actors employ different modes of valuing and therefore prioritize actions, things, ideas, and so on in different ways. This notion of value regimes strongly resonates with the discussion of postsocialist property dynamics above, as the move toward capitalism exposes people to new systems of value (Tompson 1999; Humphrey 2002; Verdery 2003). At the same time, people adhere to some of the socialist values and moralities of the past as they display a "gut loyalty to this former everyday life" (Humphrey 1999: xii). As noted by many scholars, people in postsocialist societies have been engaged in intensive debates about social values and different economic value regimes (Hann 1993; Humphrey 1995; Smith 2000, 2002a, 2002b; Verdery 1998, 1999).

Negotiations over value often connect with contestations over social identities, such as ethnic and national identities.[18] Deema Kaneff, for example, shows in her research on Bulgaria how different notions of social identity surface in the restitution of agricultural land (Kaneff 1998).[19] The restitution of agricultural land to historical owners leads villagers to emphasize ethnic cohesion as a primary social value to guide village affairs. Further, the growing attention to ethnic identities (Bulgarian, Macedonian, Turk, Pomak, Gypsy) shapes people's evaluations of land claims as being either legitimate or illegitimate—in stark contrast to national legislation that accords equal rights to all citizens. In this way, land takes on value as ethnic territory, because the restitution of agricultural land connects with contestations over social identities.

Value regimes are also in direct relationship to different views of the landscape and proper practices of land management, as Janet Sturgeon reveals in her research in China (Sturgeon 2005). Villagers' views emphasized flexibility and diversity, whereas officials sought to homogenize and stabilize the landscape through their projects. As a result, villagers and officials recognized different landscape elements as meaningful and valuable. Their different landscape visions resulted in different conceptions of what kinds of resources were "up for grabs" (Sturgeon 2004)—that is, available for property claims.

Value, we also assert, refers to the benefits attached to particular objects. Value understood in this way involves the ranking of particular objects within a value regime. Since these benefits are specific to value regimes, an object may be attributed high value in one regime but given no or low value in another. Consequently, land may possess a high symbolic value to rural people, but many may discover that it generates only low financial benefits according to the rules of the monetized economy, as highlighted in the work of Adrian Smith discussed above (Smith 2000, 2002a, 2002b). The same insight applies to particular components of rural landscapes, because each may be considered valuable in one value regime but be of little benefit in another, as illustrated in the work of Katrina Schwartz (2006) discussed above. Latvians are involved in intense debates about protected areas and rural environments, in part because they value different landscape components: where the agrarians see large fields the Europeans look out for footpaths.

The rankings of particular objects within a value regime are not a given. Instead, they are the subject of often intense negotiations, particularly within newly emerging value regimes. As David Stark writes on the privatization of Hungarian industry, managers of privatized state enterprises react to the changes in the values of their assets due to market liberalization and new accounting rules (Stark 1996). The managers renegotiate companies' rights and obligations by recombining the privatized assets in new ways. Their responses affect the valuation of companies, as managers succeed in shifting liabilities onto the shoulders of the public and retain valuable assets in reorganized companies. By the end of the privatization process managers have unpacked and repacked assets in surprising ways, repositioning the assets under their control within the new value regime.

The shift from one value regime to another can lead to serious devaluation or virtually complete annihilation of the value they attribute to an object. People may end up holding property rights to some resources but derive little or no benefit from them, something that Verdery calls a lack of "effective ownership." Studying smallholders in Transylvania, she finds that property titles do not enable people to "realize the values they saw in their new property object" (Verdery 2003: 104). Lack of machinery and inputs as well as unfavorable terms of trade make people's farming unprofitable in the terms of the new market economy. More generally, property rights do not grant an automatic share in the overall benefits attached to a particular object. Other social actors may be in a better position to generate profits from an object, even though they do not hold property rights.[20]

From this brief review, then, we learn that negotiations over property involve negotiations over value. As social actors make claims on resources, they do so within particular value regimes and attribute specific benefits to particular objects. Value regimes and benefits are both subject to the very same struggles over property, as are the rights and obligations attached to particular objects. Propertizing projects, by implication, involve negotiations over the kinds and levels of value that people attach to objects. The designers and implementers of propertizing projects cannot assume that these values are fixed.

Authority, Property and the State

Next, we discuss the issue of authority, the second defining criterion of property. Authority relates to property because rights and obligations require sanctioning in order to be considered more than a claim. This sanctioning results from politico-legal institutions of recognized authority (Benda-Beckmann 1995; Lund 2002).[21]

Authority, we suggest by way of a simple definition, is power considered legitimate. In the words of Max Weber, authority refers to an instance of power that is associated with at least a minimum of voluntary compliance, making it likely "that a command with a specific content will be obeyed by a given group of persons" (Weber 1976: 28). Authority characterizes the capacity of politico-legal institutions, such as states and their constituent institutions, village communities and religious groupings (as well as customary arrangements, moral conventions, and other social norms), to influence other social actors in ways considered legitimate. It is similar to power in the sense that it does not refer to any organization itself, but emerges from social practices and becomes a feature inherent to certain kinds of social relationships.[22] It is different from power, because the latter involves all forms of coercion, whether considered legitimate or not.

Authority is neither inherently stable nor a fixed attribute of a particular institution. Instead, authority is unstable and volatile since it requires ongoing legitimization vis-à-vis specific constituencies, and because this legitimization waxes and wanes in the wake of ongoing struggles over legitimacy (Moore 1988; Lentz 1998). The legitimacy attributed to any institution results from continuous practices of legitimization. Implied in this is the idea that an institution's authority always relates to particular constituencies and fields of social action, such as a government agency's jurisdiction over land matters vis-à-vis citizens. Authority may travel from one field of social action, such as control over land matters, to control over labor affairs, but that is far from automatic. Authority is about social relations, relations that tend to be contested. In many situations authority relations are highly contested as multiple politico-legal institutions attempt to turn power into authority by gaining and sustaining legitimacy in the eyes of their constituencies. This is a situation characteristic of postsocialist and postcolonial settings (Shipton and Goheen 1992; Verdery 1996; Humphrey 2002; and Sikor and Lund 2009b).

Claims and property rights feed into these contestations over authority. As we have seen, claims on resources require authorization by institutions of authority. In addition, claims on valuable objects simultaneously help to constitute authority. When someone asserts rights to a particular object then they also tend—explicitly or implicitly—to invoke an institution that they expect to sanction their claim as legitimate. By making their claim they simultaneously attribute authority to an institution. This intimate, two-way connection between property and authority finds illustration in Katharine Verdery's research on land restitution in a Romanian village (Verdery 1996, 1999, 2002). Verdery observes that every villager is busy making demands for the restitution of agricultural plots. The demands refer to various institutions as the ones sanctioning them as legitimate rights. Most, but not all, invoke the state in some form or other. One of the most active participants in this claim-making is the local mayor, because he positions himself between villagers and the central government. Nevertheless, not all claims invoke state discourses, laws or practices, and the claims invoking the state do not refer to a single, coherent set of state rules and practices. This observation leads Verdery to conclude that people's claims have not gravitated into a clear and coherent set of "routinized rules and crystallized practices of exclusion and inclusion" (Verdery 1999: 55). Many of the land disputes she witnesses are due to ongoing contestations over authority, and not simply direct competition for particular plots of agricultural land.

The state is often a key politico-legal institution invoked in social actors' claims on resources.[23] It figures in property dynamics in two ways. First, the state appears in claims on valuable objects and property rights as a unitary politico-legal institution or "idea" (Abrams 1988). People appeal to the state to provide the required backing for their claims, such as when the beneficiaries of land restitution hold up their ownership titles in opposition to encroachment on their land. However, the authority attributed to the state as a politico-legal institution may be in contest with competitors such as religious groupings or customary arrangements (Tilly 1985; Lund 2008). In Albania, for example, Clarissa de Waal finds in the research discussed above that many people no longer call upon the state to sanction their claims on agricultural land and forest (de Waal 2004). Many refer to customary arrangements and not state law when they seek authorization for their claims on resources.

Second, we consider it helpful to examine the state as a forum in which multiple social actors contest the exercise of state authority (Migdal 2001; Corbridge et al. 2005).[24] The contestations are not only about the jurisdictions held by particular state entities, such as a Ministry of Forestry's control over a share of the national territory; they are also about the applicable procedures recognized as legitimate. For example, Allina-Pisano finds that local government officials exert a strong influence on the implementation of land reforms in Russia and the Ukraine (Allina-Pisano 2008). They create Potemkin villages by distributing land on paper but prevent the presumed beneficiaries from effectively claiming their new land rights. The local officials support the land claims of powerful actors, such as collective farm managers and private entrepreneurs. Local officials thereby exercise an understanding of applicable rules and procedures that is radically different from national legislation and land regulations. The difference reflects ongoing struggles of authority within the state, in this case between local officials and the central governments.

Negotiations over property, therefore, connect with contestations about authority and the state. As social actors make claims on what they consider valuable, they do so in reference to particular politico-legal institutions of authority and to specific sets of rules and practices. Institutions, rules, and practices of authority are an integral part of struggles over property. The implications for propertizing projects are clear: their designers and implementers cannot assume the institutions, rules, and practices to be fixed.

Studying Property Dynamics

With the above set of concepts in mind, we will begin our empirical inquiry into propertizing projects. The challenging nature of such an endeavor becomes immediately apparent even if the spatial dimensions alone are considered, and even though we limit the scope of our empirical inquiry to postsocialist land reforms. The latter have taken place in large parts of Eastern Europe, Central Asia, and East Asia, as well as some countries of Africa and Latin America. The transformations experienced by societies undergoing property reforms involve changes in multiple and overlapping dimensions. Therefore, it is useful to discuss the method that has informed our research and the choice of the three countries—Albania, Romania and Vietnam—in which we conducted our empirical work.

A Few Words on Method

Our inquiry into property dynamics uses an ethnographic approach. Ethnography helps to show the issues rural people confront, and how they react to changes in their political-economic and biophysical environments. Ethnography of economic, political, and environmental change in specific geographical locations indicates the key elements and processes of societal transformations, together with how the transformations reflect particular histories and local conditions. In the spirit of Verdery's suggestion that "any instance provides insights," ethnographic monographs have developed new original frameworks for understanding societal transformations (Verdery 2003: 30). They show how people negotiate their way through turbulent times, refuting teleological ideas about singular and uniform transitions, such as the transition from public to private ownership.[25]

We present multiple ethnographies of change in eight villages of Albania, Romania, and Vietnam. The value of multiple cases and coordinated ethnographies has long been highlighted in commentaries on various fields of research. Nonetheless, ethnographic studies involving multiple cases remain confined to a few rare exceptions such as the volume jointly authored by Chris Hann and the Property Relations Group (2003). For our own purposes, we believe that drawing together eight case studies will allow us to illustrate the political-economic and environmental complexities of change better than if examined separately. Including them in a single book builds a stronger analysis of property dynamics, highlighting the open-endedness and, to a certain degree, indeterminacy of the societal transformations accompanying propertizing projects.

Our ethnographies communicate with each other around the set of basic concepts introduced above. These shared concepts allow us to generate a grand narrative on propertizing projects from the data and insights produced in the case studies. By putting ethnographies into communication with each other—between the two covers of a single, co-authored book—we hope to learn about property projects in general: their characteristic features, key processes, and historical significance.

Communicating ethnographies helps us to narrow the gap between the apparent complexity of single ethnographies and the striking simplicity of grand narratives. Coordinated studies generate valuable empirical insights into wider societal transformations, highlighting their complexity and ambiguity. They also demonstrate the tremendous variation among transformations in particular locations, and indicate the continuum of possible trajectories of change.[26] The goal is not to produce empirical typologies, but to reveal underlying dynamics producing economic, political, and environmental change through multiple analytical lenses. In other words, we build specific comparisons and contrasts into our analysis of the dynamics of property, value, and authority in particular locations.

We recognize that our approach of communicating ethnographies is unusual. Multiple ethnographies are rarely found in a single monograph, since they usually come in the form of edited volumes. Ethnographically minded readers may question the comparisons, which may appear overly reductionist to them. The comparatively inclined readers may find the empirical detail offered in the ethnographic chapters atypical. Our approach presents a response to what we perceive as a significant methodological tension in research on property. Ethnographic research is at its strongest when highlighting the specificity of local people's claims on resources in response to changes in their political-economic and biophysical environments. The emphasis is on open-endedness and process. Comparative analysis, in contrast, focuses on similarity and difference. Highlighting variation across space and/or time, it often tends toward rather static depictions of isolated instances or variables. By way of communicating ethnographies, we hope to weigh ethnographic inquiry and comparative analysis against each other in a productive manner.

Albania, Romania, and Vietnam

The book draws on eight village studies from Albania, Romania, and Vietnam, situating them in relation to broader economic, political, and cultural changes. Our choice of the three countries is a deliberate one. We want to critically interrogate the distinction between societal transformations in Europe and those taking place in East Asia. The distinction has been axiomatic in the political sciences and a defining element of area studies, effectively preventing a more analytical approach to comparisons and distinctions between Europe and East Asia.[27]

We understand that putting Albania, Romania, and Vietnam into the same mix and labeling them "postsocialist" is a contentious decision. It may not raise concerns if we refer to the political regimes of Albania, Romania, and Vietnam in the decades leading up to 1990 as socialist.[28] All three countries called themselves Socialist Republics under the leadership of a Communist avant-garde party. The party-state managed the economy through a centralized regime of economic planning. State enterprises and collectives controlled production in all sectors, the former taking on a prominent role in forestry, and the latter being widespread in agriculture.

Yet, we are aware that referring to contemporary Albania, Romania, and Vietnam as "postsocialist" provokes dissent (e.g., see Reid-Henry 2007). Whereas Albania and Romania now possess constitutions as liberal democracies, Vietnam continues to pride itself as a Socialist Republic. Vietnam's Communist Party remains firmly in charge of the party-state, in sharp contrast to the multiparty systems in the other two countries. Still, all three countries have embarked on fundamental economic reforms. Control over production has shifted from state and collective entities toward private actors. Markets have replaced administrative decisions as the major mechanism for allocating products and productive resources. All three countries have opened up their economies to international trade and investment. There are sufficient similarities, we are convinced, that warrant comparisons. It is useful to put village cases from the three countries into the same mix in order to identify their distinctive features in the process of comparison.

The three countries have embarked on massive propertizing projects to reform rural relations, as have many other countries in the previously socialist world.[29] The Albanian parliament passed a "Law Concerning the Land" in 1991, the Romanian parliament passed Law 18 in the same year, and Vietnam's National Assembly instituted a new Land Law in 1993. The laws signaled the beginning of enormous land reforms, as is widely noted in the literature. Far-reaching programs distributed agricultural land held by state and collective units to households and other private entities. The stated objective in all three countries was to achieve an egalitarian distribution of agricultural land, either by limited restitution to historical owners or their heirs (Romania), or distribution to the current population (Albania and Vietnam). The same land reform laws also extended to forests, but have not resulted in the massive privatization seen in agriculture. Property reforms in forestry have granted many rural households and other private entities ownership titles to forest, but on a smaller scale than in agriculture. In forestry, much of the propertizing has taken the form of legislative initiatives aimed at revamping the relations between the state and other actors, involving changes in regulatory control and the meaning of state ownership.

The three countries resemble each other in two additionally important ways. First, at the onset of the property reforms, land and forest were important resources for rural livelihoods in Albania, Romania, and Vietnam. Rural people derived a major part of their income from agriculture and forestry as living standards in the three countries remained low. Productive uses such as cropland, meadows used for grazing, and actively managed forests dominated rural landscapes in 1990. Second, all three countries harbor significant ethnic diversity even though one ethnic group in each country—the Albanians in Albania, the Romanians in Romania, and the Kinh in Vietnam—accounts for the majority of the population and dominates national identity and culture. In addition, there are other ethnic groups with their own distinct identities and cultures, including: Greeks, Macedonians, Vlachs, and Roma in Albania; Hungarians, Roma, and Rudari in Romania; and Muong, Tay, Nung, Thai, Hmong, and Dao in Vietnam.

Nevertheless, there are significant historical differences among the three countries. First, Albania, Romania, and Vietnam have found themselves in very different geopolitical positions for much of their recent history. Albania gained national independence in 1912 after a protracted struggle against the Ottoman Empire, and concerns for national independence strongly influenced socialist policy. Romania grew into its contemporary shape after World War I and joined the Soviet bloc after World War II. Vietnam, in turn, was a French colony until World War II and only gained independence and national unity after protracted wars against France and the United States. Second, socialist regimes displayed distinct features in the three countries. In Albania, the Hoxha regime not only held a firm grip on the economy and society but also isolated the country from the rest of the world. The Ceaușescu regime in Romania established totalitarian control over economic, social, and cultural life. In contrast, revolutionary leaders in Vietnam were never able to centralize power to the same degree. Third, the socialist regimes promoted different policies for the countryside. The Hoxha regime wanted to achieve national self-sufficiency in basic staples at any cost, together with the limited development of basic rural industries. Ceaușescu sought to transform the countryside by pushing rural industrialization, export-oriented agriculture, and rural–urban migration. Vietnam's policies for rural areas granted agricultural collectives significant power over production but channeled a large share of agricultural surplus into cities and industries.

We argue that solid foundations exist for productive comparisons among the eight villages in Albania, Romania, and Vietnam. All three countries implemented radical propertizing projects as part of broader efforts to refashion economies, polities, and environments. Their relative similarities help us to set aside questions about the effects of living standards, kinds of land use, and ethnic heterogeneity as causes of potential variation. At the same time, ongoing differences among the three countries enable us to explore the significance of historical influences on contemporary transformations.

The Argument: Propertizing Projects and Societal Transformations

Our argument, as presented in the chapters of this book, asserts that propertizing projects have led to radical changes in property, value, and authority in Albania, Romania, and Vietnam. Agriculture, the subject of Part I, underwent fundamental processes of devaluation and revaluation. The new landowners faced drastic changes in the relative prices of agricultural output. Furthermore, new opportunities of migration and non-farm activity revalorized the relative returns achieved in agriculture, as did a rapidly growing urban demand for rural tourism and weekend homes. More broadly, villagers became exposed to new social values and visions of a desirable life. The new landowners responded to these changes in different ways. Chapter 1 shows how some Albanians moved abroad in search of employment and a better life, while others tried to make a living in agriculture. Chapter 2 conveys how some Romanians sought to generate profits by commercializing production, while others focused on subsistence crops and livestock. Chapter 3 recounts the stories of some Vietnamese landowners who sold their land to tourism entrepreneurs and urban residents for recreational purposes, and others who acquired additional land to expand agricultural production.

The central elements in these varying reactions were people's efforts to gain property titles and to attach monetary or new symbolic value to them. As much as people valued the new land titles for their political significance in the 1990s, they subsequently looked for new monetary values inside and outside agriculture. Postsocialist negotiations over property, therefore, coincided with intense struggles over value. People valued land for the associated monetary returns, as a basis of subsistence, and as a source of social prestige or a signifier of identity. Their valuations sometimes reflected events far away from their villages, locating them within transnational processes that revalorized property rights, such as migration flows conditioned by immigration policy in other countries. The valuations also revealed the influence of local livelihood traditions that had proven effective under socialism and even prior to it. The values people attached to land also connected with the ideas they had about themselves and others, and about the lifestyles and futures they wanted for themselves and their children. In doing so, the land reforms did not benefit all new owners equally; of course, some people experienced significant improvements in the material and symbolic values attached to their land, while others witnessed dramatic declines, which deprived the land of any kind of value.

In contrast, forests, the subject of Part II, experienced nothing less than a frenzied grab for property rights and other forms of access. Our ethnographies show how many different social actors made claims on forests, which turned out to be the most valuable resource available in many locations. People struggled over the distribution of ownership titles, providing various justifications for their claims. Those who received titles contested the restrictions and obligations imposed on them by state regulation. Many others made claims on forests even though they had not received any titles. In the Albanian villages, covered in Chapter 4, many people claimed rights to forest with reference to state law or various kinds of customary arrangements, or they rushed on the forest without further justification. In Chapter 5, we explain how, in the Romanian villages, the new forest owners lost out to local state officials and other powerful actors who forced owners to sell at low prices, traded wood illegally, or rigged timber auctions. Finally, in Chapter 6, we see how, in Vietnam, local officials manipulated or ignored central government programs to derive personal benefits from timber logging and forest protection.

The ethnographies in Part II show how property struggles intersected with contestations over authority along several dimensions. One dimension was the kind of politico-legal institution to which people attributed the authority to sanction claims on resources as property. In some places, various kinds of customary arrangements became the main points of reference for property rights to land and forest. In others, it was mostly state law and practices that sanctioned claims as property. In yet others, multiple institutions offered competing authorizations for claims on resources. Another dimension in these contestations involved the procedures by which state authority was to be exercised. Where the state was the dominant politico-legal institution, the exercise of authority varied between rule-based and personalized forms. A third dimension in contestations over authority was the struggle between different state actors. Local officials and central governments often ended up competing over who was to set the rules and make decisions on forestry matters.

We revisit the premises underlying property projects in the Conclusion. Insights from postsocialist land reforms demonstrate that propertizing is not simply about states allocating objects of known value to social actors, a finding that possesses direct relevance for propertizing projects beyond postsocialist settings. Instead, negotiations over property simultaneously deal with competing sources of value and contestations over authority. Property dynamics reflect the influence of broader economic, political, and cultural processes, as well as feeding into wider societal transformations that involve simultaneous changes in property, value, and authority. The grandness of the propertizing projects and their societal effects may not be as fundamental elsewhere as the ones we describe in postsocialist contexts. Nevertheless, propertizing projects always involve simultaneous negotiations over property, value, and authority, making their outcomes much less predictable than their designers and implementers like to believe. This lack of predictability was particularly striking in the postsocialist moment, reflecting the exceptional open-endedness of postsocialist transformations.

We conclude that negotiations over property can tell us a great deal about wider societal transformations. In addition, we can gain important insights on larger economic, political, and cultural changes by looking at struggles over property in particular places, especially if our ethnographies communicate with each other. Our inquiry into property dynamics in three Albanian villages shows how twice in the 1990s it was possible that the Albanian state would collapse. Likewise, the village studies from Romania indicate how the country gained admission to the European Union in 2004—and why it took that long. Finally, our exploration of the three Vietnamese villages reveals how Vietnam's Communist Party has managed to remain firmly in power despite the evidence of widespread corruption. Property, we find, provides a special lens to examine social change.

Notes

1. The name is a pseudonym, as are all of the personal and village names used throughout the book.
2. We prefer the term "postsocialism" to "postcommunism" because the latter is tainted by its frequent usage for political abuse. In addition, socialism refers to the society-focused ideal equivalent to capitalism in the West. In contrast, communism entails a Marxist–Leninist model as, for example, applied in the Soviet Union.
3. Our term "propertizing projects" is similar to Pauline Peters's (1994) notion of propertization. While we agree with the substance of her argument, we disagree with her conclusion that property is not a useful analytical concept. Property can be useful for analytical purposes as long as we distinguish it from the legal specifications enshrined in particular legislation or the terms used by people.
4. For examples of collective organizations, consider the allocation of grazing rights to groups of herders in Central Asia (Humphrey and Sneath 1999), the restitution of forests to cooperatives in Bulgaria (Cellarius 2004), and the transfer of ownership rights on secondary irrigation canals to local organizations in Bulgaria (Penov 2004). For examples of collectivities and state agencies, see the delineation of forestland as public forest managed by a state department (Staddon 2000; Sikor 2001b), and the expansion of protected areas under the control of environmental agencies (Franklin 2002; Zingerli 2005).
5. For example, see Perreault (2005).
6. For a good, empirically informed critique of de Soto's argument, see Benjaminsen et al. (2008).

7. One could also argue that this assumption contains another one: that there is a general agreement about the nature of objects and about the ability to appropriate them as separate physical or legal entities.

8. We use the term "property relations" to highlight the social embeddedness of property (cf. Hann 1998; Verdery 2003). We speak of "property rights" only when we refer to the specific rights granted by an institution, such as the state, to a particular actor, or when we refer to particular discourses of property.

9. For the latter, see the World Bank report by Deininger (2003). For comprehensive reviews, see Heller and Serkin (1999), Akram-Lodhi, Borras and Kay (2006), Fay and James (2009) and Lipton (2009).

10. See Sachs (1990) and Manser (1993) for the boosterism found among economists and environmentalists in the early 1990s.

11. On protected areas, see Franklin (2002) and Zingerli (2005). On forests, see de Waal (2004) and Sowerwine (2004).

12. Harms (2011, 2012) provides an insightful discussion of how property practices connect with people's notions of beauty in Ho Chi Minh City, Vietnam.

13. See Baum and Shevchenko (1999) and Grzymala-Busse and Luong (2002) for insightful discussions on local governments and their relations with the central organs of the state in China and Eastern Europe.

14. On Vietnam and China, see Sowerwine (2004) and Sturgeon (2004). On Central Asia, see Anderson (1998), Humphrey and Sneath (1999) and Fernandez-Gimenez (2002).

15. On the Mafia, see Verdery (1996), Penov (2004), and Theesfeld (2004). On the influence of transnational norms, see Zingerli (2005).

16. MacPherson (1978: 3). Our approach to property draws on the works of Franz and Keebet von Benda-Beckmann, in particular their suggestion to use property as an analytical framework for looking at relationships among social actors with regard to objects of value. Among others, see Benda-Beckmann and Benda-Beckmann (1999) and Benda-Beckmann, Benda-Beckmann, and Wiber (2006).

17. For key writings on value, see Mauss (1965), Appadurai (1986), Munn (1986), and Strathern (1988).

18. Another way to put the linkage between property and identities is to look at how human subjectivities influence property claims, and are influenced by them. See Agrawal's discussion (2005) of environmentality and changes in human subjectivities underlying forest stewardship in India, and Kligman and Verdery's account (2011) of collectivization in Romania. See also Mansfield (2007) on privatization, Strang and Busse (2011) on private ownership, and Humphrey (2002) and Verdery (2003) on postsocialist property reforms.

19. See also the book she edited with Leonard (2002).

20. Here we connect with the theory of access developed by Jesse Ribot and Nancy Peluso (2003). They note that a property right to a particular resource does not necessarily create the ability to benefit from that resource, pointing out a number of "access mechanisms" that enable other social actors without property rights to benefit from resources. These insights, we suggest, may be usefully extended by considering multiple value regimes, particularly non-monetary ones, and attention to processes creating value.

21. What follows is a synthesis of the argument developed in Sikor and Lund (2009a).
22. This is a possible point for confusion, as many people commonly refer to particular organizations, such as a central or local government, as "authorities." However, we think it is useful to distinguish between politico-legal institutions (which may or may not be embodied in organizations, and which take on a fixed quality), and authority as an emergent feature of social relationships.
23. The connection between property and the state has a long tradition in social theory. See MacPherson (1978) for a selection of classical writings.
24. See also Kligman and Verdery (2011) on the linkages between struggles over property and processes of state formation.
25. On postsocialism, see Burawoy and Verdery (1999) and Humphrey (2002). Kligman and Verdery (1999) develop a convincing case of how ethnographic research can help to avoid wrong generalizations.
26. Complexity, ambiguity, and diversity are also key themes in the special issue of *Conservation and Society* 2(1) (2004) on postsocialist property relations, and in Tassilo Herrschel's work (2007a, 2007b) on the geography of postsocialism.
27. Walder (1995) is a rare exception.
28. For useful discussions of the socialist regimes, see Sjöberg (1991) on Albania, Verdery (1996) on Romania, and Fforde and de Vylder (1996) on Vietnam. For overviews of the reforms, see de Waal (2005) on Albania, Weiner (2001) on Romania, and Fforde and de Vylder (1996) on Vietnam.
29. See Verdery (2003), Mathijs and Swinnen (1998), and Rozelle and Swinnen (2004) for overviews of privatization strategies and changing ownership structures in agriculture. On property reforms in forestry and nature conservation, see World Bank (2000, 2005).

References

Abrams, Philip. 1988. "Notes on the Difficulty of Studying the State (1977)." *Journal of Historical Sociology* 1(1): 58–89.

Agrawal, Arun. 2005. *Environmentality: Technologies of Government and the Making of Subjects*. Durham, NC and London: Duke University Press.

Akram-Lodhi, Haroon, Saturnino M. Borras Jr, and Cristobal Kay (eds). 2006. *Land, Poverty and Livelihoods in the Era of Globalization: Perspectives from Developing and Transition Countries*. London: Routledge and Chapman & Hall.

Allina-Pisano, Jessica. 2008. *The Post-Soviet Potemkin Village: Politics and Property Rights in the Black Earth*. New York: Cambridge University Press.

Anderson, David G. 1998. "Property as a Way of Knowing on Evenki Lands in Arctic Siberia." In *Property Relations: Renewing the Anthropological Tradition*, ed. Chris M. Hann. Cambridge: Cambridge University Press, 64–84.

Appadurai, Arjun. 1986. "Introduction: Commodities and the Politics of Value." In *The Social Life of Things: Commodities in Cultural Perspective*, ed. Arjun Appadurai. Cambridge: Cambridge University Press, 3–63.

Baum, Richard, and Alexei Shevchenko. 1999. "The 'State of the State' in Post-Reform China." In *The Paradox of China's Post-Mao Reforms*, ed. Merle Goldman and Roderick MacFaruhar. Cambridge, MA: Harvard University Press.

Benda-Beckmann, Franz von. 1995. "Anthropological Approaches to Property Law and Economics." *European Journal of Law and Economics* 2: 309–36.

Benda-Beckmann, Franz von, and Keebet von Benda-Beckmann. 1999. "A Functional Analysis of Property Rights, with Special Reference to Indonesia." In *Property Rights and Economic Development: Land and Natural Resources in Southeast Asia and Oceania*, ed. Toon van Meijl and Franz von Benda-Beckmann. London and New York: Kegan Paul International, 15–56.

Benda-Beckmann, Franz von, Keebet von Benda-Beckmann, and Melanie G. Wiber. 2006. "The Properties of Property." In *Changing Properties of Property*, ed. Franz von Beckmann, Keebet von Beckmann, and Melanie G. Wiber. New York: Berghahn Books, 1–39.

Benjaminsen, Tor A., et al. 2008. "Formalisation of Land Rights: Some Empirical Evidence from Mali, Niger and South Africa." *Land Use Policy* 26: 28–35.

Bridger, Sue, and Frances Pine. 1998. *Surviving Post-Socialism: Local Strategies and Regional Responses in Eastern Europe and the Former Soviet Union*. London: Routledge.

Burawoy, Michael, and Katherine Verdery. 1999. "Uncertain Transition: Ethnographies of Change in the Postsocialist World." Lanham, MD: Rowman & Littlefield.

Cellarius, Barbara A. 2004. "'Without Co-Ops There Would Be No Forests!': Historical Memory and the Restitution of Forest in Post-Socialist Bulgaria." *Conservation and Society* 2(1): 51–73.

Corbridge, S., et al. 2005. *Seeing the State: Governance and Governmentality in India*. New York: Cambridge University Press.

Deininger, Klaus. 2003. "Land Policies for Growth and Poverty Reduction." *World Bank Policy Research Report*. Washington, DC: World Bank and Oxford University Press.

Fay, Derick, and Deborah James (eds). 2009. *The Rights and Wrongs of Land Restitution: "Restoring What Was Ours"*. Abingdon: Routledge Cavendish.

Fernandez-Gimenez, Maria E. 2002. "Spatial and Social Boundaries and the Paradox of Pastoral Land Tenure: A Case Study from Postsocialist Mongolia." *Human Ecology* 30(1): 49–78.

Fforde, Adam, and Stefan de Vylder. 1996. *From Plan to Market: Economic Transition in Vietnam 1979–1994*. Boulder, CO: Westview Press.

Fitzpatrick, Daniel. 2005. "'Best Practice' Options for the Legal Recognition of Customary Tenure." *Development and Change* 36(3): 449–75.

Franklin, Stuart. 2002. "Bialowieza Forest, Poland: Representation, Myth, and the Politics of Dispossession." *Environment and Planning A* 34: 1459–85.

Giordano, Christian, and Dobrinka Kostova. 2002. "The Social Production of Mistrust." In *Postsocialism: Ideals, Ideologies and Practices in Eurasia*, ed. C.M. Hann. London and New York: Routledge, 74–91.

Graeber, David. 2001. *Toward an Anthropological Theory of Value: The False Coin of Our Own Dreams*. New York: Palgrave.

Grzymala-Busse, Anna, and Pauline Jones Luong. 2002. "Reconceptualizing the State: Lessons from Post-Communism." *Politics & Society* 30(4): 529–54.

Hann, Chris M. 1993. "From Production to Property: Decollectivization and the Family–Land Relationship in Contemporary Hungary." *Man* 28(2): 299–320.

——— (ed.). 1998. *Property Relations: Renewing the Anthropological Tradition.* Cambridge: Cambridge University Press.

Hann, Chris M., and The Property Relations Group (eds). 2003. *The Postsocialist Agrarian Question: Property Relations and the Rural Condition.* London and New Brunswick, NJ: LIT Verlag.

Harms, Erik. 2009. "Vietnam's Civilizing Process and the Retreat from the Street: A Turtle's Eye View from Ho Chi Minh City." *City & Society* 21(2): 182–206.

———. 2011. *Saigon's Edge: On the Margins of Ho Chi Minh City.* Minneapolis: University of Minnesota Press.

———. 2012. "Beauty as Control in the New Saigon: Eviction, New Urban Zones, and Atomized Dissent in a Southeast Asian City." *American Ethnologist* 39(4): 735–50.

Heller, Michael, and Christopher Serkin. 1999. "Revaluing Restitution: From the Talmud to Postsocialism." *Michigan Law Review* 97: 1385–412.

Herrschel, T. 2007a. "Between Difference and Adjustment: The Re-/Presentation and Implementation of Post-Socialist (Communist) Transformation." *Geoforum* 38: 439–44.

———. 2007b. *Global Geographies of Post-Socialist Transition: Geographies, Societies, Policies.* Oxon: Routledge.

Ho, Peter. 2001. "Who Owns China's Land? Policies, Property Rights and Deliberate Institutional Ambiguity." *The China Quarterly* 166: 395–421.

Humphrey, Caroline. 1995. "The Politics of Privatization in Provincial Russia: Popular Opinions amid the Dilemmas of the Early 1990s." *Cambridge Anthropology* 18(1): 40–61.

———. 1999. *Marx Went Away—but Karl Stayed Behind.* Ann Arbor: University of Michigan Press.

———. 2002. *The Unmaking of Soviet Life: Everyday Economies after Socialism.* Ithaca, NY and London: Cornell University Press.

Humphrey, Caroline, and David Sneath. 1999. *The End of Nomadism?* Durham, NC: Duke University Press.

Kaneff, Deema. 1995. "Developing Rural Bulgaria." *Cambridge Anthropology* 18(2): 23–34.

———. 1996. "Responses to 'Democratic' Land Reforms in a Bulgarian Village." In *After Socialism: Land Reform and Social Change in Eastern Europe*, ed. Ray Abrahams. Oxford: Berghahn Books, 85–114.

———. 1998. "When 'Land' Becomes 'Territory': Land Privatisation and Ethnicity in Rural Bulgaria." In *Surviving Post-Socialism: Local Strategies and Regional Responses in Eastern Europe and the Former Soviet Union*, ed. Sue Bridger and Frances Pine. London: Routledge, 16–32.

Kerkvliet, Benedict J.T. 2005. *The Power of Everyday Politics: How Vietnamese Peasants Transformed National Policy.* Ithaca, NY: Cornell University Press.

Kligman, Gail, and Katherine Verdery. 1999. "Reflections on the 'Revolutions' of 1989 and After." *East European Politics and Societies* 13(2): 303–12.

———. 2011. *Peasants under Siege: The Collectivization of Romanian Agriculture, 1949–1962.* Princeton, NJ: Princeton University Press.

Lampland, Martha. 2002. "The Advantages of Being Collectivized: Cooperative Farm Managers in the Postsocialist Economy." In *Postsocialism: Ideals, Ideologies and Practices in Eurasia*, ed. Chris M. Hann. London: Routledge, 31–56.

Larson, Anne M., et al. (eds). 2010. *Forests for People: Community Rights and Forest Tenure Reform*. London: Earthscan.

Lentz, Carola. 1998. "The Chief, the Mine Captain and the Politician: Legitimating Power in Northern Ghana." *Africa* 68(1): 46–67.

Leonard, Pamela, and Deema Kaneff (eds). 2002. *Post-Socialist Peasant? Rural and Urban Constructions of Identity in Eastern Europe, East Asia and the former Soviet Union*. New York: Palgrave.

Lipton, Michael. 2009. *Land Reform in Developing Countries: Property Rights and Property Wrongs*. London: Routledge.

Lund, Christian. 2002. "Negotiating Property Institutions: On the Symbiosis of Property and Authority in Africa." In *Negotiating Property in Africa*, ed. Kristine Juul and Christian Lund. Portsmouth, NH: Heinemann, 11–43.

———. 2008. *Local Politics and the Dynamics of Property in Africa*. Cambridge: Cambridge University Press.

MacPherson, C.B. 1978. *Property: Mainstream and Critical Positions*. Toronto: University of Toronto Press.

Manser, Roger. 1993. *The Squandered Dividend: Free Market and the Environment in Eastern Europe*. London: Earthscan.

Mansfield, Becky. 2007. "Privatization: Property and the Remaking of Nature–Society Relations. Introduction to the Special Issue." *Antipode* 39(3): 393–405.

——— (ed.). 2008. *Privatization: Property and the Remaking of Nature–Society Relations*. Oxford: Blackwell.

Mathijs, Erik, and Johan F.M. Swinnen. 1998. "The Economics of Agricultural Decollectivization in East Central Europe and the Former Soviet Union." *Economic Development and Cultural Change* 47(1): 1–26.

Mauss, Marcel. 1965. *The Gift: Forms and Functions of Exchange in Archaic Societies*. New York: Norton.

Meurs, Mieke. 2002. "Economic Strategies of Surviving Post-Socialism: Changing Household Economies and Gender Division of Labour in the Bulgarian Transition." In *Work, Employment and Transition: Restructuring Livelihoods in Post-Communism*, ed. Al Rainnie, Adrian Smith and Adam Swain. London: Routledge, 213–16.

Migdal, J.S. 2001. *Studying How States and Societies Transform and Constitute One Another*. Cambridge: Cambridge University Press.

Moore, Sally Falk. 1988. "Legitimation as a Process: The Expansion of Government and Party in Tanzania." In *State Formation and Political Legitimacy*, ed. R. Cohen and J. Toland. Political Anthropology vol. 6. New Brunswick, NJ: Transaction Books, 155–72.

Munn, Nancy. 1986. *The Fame of Gawa: A Symbolic Study of Value Transformation in a Massim (Papa New Guinea) Society*. Cambridge: Cambridge University Press.

Penov, Ivan. 2004. "The Use of Irrigation Water in Bulgaria's Plovdiv Region during Transition." *Environmental Management* 34(2): 304–13.

Perreault, Thomas. 2005. "State Restructuring and the Scale Politics of Rural Water Governance in Bolivia." *Environment and Planning A* 37: 263–84.

Peters, Pauline E. 1994. *Dividing the Commons: Politics, Policy, and Culture in Botswana.* Charlottesville and London: University Press of Virginia.

Pickles, John. 2002. "Gulag Europe? Mass Unemployment, New Firm Creation, and Right Labour Markets in the Bulgarian Apparel Industry." In *Work, Employment and Transition: Restructuring Livelihoods in Post-Communism*, ed. Al Rainnie, Adrian Smith and Adam Swain. London: Routledge, 246–72.

Reid-Henry, Simon. 2007. "The Contested Spaces of Cuban Development: Post-Socialism, Post-Colonialism and the Geography of Transition." *Geoforum* 38(3): 445–55.

Ribot, Jesse, and Nancy Peluso. 2003. "A Theory of Access." *Rural Sociology* 68(2): 153–81.

Rozelle, S., and J.F.M. Swinnen. 2004. "Success and Failure of Reform: Insights from the Transition of Agriculture." *Journal of Economic Literature* 42(2): 404–56.

Sachs, J. 1990. "What Is to Be Done?" *The Economist* (13 January): 1–7.

Schwartz, A.H. 2006. *The Politics of Greed: How Privatization Structured Politics in Central and Eastern Europe.* Plymouth: Rowman & Littlefield.

Schwartz, Katrina Z.S. 2006. *Nature and National Identity after Communism: Globalizing the Ethnoscape.* Pittsburgh, PA: University of Pittsburgh Press.

Shipton, Parker, and Mitzi Goheen. 1992. "Understanding African Land-Holding: Power, Wealth, and Meaning." *Africa* 62(3): 307–25.

Sikor, Thomas. 2001a. "Agrarian Differentiation in (Post-)Socialist Vietnam." *Development and Change* 32(5): 923–49.

———. 2001b. "The Allocation of Forestry Land in Vietnam: Did It Cause the Expansion of Forests in the Northwest?" *Forest Policy and Economics* 2(1): 1–11.

———. 2006. "Land as Asset, Land as Liability: Property Politics in Rural Central and Eastern Europe." In *Changing Properties of Property*, ed. Franz von Benda-Beckmann, Keebet von Benda-Beckmann and Melanie G. Wiber. New York: Berghahn Books, 106–25.

Sikor, Thomas, and Christian Lund. 2009a. "Access and Property: A Question of Power and Authority." *Development and Change* 40(1): 1–22.

——— (eds). 2009b. *The Politics of Possession: Property, Access and Authority.* Oxford: Blackwell.

Sikor, Thomas, and Daniel Müller. 2009. "The Limits of State-Led Land Reform: An Introduction." *World Development* 37(8) (*The Limits of State-Led Land Reform*): 1307–16.

Sikor, Thomas, and Pham Thi Tuong Vi. 2005. "The Dynamics of Commoditization in a Vietnamese Uplands Village, 1980–2000." *Journal of Agrarian Change* 5(3): 405–28.

Sjöberg, Örjan. 1991. *Rural Change and Development in Albania.* Oxford and San Francisco: Westview Press.

Smith, A. 2000. "Employment Restructuring and Household Survival in 'Postcommunist Transition': Rethinking Economic Practices in Eastern Europe." *Environment and Planning* 23: 1759–80.

———. 2002a. "Culture/Economy and Spaces of Economic Practice: Positioning Households in Post-Communism." *Transactions of the Institute of British Geographers* 27(2): 232–50.

———. 2002b. "Imagining Geographies of the 'New Europe' Geo-economic Power and the New European Architecture of Integration." *Political Geography* 21: 647–70.

Smith, Adrian, and Alison Stenning. 2006. "Beyond Household Economies: Articulations and Spaces of Economic Practice in Postsocialism." *Progress in Human Geography* 30(2): 190–213.

Soto, Hernando de. 2000. *The Mystery of Capital: Why Capitalism Triumphs in the West and Fails Everywhere Else.* New York: Basic Books.

Sowerwine, Jennifer. 2004. "Territorialisation and the Politics of Highland Landscapes in Vietnam: Negotiating Property Relations in Policy, Meaning and Practice." *Conservation and Society* 2(1): 97–136.

Staddon, Caedmon. 2000. "Restitution of Forest Property in Post-Communist Bulgaria." *Natural Resources Forum* 24: 237–46.

Stark, David. 1992. "Path Dependence and Privatization: Strategies in East Central Europe." *East European Politics and Societies* 6(1): 17–54.

———. 1996. "Recombinant Property in Eastern European Capitalism." *American Journal of Sociology* 101(4): 993–1027.

Strang, Veronia, and Mark Busse (eds). 2011. *Ownership and Appropriation.* Oxford: Berg.

Strathern, Marilyn. 1988. *The Gender of the Gift: Problems with Women and Problems with Society in Melanesia.* Berkeley: University of California Press.

Sturgeon, Janet. 2004. "Border Practices, Boundaries, and the Control of Resource Access: A Case from China, Thailand and Burma." *Development and Change* 35(3): 463–84.

———. 2005. *Border Landscapes: The Politics of Akha Land Use in China and Thailand.* Seattle and London: University of Washington Press.

Theesfeld, Insa. 2004. "Constraints on Collective Action in a Transitional Economy: The Case of Bulgaria's Irrigation Sector." *World Development* 32(2): 251–71.

Tilly, Charles. 1985. "War Making and State Making as Organized Crime." In *Bringing the State Back In*, ed. Peter Evans, D. Rueschemeyer, and T. Skocpol. Cambridge: Cambridge University Press, 169–91.

Tompson, W. 1999. "The Price of Everything and the Value of Nothing? Unravelling the Workings of Russia's 'Virtual Economy.'" *Economy and Society* 28(2): 256–80.

Verdery, Katherine. 1996. *What Was Socialism? And What Comes Next?* Princeton, NJ: Princeton University Press.

———. 1998. "Property and Power in Transylvania's Decollectivization." In *Property Relations: Renewing the Anthropological Tradition*, ed. Christopher Hann. Cambridge: Cambridge University Press, 160–80.

———. 1999. "Fuzzy Property: Rights, Power, and Identity in Transylvania's Decollectivization." In *Uncertain Transition: Ethnographies of Change in the Postsocialist World*, ed. Michael Burawoy and Katherine Verdery. Lanham, MD: Rowman & Littlefield, 53–81.

———. 2002. "Seeing Like a Mayor. Or, How Local Officials Obstructed Romanian Land Restitution." *Ethnography* 3(1): 5–33.

———. 2003. *The Vanishing Hectare: Property and Value in Postsocialist Transylvania.* Ithaca, NY: Cornell University Press.

———. 2004. "The Obligations of Ownership: Restoring Rights to Land in Postsocialist Transylvania." In *Property in Question: Value Transformations in the Global Economy,* ed. Katherine Verdery and Caroline Humphey. Oxford: Berg, 139–60.

Waal, Clarissa de. 2004. "Post-Socialist Property Rights and Wrongs in Albania: An Ethnography of Agrarian Change." *Conservation and Society* 2(1): 19–50.

———. 2005. *Albania Today: A Portrait of Post-Communist Turbulence.* London: I.B. Tauris.

Walder, Andrew G. (ed.). 1995. *The Waning of the Communist State: Economic Origins of Political Decline in Hungary and China.* Berkeley: University of California Press.

Weber, Max. 1976. *Wirtschaft Und Gesellschaft.* Tübingen: J.C.B. Mohr.

Weiner, Robert. 2001. "Romania, the IMF, and Economic Reform since 1996." *Problems of Post-Communism* 48(1): 39–47.

Winkels, Alexandra. 2008. "Rural in-Migration and Global Trade: Managing the Risks of Coffee Farming in the Central Highlands of Vietnam." *Mountain Research and Development* 28(1): 32–40.

World Bank. 2000. "Natural Resource Management Strategy: Eastern Europe and Central Asia." Technical Paper No. 485. Washington, DC.

———. 2005. "Forest Institutions in Transition: Experiences and Lessons from Eastern Europe." Working Paper No. 35153. Washington, DC.

Zbierski-Salameh, Sulameh. 1999. "Polish Peasants in the 'Valley of Transition': Responses to Postsocialist Reform." In *Uncertain Transition: Ethnographies of Change in the Postsocialist World,* ed. Michael Burawoy and Katherine Verdery. Lanham, MD: Rowman & Littlefield, 189–222.

Zingerli, Claudia. 2005. "Colliding Understandings of Biodiversity Conservation in Vietnam: Global Chains, National Interests, and Local Struggles." *Society and Natural Resources* 18(8): 733–47.

PART I
AGRICULTURE
Negotiating Property and Value

◆ Introduction

Land reform was an issue of critical priority to the governments of Albania, Romania, and Vietnam when they began to depart from the socialist policies of the past. For example, in 1989 Romania's first postsocialist government hastily assembled three days before Christmas to announce the necessity to restructure agriculture. The announcement came on the very day that events forced the country's long-serving socialist president, Nicolae Ceaușescu, to resign from office (von Hirschhausen 1997: 55). Land reform was at the fore of the new governments' agendas for the reasons that we discussed in the Introduction: the new governments embraced private property rights in the expectation that they would provide a key pillar for economic development, a transition to democracy, and environmental protection; and they did so under the conditionalities negotiated with the World Bank, International Monetary Fund, and European Union for their assistance packages. The task of creating property rights, they and their international advisors assumed, fell to the state.[1]

Land reform was deemed necessary due to the collectivization of agriculture that had taken place a few decades earlier. Romania began agricultural collectivization in 1948, Albania in 1955, and Vietnam in 1957. In all three countries, collectivization created radical changes in property rights to land.[2] In Romania, for example, the individual members of the agricultural cooperatives lost their land rights even though they retained formal ownership rights in the absence of full-scale expropriation (Kligman and Verdery 2011). More importantly, socialist agriculture did not bring about a simple transfer of a fixed set of land rights from households to cooperatives. Collectivization fundamentally transformed the rights available to land managers and the obligations they faced. Socialist property relations were radically different from those known previously as well as those common to capitalist economies. The perceived task faced by the new governments was not merely one of transferring existing property rights; instead, new kinds of property relations had to be created (Verdery 2003).

Albania's land legislation mandated that agricultural land should be distributed among the agricultural workforce. The government issued the "Law Concerning the Land" in 1991, which specified that every member possessed equal right to the agricultural land held by agricultural collectives. The law called for the distribution of all collectivized land to the cooperative's members on an equal per capita basis. In addition to cooperative workers, other rural dwellers who were not members of cooperatives, such as state farm employees, teachers, and military personnel, received land in smaller quantities. To implement the distribution, the government established land commissions at the local level and created a specialized land administration agency to issue land titles. The titles were meant to document the new ownership rights now held by millions of rural Albanians (Cungu and Swinnen 1999).

Romania's land laws called for the restitution of agricultural land to historical owners or their heirs. The newly elected national parliament passed Law 18 in 1991, which held that land in the possession of agricultural cooperatives was to be returned to those who had owned it in 1948, as long as the returned land was not larger than ten hectares (ha). In addition, Law 18 mandated that every rural household be entitled to at least 0.5 ha of agricultural land, even if they or their families had not owned any land prior to collectivization. Similar to the new legislation in Albania, this law called for the formation of local land commissions to handle the restitution process; it also designated specialized state offices to issue new ownership titles. The second critical piece of legislation came nine years later in the form of Law 1 passed by the parliament in 2000. Law 1 confirmed the 1991 restitution of agricultural land, and the ownership status of the new land rights in general. It even expanded the allowable maximum area that could be restituted to a single owner to fifty hectares.

Similar to the tenets of Albania's law, Vietnam's land legislation endorsed the distribution of agricultural land among the present agricultural workforce. Resolution 10, issued by the Communist Party in 1988, allowed all cooperatives to devolve agricultural production to individual member households, giving them the right to use agricultural land. Further, the Land Law of 1993 recognized households' land use rights, enacted a nationwide program of land allocation to formalize the land rights, and provided the legal foundations for the creation of a new specialized land administration agency. The Land Law also granted households long-term use rights to agricultural land, including the rights of transfer and inheritance, and limited the duration of these rights to twenty years for annual crops, and fifty years for perennial crops.

Differences among the land laws enacted in postsocialist countries have received due attention in the literature. Analysts have rightly noted differences between the specific legal stipulations contained in the various land reforms and developed insightful investigations into the political and economic factors underlying the variation (e.g., see Swinnen 1997). For example, research has examined why some governments decided to restitute agricultural land to historical owners, whereas others mandated the distribution of land among the present agricultural workforce. Another example is the much-heralded difference between the formal ownership rights granted to landholders in Albania and Romania and the reference to long-term use rights in Vietnam's legislation.

However, recognition of the differences does not negate the presence of striking similarities among the three countries. The land laws of all three countries sought to give landholders not just use rights but a full set of rights equating ownership. The bundle of rights that the new owners received included the right to use the land, dispose of its products, rent it out, bequeath it to their children or dedicated heirs, or sell it. This was true for Vietnam's long-term use rights, even though the 1993 Land Law did not legally deem "long-term land use rights" as "ownership rights." In Vietnam, ownership of land remained with all "the people." Even though they were not called owners, Vietnam's new landholders could do virtually the same with the land allocated to them as their peers in Albania and Romania.

A second parallel emerges from the strongly egalitarian goals contained in the land legislation of all three countries. The effort to distribute the land equally was apparent in Albania and Vietnam, where every agricultural worker within the same village was expected to receive the same amount of land. The goal toward equal distribution of land can also be seen in two qualifications of Romania's general rule to restitute land to historical owners: the original land ceiling of 10 ha, which was later increased to 50 ha, and the amended provision to give every rural household at least 0.5 ha of agricultural land regardless of historical ownership. The underlying idea in each country was that every rural household should enjoy the same opportunity to meet their own subsistence needs or generate a basic income from agriculture, to benefit from the downfall of socialism, and to participate in the new democracies as owners of valuable assets.

The third similarity between the three countries was that their land reforms held the same vision: that of giving people the opportunity to own and cultivate specific parcels of land as smallholders. The land laws of Albania, Romania, and Vietnam did not contain provisions for people to become shareholders in reformed cooperatives or new companies, as occurred in East Germany, Hungary, and other countries of Eastern Europe and Central Asia (Swinnen 1997). Instead, the laws were expected to allow for the transfer of specific parcels of land to the new owners. This intention to create smallholders was most evident in Romania, where the legislation stipulated that historical owners should regain the very parcels that they had worked prior to collectivization.

The fourth, equally striking similarity was that all three land reforms considered agricultural land as a productive resource for smallholder agriculture. This made apparent sense in Albania and Vietnam, where 50 percent and 70 percent of the workforce remained in agriculture, and where the governments mandated the distribution of the land among the current workforce. It did not seem to reflect Romania's situation in 1990, where socialist industrialization had facilitated a decline in the agricultural workforce from 74 percent in the late 1940s to 28 percent in 1989 (Verdery 2003: 85). Yet, it was in Romania—as in many other countries of Eastern Europe—where national legislation mandated the restitution to historical owners. It was also in Romania where Cartwright (2001) observed "the return of the peasant" in debates about the countryside and agricultural policy.

Land reform proceeded at a rapid pace in all three countries despite the monumental nature of the tasks faced by their governments. Ten to fifteen years after the initial laws were passed, all three governments announced that they had more or less completed the transfer of land. In 2005, the Albanian government reported that 1,860,000 out of a total of 1,900,000 agricultural parcels in the entire country had been transferred to new owners (World Bank 2006: 33). The Romanian government estimated that, by 2001, 85 percent of the relevant land had been restituted to historical owners (Csaki and Kray 2006). In 2003, Vietnam's government declared that agricultural land allocation was complete (Ton Gia Huyen and Tran Thi Minh Ha 2009).

At the same time, observations on the ground increasingly cast doubt on the expectation that the new owners would put agricultural land to good use. Across Albania and Romania large areas of productive farmland lay idle because their owners had more pressing priorities than work the land or find someone else to work it for them (Müller and Sikor 2006; Kuemmerle et al. 2009). This caused considerable dismay to many agricultural experts, who claimed that the new owners had "abandoned" the land. The experts were frustrated that the extension of private ownership had not led to the expected productive use of agricultural land.

The discrepancy between expectations and developments on the ground provides the background for the ethnographies presented in the following three chapters. We turn our attention to seven villages in Albania, Romania, and Vietnam to chronicle how people fared once they acquired agricultural land rights in the wake of the new land laws.

Notes

1. For example, see World Bank (1992) on Albania, and World Bank (1993: esp. pp. 24–27) on Vietnam.
2. Collectivization was far from a uniform process (for example, see Meurs 1999). However, a discussion of the extent, timing, and nature of collectivization in the three countries would go beyond the scope of this introduction, as would attention to the reforms of state farms.

References

Cartwright, Andrew. 2001. *The Return of the Peasant: Land Reform in Post-Communist Romania*. Aldershot: Ashgate.

Csaki, Csaba, and Holger Kray 2006. "The Agrarian Economies of Central-Eastern Europe and the Commonwealth of Independent States." In *Environmentally and Socially Sustainable Development Working Paper* Washington, D.C.: The World Bank.

Cungu, Azeta, and Johan F.M. Swinnen. 1999. "Albania's Radical Agrarian Reform." *Economic Development and Cultural Change* 47(3): 605–20.

Hirschhausen, Beatrice von. 1997. *Les Nouvelles Campagnes Roumaines. Paradoxes D'un "Retour" paysan*. Paris: Belin.

Kligman, Gail, and Katherine Verdery. 2011. *Peasants under Siege: The Collectivization of Romanian Agriculture, 1949–1962*. Princeton, NJ: Princeton University Press.

Kuemmerle, Tobias, et al. 2009. "Land Use Change in Romania after the Collapse of Socialism." *Regional Environmental Change* 9(1): 1–12.

Meurs, Mieke. 1999. *Many Shades of Red: State Policy and Collective Agriculture*. Lanham, MD, Boulder, CO, New York, Oxford: Rowman & Littlefield.

Müller, Daniel, and Thomas Sikor. 2006. "Effects of Postsocialist Reforms on Land Cover and Land Use in South-Eastern Albania." *Applied Geography* 26(3): 175–91.

Swinnen, Johan F.M. 1997. "The Choice of Privatization and Decollectivization Policies in Central and Eastern European Agriculture: Observations and Political Economy Hypotheses." In *Political Economy of Agrarian Reform in Central and Eastern Europe*, ed. Johan F.M. Swinnen. Aldershot: Ashgate, 363–98.

Ton Gia Huyen and Tran Thi Minh Ha. 2009. "Vietnam Land Administration: The Past, Recent and for the Future." Paper presented at the 7th FIG Regional Conference, "Spatial Data Serving People: Land Governance and the Environment—Building the Capacity." Hanoi, Vietnam, 19–22 October 2009.

Verdery, Katherine. 2003. *The Vanishing Hectare: Property and Value in Postsocialist Transylvania*. Ithaca, NY: Cornell University Press.

World Bank. 1992. "An Agricultural Strategy for Albania." Report No. 11365. Tirana.

———. 1993. "Vietnam: Transition to the Market." An Economic Report, No. 11902VN. Washington, DC.

———. 2006. "Status of Land Reform and Real Property Markets in Albania." Internal Report, World Bank Office, Tirana.

1

Transnational Migration, Ethnicity, and Property in Albania

Wheat covered the land around the villages of Bagëtia, Dardha, and Kodra in southeastern Albania in the late 1980s. People planted it in the valley surrounded by rolling foothills that harbored the village of Kodra. They cultivated it in Dardha, a village located on the shores of Lake Prespa adjacent to what was then the Socialist Federal Republic of Yugoslavia. Even in Bagëtia, which lies more than one thousand meters above sea level amidst immense old-growth forests and mountain pastures in the Gorë Mountains, people grew wheat. The fields stretched from the plains along the Mediterranean Sea to the mountains bordering Yugoslavia and Greece in socialist Albania.

Wheat was ubiquitous in the country because the socialist regime gave strict priority to national food sufficiency (Pettifer 2001). This priority caused the regime to restrict internal rural–urban movements in order to retain labor in agriculture. Almost two-thirds of all Albanians remained in the countryside, while many rural residents in Western and Eastern Europe migrated to urban areas (Sjöberg 1991). In addition, the socialist regime nationalized agricultural land, ordered villagers to join agricultural cooperatives, told them to cultivate wheat, and procured the wheat for bread production.

When Johannes came to the three villages in 2004, their landscapes had become more diverse. He still found wheat in the fields around Dardha, the village on Lake Prespa. Villagers continued to grow the crop in big blocks, just as they had done during socialism. In contrast, Kodra's agricultural landscape had changed drastically. The landscape had become fragmented. The villagers worked vegetable gardens immediately around their houses, there were many small fields with various crops around the village, and pastures were farther away. Bagëtia's landscape was also different, in that villagers had given up cultivation on most of the slopes surrounding the village. There were only a few fields, and several houses were in a state of disrepair, which indicated that many of the previous residents had left.

A feature of the different changes in the agricultural landscape that struck Johannes most was that they coincided with ethnic differences between the three villages. Kodra's population was ethnic Albanian. They traced their origins back to the ancient Illyrian tribesmen who had settled in the region some three thousand years ago. Ethnic Albanians accounted for a large majority of Albania's population, and exerted a decisive influence on the country's national identity (Pettifer 2001). Dardha was one of nine Macedonian villages located across the border of what is now called the Former Yugoslav Republic of Macedonia. The villages were home to nearly 4,500 people whose origin in the region dated back to medieval empires that extended across Southeastern Europe (Apostoli 2002). Bagëtia's people, in turn, were Vlachs, an ethnic group that numbers about 200,000 people in all of Albania (Schwandner-Sievers 1999). Vlachs reside not only in Albania but also in neighboring countries, and are commonly thought to share the same historical ancestors as either Romanians or Greeks.

The villages displayed a key feature of Southeastern Europe (or 'the Balkans' as the region was commonly referred to until recently): the presence of distinct ethnic groups.[1] Additionally, life was characterized by a high incidence of migration, another main feature of villages across Eastern Europe after the demise of socialism. Millions of rural residents left their villages in Eastern Europe for other countries or urban areas after 1990. Some of the emigration consisted of ethnic Germans, Jews, Hungarians, and Russians who left for their putative home countries (Brubacker 1998; Fox 2003; Münz and Ohliger 2003). The migrants also included millions of rural residents from Southeastern Europe who left their villages after the collapse of socialism and the Yugoslav wars (Bonifazi, Conti, and Mamolo 2006). Among them, hundreds of thousands of Albanians emigrated to Greece, Italy, other countries in Western Europe, and the United States. The mass exodus gave Albania one of the highest emigration rates in the world; approximately one-fifth of its resident population were living abroad by the early 2000s (King 2005).

How did the variation in landscape changes come to coincide with ethnic differences? In this chapter we will show that migration provides the crucial link. Migration to other countries assumed an important role in villagers' livelihoods after 1990. Many villagers sought to make a living by engaging in various forms of migration.[2] However, the opportunities for jobs and social advancement abroad as well as villagers' responses to such opportunities varied with their ethnicity. Consequently changes in land use practices differed between the villages. In the process, livelihoods and land use became transnational in the sense that they reflected events not only in the villages but also in various places abroad. Livelihood and land use practices were no longer determined by events in Albania but occurred within "multi-stranded social relations that link together their societies of origin and settlement" (Basch, Glick-Schiller, and Blanc-Szanton 1994: 6). Villagers acted amid a new situation of transnationalism, which we argue had direct consequences on property relations in the three villages.[3]

Vlachs Emigrating to Greece: The Exodus from Bagëtia

The people of Bagëtia worked hard to make a living during socialism. The Vlach villagers formed an agricultural producer cooperative together with ethnic Albanians from two nearby villages as part of the collectivization drive in 1967.[4] Although the mountainous terrain was not suitable for crop production, central planning required the cooperative to produce wheat, rye, and corn for the sake of national food security. The socialist regime's aim was to "make the mountains and hills as fertile as the fields."[5] As a result, agricultural fields covered large parts of the slopes surrounding the village, facilitated by an elaborate structure of terraces that villagers built over time. Each year the cooperative had severe difficulties in meeting the production quotas set by the Ministry of Agriculture. Livestock husbandry had to make up for the low productivity of crops, producing meat, wool, and dairy products.

Despite these difficulties, Bagëtia was on a relatively equal footing with villages located in more favorable biophysical conditions.[6] Massive state support of crop cultivation made this possible, such as support given in the form of machinery, services, and inputs. In addition, the state invested in the village's infrastructure. It built a road to connect Bagëtia to the lowlands, constructed a cultural center, created a small irrigation system, erected livestock shelters and two large grain depots, and operated an elementary school and a store, which sold consumer goods. The state investment

was part of a wider effort by the socialist regime to reduce economic differences among rural villages.[7] The regime wanted to ensure that every village in Albania was accessible by road, and possessed irrigation, a school, and a cultural center, even if it was located high up in the mountains like Bagëtia. This was something that Vickers and Pettifer have referred to as a form of "extreme, spartan egalitarianism" (Vickers and Pettifer 1997: 12).

Agricultural production and public infrastructure quickly collapsed in Bagëtia after the cooperative was dissolved in 1991. As the Albanian state liberalized domestic markets and international trade, the cultivation of basic grains was no longer profitable.[8] Cultivation did not pay because output prices dropped and input prices soared. At the same time, the gravel road that once connected Bagëtia to the lowlands became impassable due to lack of maintenance.[9] By the time Johannes arrived in 2004, the closest place to catch a minibus to a lowland market was now an hour's walk along a narrow and rugged mountain path. In addition, the village possessed only three public faucets, and in the winter was often cut off from electricity for days at a time. The villagers could no longer receive Albanian radio or television programs—the satellite dishes on their houses allowed them to receive Greek, German and Italian channels but no Albanian station. If they wanted to make a phone call, they had to walk up a mountain about five hundred meters before their mobile phones reached a network connection.

As living conditions deteriorated at home, new opportunities arose for the villagers across the border. Available jobs and decent living conditions in Greece proved highly attractive to many people from Bagëtia. Greece experienced a period of economic boom in the late 1990s and early 2000s, spurred in part by the building of new infrastructure for the 2004 Summer Olympics. According to the returning migrants Johannes met in 2004, an unskilled laborer could earn twenty-five euros a day in agriculture or fifty euros a day in construction in Greece. At the same time, in the lowland towns around Bagëtia there were few jobs available in agriculture, and in construction a laborer could only make between eight and fifteen euros a day. Moreover, as villagers stressed, Greece promised them the opportunity to establish a modern life, which was an opportunity many did not find available in Albania.

Migration to Greece was not only attractive for economic and social reasons—it was also made easy by Greek immigration policy. The Greek state granted Vlachs three-year visas for a small fee that allowed them to work in Greece. In addition, Greek legislation allowed Vlachs older than sixty-five to register as residents, which entitled them to a monthly pension of 200 euros. The Greek state provided Vlachs this preferential treatment because it considered them to be of Greek origin on the basis of their Greek Orthodox religion (Schwandner-Sievers 1999; Konidaris 2005). In the Greek view, Hellenic heritage was passed on through Byzantine culture to contemporary practitioners of the Greek Orthodox religion. That was not a view many villagers in Bagëtia shared because they considered themselves to be an autochthonous people unrelated to the Greeks.[10] Notwithstanding their convictions, they eagerly embraced the opportunity to apply for visas and pensions, despite the different interpretation of their origins and culture underlying the Greek policy.

The new opportunities in Greece dramatically affected livelihood practices in Bagëtia. Between 1991 and 2004, almost two-thirds of the original seventy households permanently left the village.[11] Only twenty-four households remained in the sense that they still had at least one person who lived in the village, kept up the house, and maintained some agricultural activities. However, twenty of these households included at least one member who worked in Greece on a permanent or seasonal basis. The money sent from Greece significantly boosted the villagers' income, allowing many of them to build a second home in the lowlands. In 2004, only four households stayed entirely in Bagëtia. They lived off the occasional sale of livestock as well as from pensions and social assistance paid by the Albanian state, which barely exceeded a couple of hundred euros per year.

Maks and Lisa Dulellari ran one of the households remaining in the village. They lived a comfortable life because their two sons and a daughter lived near Athens. The children regularly sent money home. This made Maks and Lisa well-off. Maks told Johannes that he missed his children and grandchildren, but he also emphasized that he was generally happy with his life as a shepherd. Lisa, however, felt increasingly lonely. She said she missed, "the sound of children shouting: their happy voices." After their children left, the house had become "silent, [you hear] only the sound of livestock when it comes in from the pasture." To make the house livelier, they offered Johannes a place to stay during his fieldwork.

Some of the people who had emigrated to Greece returned to Bagëtia on special occasions. For instance, Frosina Geri, a vigorous woman of sevety-three, visited Bagëtia three times a year—at Christmas, Easter, and on the Assumption of Mary. When Johannes met her around the Assumption of Mary holiday she said, "Here [in Bagëtia] I have my dead father, my sisters and brothers, and as long as I can still walk I want to come and see them!" Yet her connections with Bagëtia did not extend much beyond this. She barely managed to maintain her house and had long given up any interest in working the land.

The exodus from Bagëtia changed the value that people attached to land. Land was no longer primarily a productive resource, even though the remaining villagers worked some agricultural fields and grazed their livestock on the pastures surrounding the village. Instead, villagers increasingly appreciated land for its symbolic values. For example, Frosina Geri returned to Bagëtia three times a year because this is where she grew up, where her parents and grandparents had lived, and where they were buried. Lisa and Maks Dulellari decided to stay in Bagëtia because this was where they had lived their entire lives and where they wanted to die. Land became a signifier of belonging, and assumed a new meaning for them within an environment characterized by transnational migration.

The new value people attached to land had a strong bearing on property relations in Bagëtia. Because they began to view land more as a signifier of belonging and less as a productive asset, villagers changed the claims they made on the land. The changing nature of claims on agricultural land and the implications for property relations is illustrated through a story that Maks told Johannes during his stay with the family.

From Land Distribution to Restitution: The Story of Maks Dulellari

In the 1950s and 1960s, Maks recalled, his father owned approximately ten hectares (ha) of agricultural land. As a young man, Maks worked his father's land for twelve years before it was collectivized in 1967. He and his father did not want to join collective production and did not render their land to the cooperative leadership voluntarily. Throughout collective agriculture Maks never forgot the bitter moments of collectivization, and he felt like an outsider in the village. Therefore, when villagers dissolved the agricultural producer cooperative and distributed the agricultural land among themselves in 1991, Maks thought the time had come for him to reclaim his father's land.

The problem for Maks was that Albania's Land Law of 1991 mandated an egalitarian distribution of all land among the agricultural population of villages. The law stipulated not only that all collective farmland was to be distributed on an equal basis to the rural population, but also that this rule applied to the entire country, irrespective of distinct local histories and conditions. It took into account "neither former ownership, nor the land boundaries and sizes before collectivization" (Article 8). Instead, it stipulated the full distribution of all collectivized land on a per capita basis to the members of former agricultural cooperatives (Article 5). This unwavering concern for economic and social equality reflected the egalitarianism of the past, causing its critics to label it a "Communist law." Maks could not have agreed more with their assessment.

In Bagëtia, three land commissions set out to distribute the cooperative land according to national policy. By order of the socialist regime, the village leaders established a first commission to distribute small parcels of 0.15 ha each to households, which would have retained the majority of land in cooperative management. The commission had worked on this process for less than a week before the next order came to dissolve the cooperative entirely and distribute all cooperative land to individual households. A year later the village leaders set up a second land commission to implement the "Law Concerning the Land" issued by new government.[12] Headed by the former chief of the cooperative, the second commission ignored the distribution that had already been put into effect by the first commission, and drew up an entirely new plan for distributing 0.13 ha per capita. This was the maximum land area per capita that a household could own while remaining eligible for social assistance, according to Albania's laws. However, before the second commission was able to issue any *tapitë* (land certificates), the head of the commission left Bagëtia for Greece. Responsibility then fell to a third commission to issue provisional *tapitë* to all seventy households. These documents remained the only legally valid form of land ownership in Bagëtia for a long time, since cadastral officers never made their way up the mountain to confer formal land titles to villagers.

The distribution quickly encountered open opposition in Bagëtia. Families with few members and claims to large areas of ancestral land resisted the egalitarian distribution and did not shy away from threatening the use of physical force. Four or five households occupied their historical land. They did not seek the endorsement of the land commissions or fellow villagers, nor did they mind the fact that their acts were in apparent conflict with the law.

Maks was one of the staunchest and most vocal advocates for returning land to its historical owners. He fiercely resisted the idea that the land should be distributed equally among the current population. He did not want to accept yet another intervention by the state, socialist or not, that would prevent him from claiming ownership to the land his father had worked. He proclaimed to his fellow villagers: "When the cooperative came, you stole my land, my father's land and my grandfather's land. Now I take it back!"

As he proudly told Johannes in 2004, Maks had to fight to get his land claims recognized by his fellow villagers. When the land commissions assigned 2.5 ha of his father's historical land to other families in the village, he went out with his wife and children to plant wheat on it. To reinforce his determination, Maks declared to anyone who would listen, "I will not give my land back." Moreover, he did not hesitate to threaten fellow villagers, telling them, "If someone dares to plant something on it I will kill him!" To back up his words, he bought an old German carbine, which he always carried with him.

In response to Maks's actions and proclamations, the proponents of distribution called the police. According to his recollection, Maks was arrested and jailed twelve times. The police confiscated his carbine, the family's new television set, and their radio and carpets. Once, after a bitter night in jail, Maks remembered one of the policemen threatening him: "Return the land, or I will crash this chair on your back!" But none of the pressure or threats worked. Before his resistance could weaken, the other families in the village followed Maks's example and occupied their historical landholdings.

Maks and the other proponents of restitution were successful because many of the villagers did not want to put up a fight. Initially, some of them tried to resist the return of land to historical owners, but ultimately shied away from open conflict. Moreover, the unfolding emigration eased many potential conflicts. For example, one family sold their house and left to live in a lowland village after a pre-collectivization owner had seized a small garden plot from them. Since the family wanted to leave Bagëtia anyway, they did not see any point in putting up a fight. Villagers eventually settled on restituting the land, even though it left some households with very little or no land. Maks and Lisa successfully reclaimed the ten ha that Maks's father had worked prior to collectivization. The original distribution of the land certified in the *tapitë* that was issued by the third land commission was no longer valid in practice.

Thus, the exodus from Bagëtia influenced the property relations that emerged after the demise of the socialist regime. The departure of many households gave considerable maneuvering space to local negotiations over property, because they did not put much effort into asserting land claims. In addition, those who stayed behind felt differently about life in Bagëtia than the ones who left. Many of them continued to live in the village because they felt attached to the place, which provided a sense of belonging. Furthermore, the people remaining in the village included many elderly people who cherished the idea of reclaiming the land that they or their parents had worked prior to collectivization. Like Maks, they saw the return of the land as an issue of historical justice. Land was no longer primarily a productive resource for most of the remaining villagers but a signifier of belonging and historical justice.

These changes in the values attached to land may also explain why many villages in Albania restituted land to its historical owners or their heirs after 1991 (de Waal 1998). Particularly in the north of the country and in the mountainous areas of the south, people ignored the legal mandate to distribute the land equally among the current population and restituted land to its historical owners. In total, some 15 to 20 percent of Albania's agricultural land may have been restituted to historical owners (Kodderitzsch 1999: 33). The insights we gained in Bagëtia suggest that these restitutions did not occur due to local preferences or historical attachments alone, but also because migration transformed the values that the remaining residents attached to land.

Macedonians Working in Macedonia: The Migrants of Dardha

Compared to villagers in Bagëtia, it was easier for the people of Dardha to work their land during socialism. Dardha excelled in high agricultural productivity, a fact that villagers proudly related to Johannes. The village's location, next to a large plain on the shores of Lake Prespa, had allowed villagers to develop a simple irrigation system for approximately 60 ha out of about 100 ha of fields and pastures belonging to Dardha. The villagers used the plain to cultivate wheat and corn as part of the agricultural producer cooperative that they had formed together with the inhabitants of surrounding villages. Additionally, they raised growing herds of cattle, sheep, goats, and oxen from the early 1980s onward. A battery farm operated by the cooperative in the village contained more than a thousand chickens. A book about the Prespa region that covered Dardha lauded its inhabitants, noting that "[t]he duties of the plan were realized ... in agriculture and livestock, and even more was produced" (Apostoli 2002: 43).

Even though this strong economic performance set it apart, Dardha was similar to other villages in southeastern Albania in terms of amenities. In fact, its infrastructure was comparable to that of Bagëtia. Like Bagëtia, Dardha had a cultural center, an elementary school, a cistern for storing drinking water, an irrigation system, stores selling consumer goods, shelters for livestock, and grain depots. The only significant difference between the villages was the chicken farm in Dardha, for which there was no equivalent in Bagëtia. Otherwise, most of the villagers worked in the agricultural cooperative, cultivated small household plots, and raised some animals on their own initiative.

After decollectivization, the conditions for viable commercial agriculture rapidly deteriorated in Dardha just as we observed in Bagëtia. People recalled that much of the village's vital irrigation infrastructure was looted in the upheavals of 1991. Thieves came at night to dismantle the pumps vital to the village's water supply. Villagers subsequently failed to maintain the canals that were no longer of use to them. The lack of water seriously diminished the productivity of the once fertile land. Another major impediment to viable agricultural production was the lack of market access since it took three hours on a bumpy gravel road to reach the nearest Albanian market, and farmers had to rely on public transportation for marketing. Furthermore, Dardha's farmers noticed that they suddenly faced competition from imported agricultural products, which were of good quality and sold at cheap prices. In fact, many of the trucks driving through Dardha on the road connecting Albania with Macedonia and carrying contraband in both directions brought Macedonian agricultural products into Albania.

Since agriculture was no longer a profitable activity, villagers sought new opportunities across the border. Not only was the Macedonian border closer than the next urban center in Albania, but the villagers did not face restrictions in migrating to Macedonia and taking up employment there (King and Vullnetari 2003: 32). Being ethnic Macedonians, they received preferential treatment by the country after it became independent from

Yugoslavia in 1991. Their ethnicity entitled them to unrestricted labor migration because of the weight the Former Yugoslav Republic of Macedonia accords to ethnic identity. From the viewpoint of the Macedonian state, an ethnic Macedonian was someone who was an Orthodox Christian, spoke Macedonian, and identified as Macedonian. The constitution of Macedonia specifically mentioned the "concern for the status and rights of persons belonging to the Macedonian people in neighboring countries" (Article 49).[13] It became common practice for the Macedonian state to grant citizenship to ethnic Macedonians living in Albania. This meant that virtually all of the villagers in Dardha had acquired dual citizenship by the time Johannes visited them in 2004.

The jobs available across the border proved highly attractive to the people of Dardha. Over the course of the 1990s a growing number of households began sending a member or two to Macedonia for seasonal employment. They took on jobs as masons, master bricklayers, and day laborers in agriculture. Although wages in Macedonia were not much higher than in Albania, it was much easier to find work there. By 2004, seasonal labor migration to Macedonia had become the most popular way to make a living in Dardha. The migrants usually worked in Macedonia for between three and eight months per year, and returned home during the winter. Of the eighty-one households in the village, forty-five had one or more members working seasonally in Macedonia and twelve had somebody working seasonally in Greece. The village population remained virtually unchanged after 1990, although many villagers were away in the summer.

When he became acquainted with Sterjo Shumka and his family, Johannes came to understand that the jobs in Macedonia afforded households a decent living but also imposed a heavy burden on the adults. Sterjo lived for nine months a year in Monastir, Macedonia, where he worked as a bricklayer or farm worker. His wife Drita stayed in Dardha together with their thirteen-year-old son. It took Johannes several attempts to meet her because she was extremely busy with agricultural work. Drita told him that she oversaw nearly all farm activities, including the cultivation of one hectare of agricultural land, and cared for more than a dozen sheep and goats. She told Johannes how difficult it was for her to tend to the land and the livestock alone, which typically required the work of more than one person, but she managed somehow, as did the other migrant households in Dardha. Her husband's income in Macedonia, some 500 euros a month, was important to finance their other children's education in Macedonia and Albania. The couple's three daughters lived with their father in Monastir, where they attended high school and university. In addition, Sterjo's income had allowed them to improve their house in Dardha, which appeared modern, with recently purchased furniture in the living room.

Less than one-third of all village households did not engage in seasonal labor migration because they had found ways to make a living in and around Dardha. Since agriculture was no longer profitable, they turned to different livelihood activities. For example, Jorgji and Para Andoni, a couple in their mid-60s who lived together with their 45-year-old son and daughter-in-law, enjoyed a good income from running a popular restaurant on the road leading to the Macedonian border. The restaurant had gained a regional reputation for the delicious carp it served. It opened every day in the early morning and always stayed open until late at night. It sold wine and raki (a locally distilled liquor), which the Andonis produced from their own small vineyard. The income from the restaurant was enough to send one of their grandchildren to university in the capital Tirana, and the other one to high school in a nearby town. It also allowed them to build and furnish a beautiful new house. Additionally, they were able to purchase a personal computer in 2004, the first one in the village—something that Jorgji repeatedly told Johannes.

The devaluation of agriculture caused people to look for new kinds of value they could attach to agricultural land. Despite the lack of profitability, not a single household gave up cultivation entirely. Instead, people looked to agriculture to provide a source of subsistence and a safety net. They understood that seasonal labor migration could carry significant risks as a key source of income, such as the possibility of no longer finding employment. To counterbalance the risks, they continued to engage in agriculture. They cultivated their fields to produce wheat for their own consumption. They also planted corn to feed their livestock, which they could then use as a source of meat. Agricultural production reverted back to subsistence.

Thus, the livelihoods of Dardha's villagers became just as transnational as those of their peers in Bagëtia. In both villages, opportunities and challenges arose due to increases in the flow of people and goods between Albania and other countries. On the one hand, the opening of the border provided unprecedented opportunities for employment and social advancement to villagers. On the other, it led to the influx of cheap agricultural products, which made agricultural production in the villages unprofitable and led villagers to revert to subsistence production. This was a particular irony in Dardha; some of the products making their way from Macedonia into Albania originated from the very sectors in which Dardha's migrants had found employment across the border. The link between the migrant's work abroad and the possibilities for making a living at home was immediate. Villagers' work as cheap farm labor abroad helped to keep the price of agricultural products from Macedonia low, thereby undermining the competitiveness of Albanian products—including their own.

Their transnational lives imposed a heavy burden on villagers, despite the amenities and educational opportunities migration afforded. The problem was that most households no longer had the labor to cultivate their land and raise livestock. Most adult men spent much of the year, and particularly the agricultural season, in Macedonia. Labor was chronically short in migrant households, a dilemma demonstrated by the Shumkas' experience discussed above. Drita and her thirteen-year-old son were on their own for most of the year, as Sterjo and the daughters lived in Macedonia. Nevertheless, the Shumkas found a way to overcome the labor constraint, as did other migrant households that we address in the following section.

Individualizing Land Ownership, Cooperating in Land Management

Unlike in Bagëtia, the implementation of the land reform in Dardha followed the legal stipulations of the 1991 Land Law. The villagers formed a land commission in 1991 and distributed the collective farmland on a per capita basis. Every household received approximately six parcels of land, although the exact land area depended on the number of people living in the household. The six parcels included cropland of different qualities and a vineyard. The result of this distribution was a highly fragmented structure of landholdings. The typical parcel of farmland was a thin stretch of land 15 meters wide and 150 meters long, dissecting the large plain on the shore of Lake Prespa into strips.

As the example of the Shumkas' experience shows, working the land was no easy feat for Dardha's households. The land commission conferred 1 ha of agricultural land to them in 1991. That was more than Drita could shoulder in her husband's absence, even though her son helped with some of the livestock husbandry. When Johannes met Drita in 2004, she told him how she and her husband had carefully considered their options and then decided what they wanted to do with their land.

Sterjo and Drita continued working the small vineyard originally planted by the cooperative and assigned to them in 1991. The vineyard was still productive, allowing them to make a significant amount of raki in 2003, most of which they sold to a bar owner in a neighboring village. The income from the raki was important because it helped them get through the winter months, when Sterjo could not find work in Macedonia. Without that income it would have been difficult for them to make ends meet. At the time Johannes met Drita, she was concerned about the upcoming winter because she expected a complete loss of grape production in 2004 due to mildew. If the harvest failed, Sterjo would have to go out on Lake Prespa and catch fish illegally to make up for the lost income.

The couple dealt with the labor constraint in two ways. On the one hand, they decided to abandon cultivation on a small parcel and allowed their fellow villagers to use it as pasture. They fenced off another small parcel, did not sow any crops, but cut the naturally growing grass for hay. Both fields had been cultivated with wheat, corn, beans, and tobacco under the cooperative. On the other hand, they managed to continue cultivating a large parcel by coordinating activities with the other villagers. Together they hired two or three tractors at the beginning of each planting season to plow all their fields at once. During the harvesting season, they repeated the practice with combine harvesters. The use of the tractors and combine harvesters helped them to reduce the labor requirements significantly.

Drita explained to Johannes that the coordination of fifty households was a difficult task. They had to come together to make the deals with the operators of the tractors and combine harvesters. Moreover, they had to be ready to react quickly on the day when the tractors and combine harvesters actually showed up in Dardha, because the drivers rarely committed to a fixed date in advance. If anyone missed them, the drivers would skip their plots and were unlikely to return later. However, working the fields individually was unfeasible for most, as the tractors and combine harvesters would not show up for the small fields of individual households, and would not even be able to access most fields without driving through neighboring fields. Without the use of machinery, the labor requirements would be egregious.

Coordination was a crucial precondition for the Shumkas so they could continue cultivating their fields, or at least part of them. Drita was able to grow wheat and corn in rotation with beans on their large parcel. However, since the destruction of the irrigation system in 1991 and because they did not use fertilizer, yields were low. Despite the low yield, cultivation was a welcome source of household subsistence to the Shumkas, just as the straw, hay, corn, and silage were important feed for their livestock. In turn, the livestock produced milk, butter, cheese, meat, and wool for consumption and use at home.

Like the Shumkas, most villagers solved the labor shortage problem by participating in the collective arrangements. Not unlike the cooperative era, this led to the recurrent sight of land that tractors plowed or combines harvested in entire blocks at once on the large plain on the shore of Lake Prespa, resembling the agricultural landscape of 1990 that villagers recalled. The large blocks worked by the tractors and combine harvesters were easily visible, unlike the fifty or so individual parcels contained in each block.

Not only did the agricultural landscape resemble the situation during the socialist cooperative but so did property relations. Property rights evolved away from the highly individualized structure implemented by the initial land distribution in 1991. Individual households continued to possess exclusive use rights to the parcels allocated to them in the sense that they were able to keep a significant share of the harvest and undertook minor work individually. At the same time, they were expected to honor collective agreements among villagers regarding crop choice and cultivation schedules and practices, which could collapse if a single household decided to do otherwise. Just a decade after the dissolution of the cooperative and distribution of land to individual households, villagers cooperated again in land management.

The villagers in Dardha did not cooperate in crop cultivation out of nostalgia for the socialist past, or out of any sense of camaraderie or unchanging collective spirit. Rather, they combined individual ownership with cooperative management because that made the most sense to them, as the transnational flows of people and goods deeply influenced livelihoods and property relations in Dardha. Property in the village reflected the combined influence of events across the border and the dynamics at home. Transnational processes similar to what occurred in Bagëtia muted the influence of Albania's Land Law on property relations in Dardha. However, unlike Bagëtia, Dardha's people never undid the initial distribution of land certificates.

Albanians Staying in Albania: Kodra

Judging from villagers' recollections, conditions in Kodra were relatively comparable to those in Bagëtia and Dardha in the late 1980s. This village of ethnic Albanians was part of a cooperative, with three neighboring villages, that produced a rich variety of agricultural products including grain, forage, fruits, vegetables, and tobacco, and which raised cows, sheep, oxen, horses, and donkeys. The cooperative infrastructure included a cultural center, an elementary school, cooperative stores, three irrigation reservoirs, half a dozen animal shelters, and two large depots to store the harvest. Adults in the village worked the collective land in brigades and looked after their own small gardens individually, just as they did in Bagëtia and Dardha.

When Johannes arrived in the village in 2004, he quickly noticed that the deterioration of economic conditions after the collapse of socialism was less pronounced in Kodra than in the other two villages. The change from state planning to market exchange had served Kodra better than the other villages due to its location in a fertile valley near a small market town. The village irrigation system had remained intact, for the most part, during the upheavals of regime change. Urban amenities and markets continued to be accessible, because the small town of Pogradec was close by and could easily be reached via a regular minibus service. Kodra still operated its own elementary school, reopened its mosque, and built a new evangelical church. The existence of four grocery stores, three bars and a restaurant, a garage, a doctor, and even a private language school testified to the dynamism of the village.

Despite the good conditions, most households were only part-time farmers and derived their main cash income from sources outside agriculture. More than half of all 312 households residing in the village in 2004 received their main cash income from jobs in the construction or service industries in Pogradec.[14] Nearly one in six households stayed in cultivation on a full-time basis; they practiced small-scale commercial agriculture, cultivating a diverse mix of cash crops, such as grapes, vegetables, and fruit trees.

Lefter and Vaçe Sherifi ran one of the enterprising households that combined cultivation with additional activities, thereby generating a sizable income. They produced wine and raki from a vineyard that they owned and from additional land rented from another household. The couple were proud of their wine and raki, and of the economic success they had achieved with their products. The wine was excellent, as Johannes was to discover when Lefter insisted that he sample several kinds of wine with him, turning the planned interview into one of Johannes's most enjoyable experiences in Kodra.

Lefter and Vaçe operated a "mini-cantina," as villagers called small wineries and distilleries. They used it to process their own grapes as well as those purchased from neighbors who undertook agriculture on a part-time basis but did not produce any wine or raki themselves. They sold their products to the owners of bars and restaurants in the surrounding area, earning an income of around 3,600 euros a year. In addition, they made money by producing onions and tomatoes in a field near their house. Similar to the small producers described by Nicholson, they sold the vegetables themselves at the agricultural market in Pogradec, making approximately 1,100 euros a year (Nicholson 2003). They also cultivated beans, cherries, apples, quinces, potatoes, and corn, and fattened a cow every year, but they used it for their own consumption only.

The Sherifis did well and did not feel compelled to pursue any employment abroad or outside their village. Their income was more than enough to sustain Lefter and Vaçe together with their two sons aged eight and fourteen, and Lefter's parents, who received a small pension. In the future, Lefter told Johannes, they wanted to expand agricultural production.

They still had another plot of land located on a steep hill in a remote part of Kodra, which they had not yet brought under cultivation. There, they planned to cultivate grapes and had saved sufficient surplus to invest back into production.

Lefter did not want to go abroad after he had worked in Greece in 1997. He had tried migration after they had been forced to sell off their entire livestock due to the declining profitability of livestock husbandry. He went to Greece to pick peaches and returned after one season, bringing back sufficient savings to fund the purchase of their winery and distillery. Yet he lost all desire to go abroad again because he disliked the vagaries of working and living abroad, and their activities back home afforded them a sizable income.

Migration was a far less significant source of livelihood for households in Kodra than in the other two villages. Overall, less than a quarter of all households reported to Johannes that income from seasonal migration or remittances constituted their main source of cash income. The low number of households living primarily on remittances indicated a comparatively low level of emigration; only slightly more than a half of all households in Kodra had one or more members permanently or seasonally working abroad—compared to 84 percent in Bagëtia and 70 percent in Dardha.

A primary cause of the comparatively low emigration rate was the Greek immigration law, which remained restrictive for most Albanians, the exceptions being the Vlach and Greek minorities. Albanians without an employment history in Greece could not obtain a visa to enter the country. Migrants who had worked in Greece previously could obtain visas for a three-month period only. Villagers pointed out to Johannes that to extend their visa for each additional three-month period they had to overcome bureaucratic hurdles and pay a fee of 150 euros, which was a substantial expense. Compared to the regulations pertaining to members of the Vlach minority, who easily obtained a three-year working visa, the disadvantage for ethnic Albanians was obvious. In addition, even if they held proper visas, Albanians were sometimes turned back at the border or had their visas cancelled by Greek police without cause (see also Nicholson 2002, 2004).

Immigration law was only one factor influencing villagers' decisions to migrate. Another factor that worked to discourage migration, or even ruled it out for some people, was the severe discrimination that ethnic Albanians faced in Greece. This was of great concern to villagers in Kodra.[15] Some migrants from Kodra reacted by leaving Greece for Italy, because they expected better conditions there. Yet, even there negative attitudes towards Albanians went hand in hand with increasingly restrictive immigration policies. The Bossi-Fini Law of 2002 was a clear expression of the growing anti-immigrant sentiments and policy in Italy; while permitting further regularization, it criminalized undocumented migration and widened the rules for expulsion.[16]

However, despite the restrictive immigration laws and discrimination, a significant number of villagers continued to find their way into Greece and other neighboring countries (see also Nicholson 2002). Many of them crossed the border to Greece illegally. Most already knew the route through the mountains from past experience. Others chose to go with local smugglers who took them to Greece via Macedonia for the price of 900 euros per person. They were ready to pay this hefty fee because they calculated that two months of good work would cover the cost of the trip. In particular, compared to working in agriculture or other sectors at home, migration was more attractive to young men. One young migrant commented to Johannes that people in Kodra "still work the land with the plow and donkeys like in the olden days." In Greece, he said, they "have money in the pocket everyday," despite Greek immigration laws and discrimination. "And thus the young go to Greece."

These insights show that agricultural land retained its value as a productive resource in Kodra to a larger extent than in the other villages. Agriculture remained a significant source of income and subsistence as a result of the impediments to migration and the comparatively favorable conditions for agriculture and off-farm employment in Kodra. Among village households, a variety of livelihood strategies emerged, each of which depended on particular combinations of migration strategies, agricultural production, and off-farm activities. Overall, villagers continued to value land for its productive functions because working the land allowed them to generate income and subsistence.[17] Because villagers stayed and land retained productive value, it also remained subject to intense contestations long after the initial distribution of 1991, as the following section shows.

Contesting the Legitimacy of Land Distribution

Similar to what occurred in Dardha, Kodra's land commission completed their work in 1991 by conferring *tapitë* to all entitled households. The commission distributed the collective farmland to the agricultural labor force in an egalitarian manner, giving households an area of land corresponding to their size. Kodra's households typically received four parcels of land: a field of the fertile land on the valley floor, a share of the collective vineyard, a plot with fruit trees, and a plot of cropland on the slopes surrounding the valley.

In contrast to Dardha, Kodra's farmers proceeded to farm their land on their own. They worked it individually because agriculture remained a primary source of livelihood which made land a valuable asset. The provisional land certificates issued by the land commission in 1991 continued to reflect the actual situation. Among the three villages, Kodra was the one in which the Land Law had been strictly implemented, and where property relations in agriculture still reflected the spirit of the land distribution mandated by Albania's first postsocialist government.

Nonetheless, the distribution effected by the land commission never found the unanimous support of the local population. When Johannes stayed in Kodra in 2004, many people asserted the legitimacy of historical rights to land. They said that land should belong to the people whose families had owned it prior to collectivization. Even though the land distribution had taken place thirteen years previously, many discussions in the village continued to center on the legitimacy of distributing land to the contemporary population. The topic remained highly controversial, as the following conversation, overheard by Johannes in a shared taxi, illustrates:

> Passenger: I'm for the return of the property that my father has left me and which belongs to me.
> Driver: But it has already been divided by the state.
> Passenger [insists]: It belongs to me because it's mine.
> Driver: What belongs to you? [Turning to the other passengers:] Hey, to whom does the land belong, to him or to God? [To the first passenger again:] The land belongs to God and He made it for Man, so it belongs to everybody.
> Passenger: My father bought it a long time ago, and the others take my land, huh?
> Driver [loud]: The state has already divided it, and if it's returned to the ex-owners, a civil war will break out, and Sali and Fatos will be declared "Enemies of the People."

At the time this conversation took place, Sali Berisha and Fatos Nano were the opposition leader and the prime minister, respectively. The driver clearly saw them as leaders in the national campaign for the restitution of land. "Enemies of the people" (*armiq të popullit*), in turn, had been a category created by the socialist regime to condemn wealthy peasants and deviants from the party line. People who fell into this category were publicly ostracized and lived a miserable life under socialism. It was the harshest treatment that the driver could think of for politicians who supported the restitution of land to historical owners. However, these strong words did not deter the passenger from insisting on his point:

> Passenger [louder]: They are assfuckers! If the state wants, it takes your land, and there is nothing you can do!
> Driver [conciliatory]: The state eats my shit, that's all it does! [But] what you want is that ten people eat and nine hundred others die. No, no, look [the taxi passes by a cemetery]; two meters belong to us, nothing more.

Contestations over property were not merely debates about what was right and what was wrong in people's dealings with land. Some villagers took things into their own hands, as Maks Dulellari had done in Bagëtia. For many years, Hassan and Mira Proni, for instance, became embroiled in a dispute over an agricultural parcel. The elderly couple, who were in their sixties, had received the parcel adjacent to their home from the land commission in 1991; the commission had certified their rights to the land in a *tapi*. However, neither the land commission's decision nor the certificate prevented Bujar Sherifi, a fellow villager, from claiming the plot for his own household. Bujar based his claims on historical rights he held to the plot, and threatened to destroy any crops planted by the Pronis. The couple responded by filing several complaints with the commune administration and the Pogradec deputy to the national parliament, but their efforts were in vain. Bujar, who had been the head of the commune council in the past, never felt compelled to concede.

Therefore, property relations regarding agricultural land remained contested in Kodra as they did in many other villages of Albania (Lemel 1998). Many pre-collectivization landowners refused to give up on the claims to their ancestral land, similar to the demands made by Maks Dulellari and other villagers in Bagëtia in 1991. Although they did not succeed in cancelling land distribution or achieving a general restitution—unlike in Bagëtia—they continued to contest the legitimacy of the 1991 distributions with some success. In some cases where people were unable to reclaim ancestral land, their claims nonetheless caused sufficient concerns or fears for the landholders, enough to cause social conflict and hamper agricultural production. This was the case with the Pronis, who could not work the field next to their house due to Bujar's threats. This also affected Lefter and Vaçe Sherifi; they did not dare to plant grapes on one of their plots because they feared restitution claims. As observed by Lemel, the same situation occurred in many Albanian villages (Lemel 1999, 2000). The ongoing contestations over the legitimacy of distribution reduced the security of property rights to agricultural land and dampened agricultural investment.

The debates over restitution continued at the national level as well, lingering for years without resolution. The political parties in power started several initiatives to consolidate the land reform. In 2004, Albania's political leaders finally agreed on a draft for a new law "On Restitution and Compensation of Property." The proposed law confirmed the validity of the 1991 distributions but instituted procedures for the compensation of historical owners. Four years later, when Johannes visited Albania for the last time, the law was still awaiting implementation (World Bank 2006; European Parliament 2008).

These ongoing local and national debates on the 1991 land distributions were not only about competing material interests but also different "ideologies of property rights" (Hann 1993).[18] People contested the legitimacy of distribution and the need for restitution so vigorously because the allocation of land was an issue of social justice to them. Moreover, they adhered to different notions of social justice. To some, such as the passenger in the taxi near Kodra and Maks Dulellari in Bagëtia, justice meant restituting land to its historical owners as a way to undo the injustices of socialism. To others, the only just form of allocating land was to distribute it among the contemporary population fairly, as noted by the driver of the shared taxi.

Transnational Property and Ethnicity in Bagëtia, Dardha, and Kodra

In 1991, land commissions in Bagëtia, Dardha, and Kodra set out to distribute the collective farmland among villagers. They began with the assumption that people would continue to value the land as a productive resource. Yet the values villagers attributed to land changed quickly and in different directions. The people remaining in Bagëtia valued land as a signifier of belonging and historical justice. Dardha's villagers came to consider land as a source of subsistence to complement the cash income they derived from employment in Macedonia. In Kodra, land retained its value as a productive resource because households used it to generate subsistence and cash income.

As we discussed at the beginning of this chapter, the changing values regarding land were reflected in the village landscapes. The people who remained in Bagëtia ceased cultivating most of the slopes surrounding the village and instead grazed sheep, goats, and cows. Some only returned to Bagëtia on occasional visits to reconnect with the place of their childhood and ancestors. In 2004, Dardha's landscape still showed the large blocks in which villagers had worked the land under the socialist cooperative. Villagers retained the blocks and planted wheat and corn as dominant crops, because it allowed them to produce subsistence products without expending much labor. In contrast, Kodra's landscape had become fragmented; villagers set out individually to make productive use of the fertile land around the village to generate income and subsistence.

The values people attributed to land emerged from their efforts to make a living in the "new situation of transnationalism" (de Rapper 2005: 192). As Albania abruptly ended the self-imposed isolation of the socialist past, many people took jobs in neighboring countries in an effort to take advantage of new opportunities for economic betterment and social advancement. The available work and the quality of life abroad were attractive due to the structural disadvantage of the way in which Albania integrated with the rest of the capitalist economy. Villagers seized on the opportunities for work and a modern life abroad, while experiencing the devaluation of agricultural production and rural life back home. Some left permanently, but most sought to combine work and life abroad with a continued residence and productive activities in their home villages. They took on transnational lifestyles, maintaining various kinds of ties with their home villages while at the same time incorporating into life abroad (see also Levitt 2001).

The radical transformations of rural property relations occurring in the villages after 1990 took place in this new transnational environment.[19] They occurred through negotiations over property in Bagëtia, Dardha, and Kodra, but were shaped by events abroad. In the process property relations became as transnational as the migration practices conditioning them. In addition, the variation in property relations between the three villages reflected differences in villagers' migration opportunities as conditioned by the immigration laws instituted by foreign governments, the channels available for non-legal migration, and the discrimination migrants experienced in the receiving societies. Consequently, the association between property relations and ethnic affiliation was not as "homegrown" as seen in other Southeast European localities (Verdery 1996, 2005; Kaneff 1998).

Ethnic identities gained transnational currency as part of the same processes. The ethnic distinctions made in foreign immigration laws and applied in societies abroad influenced local discourses about identity and ethnic affiliations in the villages. This was similar to what de Rapper observed in villages of southern Albania (de Rapper 2005). The people of Bagëtia, Dardha, and Kodra came to see themselves increasingly as ethnic Vlachs, Macedonians, and Albanians, respectively, instead of simply Albanian citizens. Only if they identified as Vlachs did Greek immigration laws accord the people of Bagëtia the right to apply for long-term visas. By virtue of their Macedonian origins Dardha's people gained the right to reside in Macedonia, something that was not available to Vlachs or ethnic Albanians. Kodra's migrants faced the risk of discrimination in Greece if they were recognized as ethnic Albanian, in sharp contrast to the reception that Vlachs experienced.

Do these findings speak to a declining role of the nation state and national legislation with regards to property? They do attest to the limited influence Albania's Land Law had on property relations in the three villages. The Albanian government's and land commissions' efforts to stipulate and implement land legislation were partly in vain. At the same time, property relations did reflect the effects of some laws—for example, the immigration laws passed by the Greek, Macedonian, Italian, and other governments. These laws appeared to exert stronger influence on property relations in the villages than Albania's Land Law. Even within the new transnational situation, national legislation mattered for people's dealings with land. However, the laws and regulations that the Albanian government had issued with the explicit purpose of regulating property relations had only limited influence.

Negotiations over property took place in a new transnational environment, making property itself a transnational field. Another key influence on property originated from people's politicized recollections of the past. Social rememberings and invocations of the past played an important role in negotiations over property and value in the three villages, as illustrated by the weight that claims of historical possession carried. This influence of the past on contemporary property relations will be the focus of the next chapter.

Notes

1. Ethnic Albanians accounted for roughly 90 percent of Albania's total population in 2003. Other ethnic groups included Bosniaks, Greeks, Macedonians, Serbian-Montenegrins, Roma, Vlachs, and Yvgjets (Lastarria-Cornhiel and Wheeler 1998; Berxholi, Doka, and Asche 2003). These ethnic categories are obviously problematic as they hide variation within each group and overstate differences between groups. In addition, they tend to naturalize ethnic distinctions that are socially constructed. For insightful discussions of ethnic identities in Albania, see Schwandner-Sievers (1999) and de Rapper (2005).
2. On transnational migration, see Portes, Guarnizo, and Landolt (1999), Levitt (2001), and Levitt and Jaworsky (2007).
3. The argument draws on Stahl and Sikor (2009). On property and transnational processes, see the special section of *Anthropologica* guest-edited by Bertram Turner and Melanie Wiber (2009). The introduction to the section and its various contributions highlight ways in which transnational processes and forces condition rural property and access to rural resources, such as legal concepts embedded in global agreements, development projects, and the advocacy of international NGOs. Our interest here is narrower, as we focus on the transnational constitution of value and its implications for property.
4. See Sjöberg (1991) for a review of the agricultural and rural policies enacted by the socialist regime in Albania.
5. 'Tu qepemi maleve dhe kodrave ti bëjmë pjellore si fushat,' in Albanian.
6. This comparison (and similar ones involving the other two case study villages) is informed by a random survey of ninety-eight villages conducted in 2004. See Müller and Sikor (2006) and Müller and Munroe (2008) for key findings from the village survey.

7. See Sjöberg (1991) and OECD (1995) on the equalizing tendencies of the socialist regime's agricultural policy.

8. See Kodderitzsch (1999: 14–20) on Albania's trade policy after 1990, particularly the massive increase in agricultural imports.

9. See Saltmarshe (2001: 173–78) for an illustration of public deinvestment played out in two other villages of Albania.

10. Similar to the villagers, some Vlach organizations in Albania deny any shared historical origins with the Greeks. They take a 'pro-Romanian' stance, locating Vlach origins there and basing their claim on the apparent linguistic affinity to Romanian (Schwandner-Sievers 1999).

11. About 40 percent of Albania's original rural population in 1990 left rural areas between 1990 and the early 2000s (King 2005).

12. See Introduction to Part I.

13. Perry (1997) argues that the emphasis on ethnic identity in Macedonia reflected not only the country's recent secession from former Yugoslavia but also the culmination of a nation-building process that the country had pursued since the end of World War II.

14. See Saltmarshe (2001: 138–48) for a rich description of non-farm activities in two other villages of Albania.

15. Villagers' concerns matched reports in the literature of continuing discrimination, despite two regularization programs in 1998 and 2002, under which more than 300,000 Albanian immigrants were legalized in Greece (Fakiolas 2003; Konidaris 2005).

16. See King and Vullnetari (2003), Kelly (2005), and Carletto et al. (2006) on Albanian migration to Italy.

17. In hindsight, we also came to understand that villagers' valuation of land as a productive resource was a key reason why we ended up with Kodra as one of our study sites. We had asked Albanian colleagues at the Agricultural University of Tirana for suggestions about where we could discuss research on changes in agriculture and land use since the demise of socialism. They were keen to introduce us to Kodra because the village had come to serve as a "model" regularly visited by foreign research and development workers on their exploratory visits to Albania. It was easily accessible and perceived to demonstrate the viability of commercial agriculture. Kodra consequently was not only the destination of our own exploratory trip but also received assistance from USAID for the foundation of a farmers' association and two American NGOs on improved livestock races and credit.

18. Katharine Verdery refers to this as "ideologies of land ownership" (Verdery 1996: 163).

19. For a general discussion of property in a transnational environment, see the special section of *Anthropologica* guest-edited by Bertram Turner and Melanie Wiber (2009). See also related work on the effects of transnational migration on rural populations (Carletto et al. 2006), economies (Horvat 2004), and identities (Fox 2003).

References

Apostoli, Stilian. 2002. *Prespa: Zhvillime Social-Ekonomike* [Prespa: Socioeconomic development]. Tirana: Flesh.

Basch, Linda, Nina Glick-Schiller, and Cristina Blanc-Szanton (eds). 1994. *Nations Unbound: Transnational Projects, Postcolonial Predicaments and Deterritorialized Nation-States*. New York: Gordon & Breach.

Berxholi, Arqile, Dhimiter Doka, and Hartmut Asche (eds). 2003. *Atlasi Gjeografik I Popullsise Se Shqiperise. Atlasi Si Shqiperise* [Demographic atlas of Albania. Atlas of Albania]. Tirana: Shtypshkronja Ilar.

Bonifazi, C., C. Conti, and M. Mamolo. 2006. "Balkan International Migration in the 1990s." Demobalk Working Paper 8. Rome: IRPPS.

Brubaker, Rogers. 1998. "Migrations of Ethnic Unmixing in the 'New Europe.'" *International Migration Review* 32(4): 1047–65.

Carletto, Calogero, et al. 2006. "A Country on the Move: Internal Mobility and International Migration in Post-Communist Albania." *Albania Migration Review* 40(4): 767–85.

European Parliament. 2008. "Property Restitution in Albania." Briefing Paper—Policy Department External Policies. Brussels.

Fakiolas, Rossetos. 2003. "Regularising Undocumented Immigrants in Greece: Procedures and Effects." *Journal of Ethnic and Migration Studies* 29(3): 535–61.

Fox, John E. 2003. "National Identities on the Move: Transylvanian Hungarian Labour Migrants in Hungary." *Journal of Ethnic and Migration Studies* 29(3): 449–66.

Hann, Chris M. 1993. "From Production to Property: Decollectivization and the Family–Land Relationship in Contemporary Hungary." *Man* 28(2): 299–320.

Horvat, Vedran. 2004. "Brain Drain: A Threat to Successful Transition in South East Europe?". *Southeast European Politics* 5(1): 76–93.

Kaneff, Deema. 1998. "When 'Land' Becomes 'Territory': Land Privatisation and Ethnicity in Rural Bulgaria." In *Surviving Post-Socialism: Local Strategies and Regional Responses in Eastern Europe and the Former Soviet Union*, ed. Sue Bridger and Frances Pine. London: Routledge, 16–32.

Kelly, Ellen. 2005. "Lifestyles and Integration of Albanian Women in Bologna: Two Steps Forward, One Step Back?". In *The New Albanian Migration*, ed. Russell King, Nicola Mai, and Stephanie Schwandner-Sievers. Brighton: Sussex University Press, 29–64.

King, Russell. 2005. "Albania as a Laboratory for the Study of Migration and Development." *Journal of Southern Europe and the Balkans* 7(2): 133–55.

King, Russell, and Julie Vullnetari. 2003. "Migration and Development in Albania." Working Paper C5, Sussex Centre for Migration Research. Brighton: Development Research Centre on Migration, Globalisation and Poverty.

Kodderitzsch, Severin. 1999. "Reforms in Albanian Agriculture: Assessing a Sector in Transition." World Bank Technical Paper No. 431. Washington DC: The World Bank.

Konidaris, Gerasimos. 2005. "Examining Policy Responses to Immigration in the Light of Interstate Relations and Foreign Policy Objectives: Greece and Albania." In *The New Albanian Migration*, ed. Russell King, Nicola Mai, and Stephanie Schwandner-Sievers. Brighton: University of Sussex Press, 64–92.

Lastarria-Cornhiel, Susana, and Rachel Wheeler. 1998. "Gender, Ethnicity, and Landed Property in Albania." Working Paper No. 18: Albania Series. Madison, WI: University of Wisconsin-Madison Land Tenure Center.

Lemel, Harold. 1998. "Rural Land Privatisation and Distribution in Albania: Evidence from the Field." *Europe–Asia Studies* 50(1): 121–40.

———. 1999. "A Glimpse of Change in Albania's Post-Communist Coutryside." *Quarterly Journal of International Agriculture* 38(1): 21–34.

———. 2000. *Rural Property and Economy in Post-Communist Albania*. New York: Berghahn Books.

Levitt, Peggy. 2001. *The Transnational Villagers*. Berkeley: University of California Press.

Levitt, Peggy, and B. Nadya Jaworsky. 2007. "Transnational Migration Studies: Past Developments and Future Trends." *Annual Review of Sociology* 33: 129–56.

Müller, Daniel, and Thomas Sikor. 2006. "Effects of Postsocialist Reforms on Land Cover and Land Use in South-Eastern Albania." *Applied Geography* 26(3): 175–91.

Müller, Daniel, and Darla Munroe. 2008. "Changing Rural Landscapes in Albania: Cropland Abandonment and Forest Clearing in the Postsocialist Transition." *Annals of the Association of American Geographers* 98(4): 1–22.

Münz, Rainer, and Rainer Ohliger. 2003. *Diasporas and Ethnic Migrants: Germany, Israel and the Post-Soviet Successor States in Comparative Perspective*. London: Frank Cass.

Nicholson, Beryl. 2002. "The Wrong End of the Telescope: Economic Migrants, Immigration Policy, and How It Looks from Albania." *The Political Quarterly* 73(4): 436–44.

———. 2003. "From Cow to Customer: Informal Marketing of Milk in Albania." *Anthropology of East Europe Review* 21(1): 149–58.

———. 2004. "Migrants as Agents of Development: Albanian Return Migrants and Micro-Enterprise." In *New Patterns of Labour Migration in Central and Eastern Europe*, edited by Daniel Pop. Cluj Napoca: AMM Editura, 94–110.

Organisation for Economic Co-operation and Development (OECD). 1995. "The Albanian Agro-Food System in Economic Transition." Paris.

Perry, Duncan M. 1997. "The Republic of Macedonia: Finding Its Way." In *Politics, Power, and the Struggle for Democracy in South-East Europe*, ed. Karen Dawisha and Bruce Parrott. Cambridge: Cambridge University Press, 226–80.

Pettifer, James. 2001. *Blue Guide: Albania and Kosovo*. London: A&C Black.

Portes, Alejandro, Luis E. Guarnizo, and Patricia Landolt. 1999. "Introduction: Pitfalls and Promise of an Emergent Research Field." *Ethnic and Racial Studies* 22(2): 217–37.

Rapper, Gilles de. 2005. "Better than Muslims, Not as Good as Greeks: Emigration as Experienced and Imagined by the Albanian Christians of Lunxhëri." In *The New Albanian Migration*, ed. Russell King, Nicola Mai, and Stephanie Schwandner-Sievers. Brighton: University of Sussex Press, 173–94.

Saltmarshe, Douglas. 2001. *Identity in a Post-Communist Balkan State: An Albanian Village Study*. Aldershot: Ashgate.

Schwandner-Sievers, Stephanie. 1999. "The Albanian Aromanians' Awakening: Identity Politics and Conflicts in Post-Communist Albania." ECMI Working Paper No.3. Flensburg: European Centre for Minority Issues.

Sjöberg, Örjan. 1991. *Rural Change and Development in Albania*. Oxford and San Francisco: Westview Press.

Stahl, Johannes, and Thomas Sikor. 2009. "Rural Property in an Age of Transnational Migration: Ethnic Divisions in Southeastern Albania." *Anthropologica* 51(1): 95–107.

Turner, Bertram, and Melanie G. Wiber (eds). 2009. "Paradoxical Conjunctions: Rural Property and Access to Rural Resources in a Transnational Environment." Special Thematic Section of *Anthropologica* 51.

Verdery, Katherine. 1996. *What Was Socialism? And What Comes Next?* Princeton, NJ: Princeton University Press.

———. 2005. "'Possessive Identities' in Post-Socialist Transylvania." In *Between East and West: Studies in Anthropology and Social History*, ed. Stefan Dorondel and Stelu Serban. Bucharest: Editura Institututului Cultural Roman, 341–66.

Vickers, Miranda, and James Pettifer. 1997. *Albania: From Anarchy to a Balkan Identity*. London: C. Hurst & Co.

Waal, Clarissa de. 1998. "From Laissez-Faire to Anarchy in Post-Communist Albania." *Cambridge Anthropology* 20(3): 21–44.

World Bank. 2006. "Status of Land Reform and Real Property Markets in Albania." Report of World Bank Office, Tirana.

2

Livelihood Traditions, Worker-Peasants, and Peasant Entrepreneurs in Romania

From Bucharest, one reaches Dragomireşti some twenty-six kilometers after the regional hub of Piteşti. The village of 2,852 inhabitants lies in a small valley in the foothills of the southern Carpathians. When Stefan visited the village for the first time in 2004, small houses built in the 1970s and 1980s lined the national road. Behind the houses, thin stripe-like fields cut through the valley, each just a few meters wide. Plum orchards surrounded the valley like a belt. The agricultural landscape was aesthetically appealing to Stefan, but it also revealed a trend of decline. Villagers had not tended the orchards well, and the fields at the back of their houses did not contain any crops that could be sold for a profit. Most notably, villagers had built very few new houses since 1990.

The entrance to Dragova is more dramatic. Visitors reach the village, which is located farther up the Carpathian range, through a narrow rocky gorge, which suddenly opens up, allowing a complete view of the village of eleven hundred inhabitants. High mountains sprinkled with dark green forests and light green pastures tower over the village, including the Piatra Craiului Mountains to the west. At the time of Stefan's visit in 2004, villagers kept cows and sheep on the pastures surrounding the village. However, maintaining livestock was not the only business in the village, nor was it their primary source of income. Newly built guesthouses and restaurants lined the village road. The village was clearly doing well, benefiting from tourists who came to enjoy the mountain landscape and the locally produced food.

The difference in village landscapes in 2004 demonstrated that the people of Dragomireşti and Dragova had fared differently after 1990, when Romania begun to divest itself of socialism. People in Dragomireşti continued to live in the small houses they had built in the 1970s and 1980s, and to work the land for subsistence. In sharp contrast, new guesthouses and restaurants crowded the center of Dragova, where many villagers had become entrepreneurs. The primary cause of the difference between the two villages was obvious: Dragova prospered because tourists came to enjoy the dramatic landscape, whereas Dragomireşti did not attract any tourists. The villagers of Dragova enjoyed opportunities that were not available to their peers in the other village.

However, the difference in opportunities did not fully explain the prosperity in Dragova or the decline in Dragomireşti. Another important factor was that Dragova's people proved able to take advantage of the new opportunities in tourism, while Dragomireşti's villagers decided to embrace subsistence agriculture. Though they both reacted to land losing its primary significance as a productive resource for commercialized agriculture, they nonetheless occupied different positions in relation to larger changes in land values, and consequently attached different kinds of new value to land. Villagers' different reactions to their new economic and political environments after 1990 are the subject of this chapter. We examine how villagers in Dragova were able to seek out new opportunities and to manage the risks of entrepreneurship, and what factors caused people in Dragomireşti to practice peasant agriculture.

We are particularly interested in understanding how local livelihood traditions conditioned people's reactions. Livelihood traditions were important because they provided a "system of dispositions" in the sense of habitus, and contained social recollections of past livelihood practices (Bourdieu 1990: 77). The people of Dragomireşti and Dragova had developed different traditions of making a living under socialism, and they harbored different social memories of what practices had succeeded or failed during the previous forty years. Livelihoods in the two villages followed distinct "practical logics" and had social memories of which ones had served people well in the past. Understanding these traditions will help us to explain differences in livelihood practices and, by extension, property relations between the two villages.

Dragomireşti: Peasants Becoming Workers

When Ceauşescu came to power in 1965, a new era began for Romania. The Ceauşescu regime aggressively pursued the industrialization of the country. It initiated massive industrial projects, such as the construction of giant steel factories and chemical plants (Casals 2002). The declared objective was to make industry the primary economic sector in Romania. Industrialization was intended to turn most of the country's millions of peasants into industrial workers, while the rest became workers in collective farms. As ambitious as the objective was, industrialization did achieve a drastic decrease in the working population employed in agriculture, from 74 percent in the late 1940s down to 28 percent in 1989 (Verdery 2003: 85).

One of the industrial projects undertaken in the 1960s was the Dacia car plant, located less than ten kilometers from Dragomirești. The plant was of great importance to the Ceausescu regime, which heralded it as the crown pearl of Romanian industry; it also held great significance for Dragomirești because it opened up unprecedented employment opportunities. Many young men took jobs at the factory, which paid well and allowed them to gain a higher social status compared to agricultural work. In the 1970s and 1980s, three large buses would arrive in the village to collect workers for every shift.

In addition, jobs at the Dacia plant were attractive because they allowed workers to make extra income on the black market. In 2004, when Stefan was in Dragomirești, people shared many stories with him about how they turned their jobs into sources of considerable wealth. Because car parts were extremely scarce in Romania's shortage economy, workers could raise their income significantly by smuggling spare parts out of the factory and selling them on the highly lucrative black market. Similarly, drivers could easily sell small amounts of the gasoline in their trucks for a premium. Of course, if caught stealing, workers risked being accused of "economic sabotage" and could consequently be sentenced to several years in jail. But that risk did not deter villagers from pilfering spare parts and gasoline. Villagers estimated that, at times, about a third of the total production was being stolen from the factory. They joked that they could build whole cars in their backyards with the pieces they stole from Dacia.

Women found employment on the collective farm, which had been established when the socialist regime collectivized agriculture throughout the country in the 1950s (Dobrincu and Iordache 2005). The farm raised bulls for the domestic market, grew fodder for the bulls in the fields around the village, and exported high quality plums from the village's orchards to Western Europe. In addition, the women worked small vegetable gardens and raised a cow or two on the land behind their houses. Even if their husbands and sons held jobs at Dacia, they still joined their family in this farm labor. The men worked alongside their wives or elderly parents before or after their shifts at the factory, helping them at home and with their duties on the collective farm.

Dragomirești prospered in the 1970s and 1980s. This was apparent to Stefan in 2004, when he walked down the village road. Following a common custom in rural Romania, the year of construction was displayed on the front of the houses. Most houses specified a year between 1970 and 1990. These two decades had been years of prosperity for the villagers because most men had jobs at the Dacia plant and most women had found employment on the collective farm. Looking back, villagers noted that it was sometimes hard to work at the factory or on the farm and then attend to the requirements of agricultural production at home. But nobody was ready to give up subsistence agriculture because it remained an important source of fresh food, which was precious in Romania's shortage economy. To villagers, industrial jobs, farm work, and subsistence agriculture together were the basis for a good life.

Villagers' lives were prosperous because they combined salaried employment with activities on the black market and subsistence agriculture. The villagers never fully met the expectations of the Ceauşescu regime to become rigidly defined socialist workers who staffed industrial plants and worked collective farms, nor did they abandon subsistence cultivation or black market activities. Instead, they made a decent living by becoming involved in multiple activities simultaneously and maintaining the ability to move back and forth between them. These kinds of livelihood practices allowed people to tap into value originating from multiple sources: the salaries and social entitlements that came along with the jobs at the Dacia plant and on the collective farm; the cash earned from the pilfering; and the agricultural products grown at home for self-consumption.

However, in the late 1990s, the villagers' advantageous situation was in danger. The Radu Vasile government sold a controlling share in Dacia to Renault as part of a larger privatization program demanded by the International Monetary Fund and World Bank in 1999 (Weiner 2001; Pop 2006). Part of the sale agreement was a reduction in Dacia's workforce from 27,000 to 16,500, which caused many people from Dragomireşti to lose their jobs. The privatization also put an end to the pilfering, because Renault quickly tightened the control of workers leaving the plant. The Dacia brand made an impressive comeback in the subsequent year with the new 'Logan' model, which Renault eventually exported to forty-one countries. Yet, in spite of this comeback, the people of Dragomireşti still suffered because Renault was no longer hiring new workers, and their livelihoods became greatly strained.

"We are Neither Entirely Farmers, Nor Completely Workers"

Villagers responded to the stress on their livelihoods by seeking out new ways to combine multiple activities. They held on to their jobs at the Dacia plant as long they could. They found new jobs in industry, services, or the state sector after the new owners of Dacia laid them off. They claimed the social pensions and unemployment benefits offered by the Romanian state, meager as they were. Yet most importantly, they all embraced small-scale agriculture. Like millions of other rural dwellers in Romania they worked the agricultural land that they had claimed in 1990, when collective farms broke up all around the country (von Hirschhausen 1997; Cartwright 2001).

In 2004, people told Stefan that nearly every villager had seized the opportunity to take up individual farming in 1990. When the collective farm of Dragomireşti broke up, no one wanted to wait for the government to pass a corresponding law that would have initiated the dissolution of the farm. Instead, just a few months after the fall of Ceauşescu, villagers took things into their own hands and decided to dissolve the collective farm. They claimed the small parcels that they or their parents had worked prior to collectivization. By the time the Romanian parliament had passed Law 18 on the restitution of land, all agricultural land in Dragomireşti had returned to its historical owners.[1] The land commission, which was set up by the commune administration, had little power and could only confirm the legality of villagers' practices. In most cases, the land certificates issued by the commission specified that households now owned several parcels of agricultural land which typically included a high-quality plot along the river, a lower-quality plot away from the river, and an orchard on the valley margins.

Thereafter, virtually all households set out to work their own land. Agriculture became a primary vehicle for them to enjoy the newly gained independence as individual producers. This is illustrated by the story of an agricultural engineer from a nearby village who tried to convince villagers to form an agricultural association. He provided sound financial reasons to do so, and told Stefan that "the work in an association is more profitable than what they [the villagers] are doing." Nevertheless, he gave up on his idea because people were not convinced on financial grounds. They did not embrace the idea of forming an agricultural association or even cooperating in small farming groups for other concerns. They refused the idea of an association; instead they argued that they would not give up their newly claimed land "for anything in the world." "I [have] had enough collective," Stefan often heard, "I want to work my own land now." Owning and working their own land meant a great deal to villagers, even if it did not generate any profit.[2]

As such, people continued to work the land even as they discovered that agriculture was not profitable. The fall of the Ceauşescu regime did away with the state support and favorable procurement system that had benefited agriculture up to 1989. Agricultural product prices fell precipitously between 1989 and 1991, and continued to decline in the following years.[3] The villagers now had to compete with cheap foreign imports (the same was true in Albania, which we discussed in Chapter 1). They realized that they could not earn any income from commercial agriculture, even though the underlying changes in agricultural markets and policy were not apparent to them.[4]

Villagers reacted by reverting to subsistence agriculture, which was a common response in many other villages in Romania and Central and Eastern Europe (Bridger and Pine 1998; Smith 2002; Meurs 2002; and Pickles 2002). They no longer exported plums to Germany or sold bulls in Romania. In 2004, only 2 out of 241 households sold any agricultural crops. The others produced crops and livestock for their own consumption only. Most raised a cow and a few chickens to supply meat, cultivated corn and grass to feed the cow, and grew potatoes and vegetables for their own consumption. A few also raised a horse to help with the heavy work, such as plowing and the harvest.

As people turned to subsistence agriculture, they began to conceive of land as a resource for the social reproduction of households. This became clear in a conversation Stefan had with Cornelia Macovei in 2004. Cornelia and her husband Mircea barely got by since Mircea had lost his job at Dacia. His unemployment benefit of thirty-two euros a month was not enough to feed them—not even in combination with the monthly welfare check of thirteen euros for their two children. They only made ends meet by engaging in subsistence agriculture. They worked the agricultural fields that they had successfully claimed in 1999, raised a cow, and tended the garden behind their house. They did not have any machinery to work the land and had to rely on their own labor. That was hard work, Cornelia said, but it produced much of the food they consumed at home.

Land sales remained rare in Dragomireşti because people held on to their land. Most of the sixty-seven recorded sales between 2001 and 2004 were for small plots that villagers bought to construct houses for their children in the future, and not for agricultural production. Land leases were unusual as well. Households would only rent out agricultural land if they no longer had the physical strength to work the land themselves. For example, Cornelia and Mircea leased a plot of 3,000 m² from an elderly couple, and in return they helped the couple with different domestic jobs, such as house cleaning and collecting firewood.

Thus, Dragomireşti became a village of "worker-peasants", resembling the village in northern Italy described by Holmes (Holmes 1989). There was, of course, great variation among villagers. Many did not find jobs in the economic depression of the early 2000s and instead hung on to meager unemployment benefits and social pensions. One villager became an agricultural entrepreneur, offering machinery services to farmers in southern Romania. But overall, Dragomireşti became a village of worker-peasants combining salaried jobs with agricultural work.

The resurgence of peasant agriculture reflected the influence of past livelihood practices. However, it was neither part of a straightforward "return of the peasant" (Cartwright 2001), nor the outcome of a simple "truncation of the household economy" (Meurs 2002). The resurgence of peasant-like practices did not reflect a simple return to livelihood practices from the 1940s because subsistence agriculture took on a new role in diversified household economies. It did not come about as a mere leftover from previously dual livelihood strategies under socialism, as villagers had tended most land as workers on the collective farm from the 1960s onward. Instead, underlying the transformation toward worker-peasant livelihoods in Dragomireşti were villagers' attempts to sustain livelihoods based on multiple activities. Pluri-active and hybrid livelihoods had proven effective under socialism, and villagers expected such livelihood traditions to provide effective guidance for tackling the uncertainties of life in a market economy. Their reactions reflected the influence of a particular set of 'practical dispositions' (Bourdieu 1990: 86), in particular the disposition to diversify sources of income and subsistence.

Looking for Value: The Social Life of *Ţuica*

The influence of people's livelihood traditions was not limited to their provision of a set of practical dispositions. Livelihood traditions were also at the center of people's rememberings of the past when they looked for new kinds of value to attach to agriculture. Agriculture no longer generated the values of the past: the orchards no longer yielded plums that could be exported, and the fields no longer produced crops that could be sold. This caused villagers to turn to subsistence agriculture to search for new material and immaterial values, something that became apparent through the role assumed by *ţuica* (locally distilled brandy) in agricultural production and social life.

Ţuica had been around for centuries in Dragomireşti. Villagers grew the key ingredient—plums—in the orchards surrounding their village. The village's men distilled the brandy using small-scale equipment in the back of their own houses. And both men and women drank it on many occasions, such as at weddings, funerals, and work exchange parties. Moreover, its production required special skills: one needed to select the best plums, maintain the fire at the right temperature, know the exact moment during distillation when *ţuica* turns sour, identify the right kind of barrel in which to keep the *ţuica*, and eventually open the barrel at the proper time.

Up until collectivization in the early 1960s, Dragomireşti had been known for its *ţuica*, as villagers proudly recalled to Stefan. Villagers grew plums in private orchards, made the wooden barrels used to store *ţuica* from the oak trees around the village, and sold it at nearby fairs. However, collectivization reduced the level of production drastically and took away much of its social significance. The collective farm took over the orchards, exporting the best plums to Germany. Farm managers confiscated all private distilleries together with other agricultural implements such as horse carts and ploughs. That did not put an end to the production of *țuica* in Dragomirești: a few men dared to produce it in small distilleries, which were now illegal. Yet most villagers stopped producing *țuica*, thereby making it a much less significant source of pride in village life.

Nevertheless, when Stefan visited Dragomirești in 2004, *țuica* was again an important part of social life. Women and men drank homemade *țuica* at important family events, particularly baptisms, weddings, funerals, and the *pomana* rituals at which a family offered food and *țuica* to honor the dead. People even believed that the dead would not depart if the *țuica* were not of the best quality at a funeral, and that the dead would be unhappy if their family failed to offer good *țuica* at a *pomana* ritual.[5] Therefore, men who had gained a reputation for making good *țuica* were welcome guests at the village's social events and were held in high esteem. More importantly, villagers expected every household to make their own *țuica*.

Home production of *țuica* became an indicator of social status in Dragomirești. When Stefan asked villagers about wealth differences between households, they repeatedly answered that poor households were those who drank *țuica*. That was puzzling to Stefan because he had observed that virtually every villager drank the brandy. During the first month of his fieldwork he was invited to several parties in the village, and witnessed that men expected each other to drink at such occasions. How could villagers claim that only the poor imbibed? It took Stefan another couple of weeks to understand that what his respondents meant was that only poor villagers drank brandy *in local bars*. They consumed *țuica* in bars because they did not own any orchards and therefore could not produce brandy at home. Many villagers would not drink *țuica* when going out because the brandy sold in the bars was cheap and of bad quality.

Not surprisingly, a member of the communal council came out at the top of the wealth ranking conducted by Stefan because he was considered to make the best *țuica* in the village. People explained that the household owned a significant number of plum trees, allowing the councilor to select the best plums for his *țuica*. He did not have to use any of the lower-quality plums, which spoilt the *țuica* made by households with small orchards. As a result, the councilor was always invited to the social functions that followed formal council meetings. He was the one who supplied the *țuica* at the functions—something no one felt in the position to contest. The councilor drew pride from his *țuica*, and his words carried considerable weight in the council's deliberations. In addition, he was considered not to have a single enemy either in the council or the village, which was an exceptional achievement in the everyday politics of Dragomireşti.

The social significance of *ţuica* explained the failure of an outside investor who sought to purchase orchards in 2002. That year a business man interested in buying a significant area of plum orchards approached a series of villagers. Since many villagers had clearly not invested money in developing their orchards, he was hopeful that he could convince the villagers to sell. Some of the plum trees had grown old, thus producing fewer plums, and plums of lesser quality. The prospective investor was ready to pay a decent price for the orchards, because he wanted to capitalize on the region's reputation for *ţuica*. In the end, not a single villager agreed to sell plum trees to him. The orchards were too important to them for the social status attached to the home production of *ţuica*.

The "social life" (Appadurai 1986) of *ţuica* indicates how villagers found new value in subsistence agriculture.[6] This value was partially material, as the self-produced food and liquor allowed villagers to save on consumptive expenditures. Yet it was also immaterial, as subsistence production became a new source of meaning and pride to villagers. As agriculture lost the values of the past, villagers revalorized the cultivation of land and livestock husbandry in a new way. Their subsistence practices may have looked like desperate strategies of household survival from the vantage point of the monetary economy (see also Standing 2002), yet they created new kinds of material and immaterial value; villagers considered subsistence agriculture as a proper and desirable productive activity, even though the work was hard and garnered little monetary reward.[7] The new kinds of value were not that "new" after all, since they emerged from people's practical expertise in the production of *ţuica* and their rememberings of the past.

The Shepherds of Dragova

In contrast to Dragomireşti, agriculture was never collectivized in Dragova. The socialist regime tried collectivization in the late 1950s but quickly gave up, just as happened in many other villages located in the hilly and mountainous regions of Romania (Rizov et al. 2001; Verdery 2003: 34). Dragova's households continued to own agricultural plots and to manage them individually as they had done for many generations. Their primary activity was to raise sheep and cattle, which they kept in stables in the vicinity of their houses. They managed pastures on the steep slopes for the production of hay, and sent their sheep up the mountain in the summer.

Paul Cornea was one of the shepherds who took people's sheep up the mountain during the last summers of the socialist regime. Additionally, until 1989, Paul had been in charge of animal health in the commune including Dragova and another two villages. When they met in 2004, he told Stefan that people looked up to him for his veterinary skills. He and five other veterinarians assumed important positions in the village because livestock were the main source of livelihood. In addition, his family owned six cows and a large number of sheep, and managed to work 5 ha of pasture.

Paul explained to Stefan why villagers' lives as shepherds had been good under socialism. The first reason was that the state procurement system had been favorable to shepherds. It had made certain that there was constant demand for villagers' livestock, milk, and wool. In addition, "the state" had guaranteed fair prices for their products in relation to the prices charged for produce purchased by villagers. The Cooperativa de Achiziție (purchasing cooperative) would purchase bulls and milk raised by villagers. Even though the stated price had been lower than what villagers could get on the black market, they had considered it a fair price because they could exchange the bulls and milk for cereals and corn at a decent rate.

The second reason was that people could sell some of their products on the black market. City people had always looked to purchase meat and cheese directly from rural producers, since these goods had been chronically short in the state distribution system. Moreover, Dragova and the surrounding villages had been famous for their smoked cheese for generations. Although there had been some risk of detection, because selling at a price above the one set by the state had been against the law and sellers could have been accused of being "speculators," people had found ways to minimize the risk. That had been easier to do for cheese, as Paul explained, because it could be kept over a long period of time. Villagers had used relatives working in large industrial enterprises to market their cheese, or developed good relations with people living in urban apartment blocks, asking them to distribute their cheese.

The marketing of meat had required villagers to develop significant entrepreneurial skills. It had been more difficult than cheese because meat was perishable. However, the difficulties had not prevented villagers from developing ways to sell meat on the black market. If villagers had wanted to sell, they would usually arrange the required car for the transport of meat in advance. Once the transport had been arranged, they slaughtered a calf or another animal, loaded it into the car in the middle of the night, and drove it straight to a black market retailer in the city. Such a deal was highly lucrative to villagers; a single calf could generate cash income in slight excess of a monthly salary in the state sector.

Paul confided in Stefan that after 1989 the villagers' situation worsened. The wool price dropped immediately after the state procurement system collapsed. "Before 1989, you could buy a car by selling the wool of a hundred sheep over two years," Paul indicated to Stefan. "Look at the prices now," he continued, and performed a simple calculation to make his point. Under the new price, a hundred sheep would yield a return of 250 euros over two years, which would not buy much more than a set of spare tires for an old Dacia. "Is this a right thing?" Paul asked, as he concluded his calculations.

Paul's family felt the pinch of the new market conditions and no longer made much profit from their seventy-five sheep. If everything worked out, they could make a small profit; but sheep were often afflicted by diseases, which could kill one out of five lambs at a time. And a significant part of his business depended on the timing of Easter. "Selling a lamb is a tricky business," he explained. "If Easter falls in early April, then you are screwed!" This was because lambs were still too small at that time of the year, and so did not earn a good price. But "if Easter falls into May," he said, "then you can gain good money."

Paul's story shows how Dragova's people had done well under socialism, as already described for other shepherds in Stewart (1998). This was true because they had been able to operate in the state procurement system and the black market simultaneously. The state system had offered them a fair rate between sales and purchases. The black market had allowed them to profitably market products in excess of what they had to sell to the state in order to finance required purchases. As was true in Dragomireşti, their livelihoods had been built on multiple sources. However, unlike in Dragomireşti, Dragova's shepherds had developed significant entrepreneurial skills in the direct marketing of their products. The sale of cheese and fresh meat on the black market had required initiative and networking skills that went way beyond those that had been required from Dragomireşti workers for the pilfering of car spare parts. These entrepreneurial skills proved very useful after 1990, as we will demonstrate in the following section.

Looking for New Value in Agriculture: Peasant Entrepreneurs

Dragova's shepherds reacted to the declining profitability of livestock husbandry in different ways. Some continued to do what they had done under socialism. Like Paul, they complained about the declining profitability of shepherding and continued to raise sheep and cattle as before. Others employed their entrepreneurial skills in the search of new sources of monetary value. They enlarged their herds, looked for new markets for their products, and hired workers to tend their growing herds, coming to constitute a new breed of "peasant entrepreneurs" in the market economy.

One of this new breed of peasant entrepreneurs was Severin Ungureanu, who was forty-three years old when Stefan met him in 2004. Severin started their conversation by talking about the history of his family. His grandfather, Nicolae, had been rich before collectivization. He had owned a mill, sawmill, bakery, some 40 ha of forest, and 50 ha of pasture. That had afforded Severin the possibility to claim 10 ha of additional pasture during the restitution process for himself and his wife Victoria, the maximum amount of land that a single household could get under Law 18.[8] In addition, his father had raised a relatively large herd of around a hundred sheep in the 1980s, allowing him to send Severin to college in the early 1990s. The land and the training meant that Severin was in a good position to compete in the new market economy after 1990.

Victoria and Severin enlarged the sheep herd they had inherited from his father to six hundred in 2002. They employed six poor men from Dragova and neighboring villages to look after the herd. The shepherds were constantly on the move with the herd because there was not enough pasture around the village. They moved the sheep over the mountain pastures of the southern Carpathians in the summers, and went to southern and southeastern Romania in the winters. The business went well, allowing Severin and Victoria to pay the shepherds around 200 euros a month, which was higher than the average salary in Romania. They also employed the workers to cut the grass on their pasture, using the hay to feed their fourteen cows.

Victoria and Severin concentrated all their efforts on the marketing of their products. Over the years, they had successfully diversified the channels through which they sold their products. Severin's greatest pride was that they had signed a lucrative contract with an Arab firm to export three hundred rams a year to Saudi Arabia. In addition, they had developed a favorable marketing arrangement for their cow and sheep cheese. They sold a large quantity of sheep cheese to a single intermediary, who would market it to supermarkets all over the country. The price they received under the deal was not the best, but it gave them a stable and secure source of income. Additionally, they sold some cow milk cheese on the market of Câmpulung, a town approximately 25 km from Dragova, and directly to tourists visiting Dragova. The threefold marketing arrangement worked well for them, as Severin explained. They had come to understand that it paid off to "sectoralize" dairy production: "I'm rich, I admit that, but I have worked hard for that."

Victoria and Severin even managed the challenges that agricultural producers faced as a result of Romania's pending accession to the European Union. They constructed a guesthouse to circumvent a new regulation from 2002 that outlawed the processing of agricultural products at home.[9] The regulation would have obliged them to use the services of government-licensed slaughter houses, which would have meant additional costs.

However, as guesthouse owners they were exempted from the regulation, which allowed them to continue making cheese and slaughtering livestock at home. They sold some of the cheese and meat to their guests, but a large part ended up on the plates of people elsewhere.

Thus, Victoria and Severin emerged as examples of a new breed of peasant entrepreneurs, similar to the "super-tenants" described in Verdery (2003).[10] They did not lease hundreds of small parcels of land like Verdery's super-tenants, but they employed several workers and had to negotiate the herd's access to hundreds of hectares for grazing. The peasant entrepreneurs did well because they knew how to detect new kinds of value and claim it them for themselves in the market economy after 1990. In addition, they were successful due to livelihood traditions in Dragova, in particular the entrepreneurship (see also Stewart 1998). Dragova's shepherds employed a more entrepreneurial approach in the search for new sources of income than villagers in Dragomireşti. The marketing practices employed after 1990 resembled the strategies that had made shepherding profitable under the socialist economy, particularly the combination of bulk sales to stable outlets with direct marketing to consumers.

Looking for New Value in Tourism: Socialist Entrepreneurs Turned Capitalist

The influence of Dragova's socialist history did not stop with villagers' general familiarity with entrepreneurship. Socialist developments also influenced villagers' individual life trajectories after socialism. For example, Severin benefited from the fact that his father had been a successful shepherd under socialism; he had gone to college, and inherited a large herd from his father. Another important source of socialist advantage was Dragova's Consume Cooperative because it allowed a few villagers to acquire skills and networks of significant personal benefit during socialism and thereafter. The cooperative's ex-managers were at the fore of villagers' increasing investment in tourism, and they became Dragova's leading tourism entrepreneurs.

Work at the Consume Cooperative in the 1970s and 1980s afforded the shopkeepers, waiters, and managers social networks and risk-taking skills not available to regular shepherds in Dragova. In the socialist shortage economy the jobs had required formidable entrepreneurial skills just to perform the regular duties assigned to them. The managers of Dragova's restaurants and guesthouses had also developed extensive networks with the managers of state units comparable to the networks developed by the directors of collective farms described in Verdery (2003). The networks had been important to the socialist managers because they helped them to source scarce items vital for their operations. Similarly, managers had developed considerable entrepreneurial skills when they ran operations "through the back door." They learned to judge who they could trust and who they could not, how to develop stable networks with purchasers, and how to hide the income they made from back-door sales.

One villager who had done very well in building such connections was Constantin Oprea. His family had a long tradition in the restaurant business. His parents had operated a small restaurant before collectivization; when it was collectivized in the late 1950s, they continued to work as managers of a bar and restaurant operated by the Consume Cooperative. They were able to send Constantin to the Economics High School, from which he graduated in the early 1980s. They also helped him to get a job at the Consume Cooperative's guesthouse, first as a cook and then as a waiter. In these positions and through the help of his parents, he acquired an extensive network of contacts and special entrepreneurial skills. Through his work he also met Cristina, whom he eventually married.

Their contacts and skills gave Cristina and Constantin a clear advantage after the state-run economy collapsed in 1990. The significance of the social networks and entrepreneurial skills became very important in the uncertainty and upheavals that characterized the early 1990s. Thanks to their business skills, they sensed early on that tourism could provide a new source of income for people in Dragova; even though only a few visitors actually came in the first years after the collapse of socialism, Cristina and Constantin recognized that the trickle could expand to a significant stream in coming years. They decided to open up a guesthouse with a capacity of fifteen visitors and a restaurant in 1993. Over time, visitors from Bucharest and other large cities filled the guesthouse and restaurant on many weekends and holidays. By 2004, when Stefan visited, visitors had to book a room well in advance if they wanted to come on a winter weekend.

When talking to Stefan in 2004, Constantin pointed out how their social networks and entrepreneurial skills had allowed them to deal with the risks of building up new businesses. Their parents' help and social networks had afforded Cristina and Constantin the possibility to take out significant bank loans on several occasions. They had started with a loan of 700 euros, but the last loan amounted to 3,200 euros. It had taken significant courage, he emphasized, to take out such big loans. The interest and repayment of principal cost them the equivalent of three fully grown pigs. Constantin explained: "That means, every month I could have bought three big pigs from the money I had to give to the bank." Yet he and his wife weathered the difficulties, which made him proud. They had become "winners of transition" because they had showed courage and worked hard.

Even though Cristina and Constantin did well, they did not give up agriculture. In 2004, they had owned a nice guesthouse and restaurant since 1993, built another, more modern guesthouse in 2005, and finally opened a third guesthouse in 2007. At the same time, they continued to raise three cows, five pigs, and twelve sheep, and worked the two hectares of pasture inherited from his father. They did not want to abandon livestock husbandry because it provided them with good meat for their own consumption and for their tourism business. Maintaining agriculture also allowed them to sustain multiple sources of income. Although both Constantin and Cristina had worked in the tourism business for almost twenty years, they had never entertained the idea of withdrawing from agriculture.

Cristina and Constantin exemplified another kind of entrepreneurship: one that reflected the influence of livelihood traditions similar to the peasant entrepreneurs discussed previously. Tourism looked like a new sector in the village economy, yet under socialism some tourists had already arrived, and a guesthouse and a restaurant had offered their services. The villagers taking a leading role in tourism investment had managed the Consume Cooperative's guesthouse and restaurants up to 1989, giving them an advantage over others when the new opportunities opened up after 1990. Comparable to the collective farm managers in Transylvania and Hungary discussed by Verdery (2003) and Lampland (2002), Dragova's socialist managers had acquired practical dispositions of taking risks, evaluating situations for business opportunities outside agriculture, and making decisions under uncertainty. They had also developed the social networks necessary to obtain critical resources, such as bank loans, and to access new opportunities outside agriculture. These skills and networks prepared them well for the new market economy.

Renegotiating the Meaning of Property

The turn towards tourism as a new source of value revalorized the land of Dragova. Its productive value for agriculture was still important to villagers, yet what came to matter more in terms of financial value was whether the land was suitable for tourism investment. All land located along the paved village road experienced a sharp hike in price because it was suitable for the construction of guesthouses, restaurants, and bars. The location of land took on a new significance as the price differential between accessible and non-accessible parcels rose dramatically.

The revalorization of land led to significant changes in property relations going beyond the observation that some villagers sold land and other villagers or outsiders purchased it. Land sales became increasingly common. A growing number of people from Bucharest and other cities came to Dragova to purchase land for the construction of guesthouses or speculative purposes. By 2004, nearly one out of every three households in the villages had been involved in a land sale registered with the mayor's office.

The rising incidence of land sales led people to renegotiate how property was defined in relation to land, as a heated conflict between two neighbors revealed to Stefan in 2004. The conflict had come about when the Mateescu family decided to construct a guesthouse on their land. Since the land was located close to the village road, the family wanted to take advantage of the rising number of tourists. In the process, they wanted to upgrade the dirt tracks connecting their land with the village road so that tourists could drive their cars straight to their house without getting their shoes dirty.

The conflict erupted when they told their neighbors, the Boerus, that they could no longer use the tracks that they had used since they were first made in 1903, and which were vital for them to move their cows to and from their house. The tracks were also crucial because of the possibility for the Boerus to enter the tourism business at some point in the future. In reaction, the Boerus simply refused to accept the attempted exclusion, as they needed the few meters of tracks to connect with the village road. The conflict had not arisen between the two families previously, even though the applicable legislation had changed thirteen years earlier. Law 18, passed by Romania's parliament in 1991, stated clearly in Article 108 that the occupation or trespassing of private property was a felony and punishable with a prison sentence of one to five years. The legal stipulation became relevant only after the Mateescus decided to construct a guesthouse.

When Stefan went with Dragova's vice-mayor to visit the families, he noticed that Tina Mateescu argued her family's case in terms of the law: they could do with their land as they pleased. Being a law student, she applied the concepts and employed the reasoning she had learned at college. Because her family possessed legal title to the land, Tina argued, they could decide its desirable use. They needed to have a good and clean access road to make their guesthouse inviting to tourists. They had already spent some 1,600 euros to hire a caterpillar for flattening the terrain, and they wanted to pave the new road. If they allowed them to trespass on a regular basis, their neighbors' cows would soil the new road and destroy it over time. "It is not an aesthetic view when you see dung on the road," she said in anticipation of tourists' perception.

Tina's motivations were not just about property but also invoked broader justifications of entrepreneurship and individualist capitalism. Tina said that she wanted to be sure that if the Mateescus invested, they actually did so on land that was their own and to which they held exclusive title. They did not want to spend money on "somebody else's property." There was a need to "individualize their property," she explained to Stefan. Her notion of land ownership was a thoroughly exclusive idea—one that bundles all rights to land within the hands of a single actor, the landowner.

Maria Boeru, her neighbor and distant relative, argued her family's case for using the tracks by asserting an inclusive notion of land ownership.[11] To her, the ownership of a particular parcel of land by one person did not exclude the possibility for other people to enjoy specific use rights to the land. She admitted to the vice-mayor and Stefan that the Mateescus owned the tracks according to the Agricultural Register. Nonetheless, she also showed them a document that had been signed by the two families in October 1973, which specified that her own family gained possession of the land underneath the tracks. Her family in turn had to help the Mateescus to build separate access tracks on their land, using their horse and cart to bring the necessary rocks. The signed agreement stated that it would be binding for all future generations. In addition, Maria said, one should consider that their great grandfathers had built the disputed tracks together back in 1903. Until today, the families had always maintained a good relationship. But if the Mateescus prevailed, she concluded in a dramatic ending, the Boerus would not even be able to move her old mother's dead body from the house to the churchyard.

The conflict between the two families shows that changes in property involved contestations over the symbolic meaning of property and the function of individual property rights in economic and social life, similar to the disputes witnessed in the Albanian village of Kodra (see Chapter 1). The conflict was as much about access to the tracks as about competing ideologies of property (see also Hann 1993 and Verdery 1996). The contestations in Dragova centered on the degree to which land ownership was able to accommodate overlapping claims by multiple persons—that is, to be inclusive of multiple actors' claims or exclude these in favor of a single owner. Some argued for the exclusive notions of individual ownership as stipulated in Romania's land legislation. Others made a case for an inclusive understanding of ownership, supporting the possibility that more than one person may hold rights to a particular piece of land, as was the practice in the past.[12]

Livelihood Traditions and Property Relations in Dragomirești and Dragova

Like their peers in Albania in the early 1990s, the villagers of Dragomirești and Dragova set out to cultivate their land. The people of Dragomirești filed their restitution claims with the land commission to get back the land lost during collectivization. In the absence of collectivization (and hence the need for restitution), the people of Dragova held on to their land. However, within a few years many villagers changed the values they attributed to land in reaction to the new political and economic environments. Facing a drastic decline in the profitability of commercial agriculture, they sought to use land in new ways that were beneficial, proper, and desirable to them. The people of Dragomireşti increasingly valued land as a source of material subsistence and pride derived from skillful production. Dragova's villagers went into large-scale livestock husbandry and tourism as new sources of value for land.

Livelihood traditions influenced people's search for new sources of value. Socialist livelihoods, as remembered by villagers, provided them with specific sets of "intuitions of the practical sense" (Bourdieu 1990: 86), in particular the shared tendency to engage in multiple activities simultaneously. In addition, the practical dispositions acquired under socialism caused villagers in Dragomireşti to seek out salaried jobs, whereas people in Dragova tried their luck in entrepreneurship. Another critical influence on people's livelihood traditions became manifest in villagers' representations of the past, particularly in rememberings about what constituted value. Local products such as *ţuica* and cheese emerged as key symbols in people's efforts to make sense of their changed economic and social lives. They took on a central role in production and village life because they provided people with a powerful way of knowing about the past and of constructing a present that possessed positive meaning to them.

Variation in livelihood traditions contributed to the emergence of "multiple geographies of economic practices" in the two villages (Smith and Stenning 2006). Dragomireşti turned into a village of worker-peasants as many villagers retained the preference for salaried jobs from socialism. They became worker-peasants because they appreciated the benefits of livelihoods drawing on multiple sources of income and subsistence. Dragova's villagers came to seek out new opportunities in commercial agriculture and tourism. The peasant entrepreneurs of Dragova combined new business ventures with subsistence agriculture, similar to the ways that had proven successful for them during socialism. A common trait of livelihoods in both villages was that they cut straight across the multiple geographies of economic practices. Dragomireşti's people were neither solely workers nor entirely peasants, while Dragova's inhabitants were neither exclusively peasants nor fully entrepreneurs.

The changes in value generated different effects on property relations in the two villages. Agricultural land was distributed relatively equally among households in Dragomireşti, as people valued it largely as a source of subsistence. In addition, there were very few sales, and the few rentals occurred between villagers. In contrast, there was greater inequality in land ownership in Dragova based on who owned land by the road and who did not. As villagers and a few outsiders came to value land located along the village road for its tourism potential, a lively land market developed. The price of land situated along the road increased, and this created opportunities for significant financial benefits for some but not others.

The revalorization of land profoundly transformed the meaning of property rights to agricultural land in the two villages. In Dragomireşti, rights to use land were closely tied to the obligation to cultivate the land as Verdery (2004) shows in another Romanian village. Once a household was no longer able to work their land, they felt obliged to pass it on to younger people who needed it to secure their subsistence. In Dragova, land was increasingly sold and bought between villagers and outsiders alike. Villagers viewed land more and more as a source of individual profit, and came to favor exclusive notions of ownership.

More generally, these insights demonstrate the many ways in which socialist pasts influenced contemporary property relations. As noted in the literature, recollections of the socialist past exerted direct influences on negotiations over property after 1990 (Verdery 1996; Cellarius 2004a, 2004b). Conceptions of proper dealings with land influenced by socialist ideas and practices influenced postsocialist claims on resources (Verdery 2003). Social networks and power relations developed during socialism conditioned access to land and other assets in the postsocialist countryside (Verdery 2003; Mungiu-Pippidi 2010). In addition, on the basis of the insights gained in this chapter, we suggest socialist pasts influenced contemporary property relations in more indirect but equally critical ways through the livelihood traditions that people had acquired under socialism. People's practical dispositions and their representations of socialist livelihoods exerted significant effects on negotiations over property after 1990.

Another central element in negotiations over property and value that we have raised in this chapter was the influence of people's ideas about their own personhood and identities. For example, the social life of *ţuica* was intimately connected with negotiations of male identities. Similarly, people's ideas about personhood were at stake when Tina Mateescu made her family's case for the contested land. Tina implicitly portrayed herself as an individualist capitalist, revealing the powerful influence of new ideas about how people ought to behave in Romania's market economy. It is this influence of ideas about personhood and identities on postsocialist negotiations over property and value that we explore in the following chapter.

Notes

1. Our account matches the one in von Hirschhausen (1997) about other Romanian villages where local-level decollectivization had preceded national legislation. Von Hirschhausen attributes much significance to these events at the local level, as they forced national policy makers to adjust legislation accordingly.

2. Another possible reason was that villagers kept up hopes that Romania's pending access to the European Union would bring about the disbursement of plentiful subsidy payments to them. Romania submitted an official application for membership of the European Union in 1995, and joined on 1 January 2007.

3. Macours and Swinnen (2000). The drastic fall in the agricultural terms of trade—the relations between agricultural output prices and the general price index—was due to various factors, such as runaway inflation, currency devaluation, removal of subsidies, and the liberalization of food marketing (OECD 2000; Weiner 2001; Csaki and Kray 2005; Csaki, Kray, and Zorya 2006). Total producer support decreased from around 50 percent in the 1986–90 period to a mere 3 percent in 1997 (OECD 2000).

4. Small producers did not compete on a level playing field. In international comparison, total producer support in Romania was well below the average support in OECD countries (OECD 2000). Domestically small producers faced significant hurdles in accessing state support, even after the termination of state subsidies to state farms and agricultural associations (OECD 2000; Csaki and Kray 2005).

5. See Dorondel (2004) on funeral customs in Romania.

6. Furthermore, these insights demonstrate people's uneven participation in this process. Social differences emerged between households, as illustrated by the ability of some to possess larger orchards and produce better *ţuica* than others. Differences also arose from different gender roles in the production of *ţuica*. The making of *ţuica* was closely connected with ideas about desirable male behavior and manhood. The social significance of *ţuica* obliged men to get involved in the distillation of brandy. Villagers also expected men to drink heavily at social events and work parties, something that was not expected from women, even though they often enjoyed a glass or two. It was perfectly acceptable for men to be drunk in public, which would have been considered highly inappropriate behavior in the case of a woman.

7. More generally, villagers emphasized the significance of good land husbandry, and judged each other in these terms. When Stefan asked villagers about a particular household, they would typically state if they considered them to be good land managers (*gospodar*) or not. See also Verdery (2004) and Sikor (2006).

8. Although agriculture in Dragova was not collectivized under socialism, villagers lost some meadows located near forests during the nationalization of forests (see Chapter 5).

9. See Fox (2011) for a discussion of new EU regulations regarding food processing in accession countries.

10. There were another four or five shepherds in the whole commune who had successfully enlarged their herds like Victoria and Severin.

11. See Sikor and Tran (2007) on the distinction between inclusive and exclusive notions of property. Verdery (2003) argues more generally that socialist conceptions and practices of property were highly inclusive.
12. The conflict between the two families lingered on after Stefan finished his fieldwork. He heard years later that one of the families had taken the other to court over the issue.

References

Appadurai, Arjun. 1986. "Introduction: Commodities and the Politics of Value." In *The Social Life of Things: Commodities in Cultural Perspective*, ed. Arjun Appadurai. Cambridge: Cambridge University Press, 3–63.

Bourdieu, Pierre. 1990. *In Other Words: Essays Towards a Reflexive Sociology*. Cambridge: Polity Press.

Bridger, Sue, and Frances Pine. 1998. *Surviving Post-Socialism: Local Strategies and Regional Responses in Eastern Europe and the Former Soviet Union*. London: Routledge.

Cartwright, Andrew. 2001. *The Return of the Peasant: Land Reform in Post-Communist Romania*. Aldershot: Ashgate.

Casals, Felipe Garcia [Pavel Câmpeanu]. 2002. *Societatea Sincretica* [The Syncretic Society]. Iasi: Polirom.

Cellarius, Barbara A. 2004a. *In the Land of Orpheus: Rural Livelihoods and Nature Conservation in Postsocialist Bulgaria*. Madison: The University of Wisconsin Press.

———. 2004b. "'Without Co-Ops There Would Be No Forests!': Historical Memory and the Restitution of Forest in Post-Socialist Bulgaria." *Conservation and Society* 2(1): 51–73.

Csaki, Csaba, and Holger Kray. 2005. "The Agrarian Economies of Central-Eastern Europe and the Commonwealth of Independent States." Environmentally and Socially Sustainable Development Working Paper. Washington, DC: The World Bank.

Csaki, Csaba, Holger Kray, and Sergiy Zorya. 2006. "The Agrarian Economies of Central-Eastern Europe and the Commonwealth of Independent States: An Update on Status and Progress in 2005." Environmentally and Socially Sustainable Development Working Paper. Washington, DC: The World Bank.

Dobrincu, Dorin, and Constantin Iordachi. 2005. *Țărănimea și puterea: procesul de colectivizare a agriculturii în Romania, 1949–1962* [The peasants and the power: The collectivization of agriculture in Romania, 1949–1962]. Iasi: Polirom.

Dorondel, Stefan. 2004. *Moartea și Apa. Ritualuri funerare, simbolism acvatic și structura lumii de dincolo în imaginarul țărănesc* [Water and death: Funerary rituals, water symbolism and the otherworld peasant structure]. Bucharest: Paideia.

Fox, Katy. 2011. *Peasants into European Farmers? EU Integration in the Carpathian Mountains of Romania*. Zurich: LIT Verlag.

Hann, Chris M. 1993. "From Production to Property: Decollectivization and the Family–Land Relationship in Contemporary Hungary." *Man* 28(2): 299–320.

Hirschhausen, Beatrice von. 1997. *Les Nouvelles Campagnes Roumaines. Paradoxes D'un "Retour" paysan*. Paris: Belin.

Holmes, Douglas R. 1989. *Cultural Disenchantments: Worker Peasantries in Northeast Italy*. Princeton, NJ: Princeton University Press.

Lampland, Martha. 2002. "The Advantages of Being Collectivized: Cooperative Farm Managers in the Postsocialist Economy." In *Postsocialism: Ideals, Ideologies and Practices in Eurasia*, ed. Chris M. Hann. London: Routledge, 31–56.

Macours, Karen, and Johan F.M. Swinnen. 2000. "Causes of Output Decline in Economic Transition: The Case of Central and Eastern European Agriculture." *Journal of Comparative Economics* 28: 172–206.

Meurs, Mieke. 2002. "Economic Strategies of Surviving Post-Socialism: Changing Household Economies and Gender Division of Labour in the Bulgarian Transition." In *Work, Employment and Transition: Restructuring Livelihoods in Post-Communism*, ed. Al Rainnie, Adrian Smith, and Adam Swain. London: Routledge, 213–26.

Mungiu-Pippidi, Alina. 2010. *A Tale of Two Villages: Coerced Modernization in the East European Countryside*. Budapest: Central European University Press.

Organisation for Economic Co-operation and Development (OECD). 2000. "Review of Agricultural Policies: Romania." Paris.

Pop, Liliana. 2006. *Democratising Capitalism? The Political Economy of Post-Communist Transformations in Romania, 1989–2001*. Manchester and New York: Manchester University Press.

Pickles, John. 2002. "Gulag Europe? Mass Unemployment, New Firm Creation, and Right Labour Markets in the Bulgarian Apparel Industry." In *Work, Employment and Transition: Restructuring Livelihoods in Post-Communism*, ed. Al Rainnie, Adrian Smith, and Adam Swain. London: Routledge, 246–72.

Rizov, Marian, et al. 2001. "Transition and Enterprise Restructuring: The Development of Individual Farming in Romania." *World Development* 29(7): 1257–74.

Sikor, Thomas. 2006. "Land as Asset, Land as Liability: Property Politics in Rural Central and Eastern Europe." In *Changing Properties of Property*, ed. Franz von Benda-Beckmann, Keebet von Benda-Beckmann, and Melanie G. Wiber. New York: Berghahn Books, 106–25.

Sikor, Thomas, and Tran Ngoc Thanh. 2007. "Exclusive versus Inclusive Devolution in Forest Management: Insights from Forest Land Allocation in Vietnam's Central Highlands." *Land Use Policy* 24(4): 644–53.

Smith, A. 2002. "Culture/Economy and Spaces of Economic Practice: Positioning Households in Post-Communism." *Transactions of the Institute of British Geographers* 27(2): 232–50.

Smith, Adrian, and Alison Stenning. 2006. "Beyond Household Economies: Articulations and Spaces of Economic Practice in Postsocialism." *Progress in Human Geography* 30(2): 190–213.

Standing, Guy. 2002. "The Babble of Euphemisms: Re-Embedding Social Protection in 'Transformed' Labour Markets." In *Work, Employment and Transition:*

Restructuring Livelihoods in Post-Communism, ed. Al Rainnie, Adrian Smith, and Adam Swain. London: Routledge.

Stewart, Michael. 1998. "'We Should Build a Statue to Ceaucescu Here': The Trauma of De-Collectivisation in Two Romanian Villages." In *Surviving Post-Socialism: Local Strategies and Regional Responses in Eastern Europe and the Former Soviet Union*, ed. Sue Bridger and Frances Pine. London: Routledge, 66–79.

Verdery, Katherine. 1996. *What Was Socialism? And What Comes Next?* Princeton, NJ: Princeton University Press.

———. 2003. *The Vanishing Hectare: Property and Value in Postsocialist Transylvania*. Ithaca, NY: Cornell University Press.

———. 2004. "The Obligations of Ownership: Restoring Rights to Land in Postsocialist Transylvania." In *Property in Question: Value Transformations in the Global Economy*, ed. Katherine Verdery and Caroline Humphey. Oxford: Berg, 139–60.

Weiner, Robert. 2001. "Romania, the IMF, and Economic Reform since 1996." *Problems of Post-Communism* 48(1): 39–47.

3

 Modernity, Fantasies, and Property
in Vietnam

Introduction

Anyone who traveled into the hills surrounding the Red River Delta in the mid-1990s would see that the two Dao villages of Than Con and Ho So had made productive use of their surrounding land.[1] Although the villages were some forty kilometers apart, people used the land in a relatively similar manner. Wet-rice fields sculpted the small valleys adjacent to people's houses into delicate structures of staggered terraces. Rice and cassava fields extended far up the slopes of the Luoi Hai and Ba Vi mountains towering over the villages. The fields and forest at various states of regeneration created a complex mosaic of different land uses on the slopes. Home gardens grew around people's houses, including a variety of food crops, medicinal plants, and fruit trees. The houses themselves were rather simple, constructed with wooden panels for the walls and palm leaves for the roof.

Ten years later, when Phuc traveled to the villages in the mid-2000s, he saw that these landscapes had changed drastically. In Than Con, rice fields and forest patches had all but disappeared from the slopes. The complex mosaic of fields, bushes, young trees, and forests had given way to a much more simplified and compartmentalized landscape. Tea plantations had popped up near people's houses and tree plantations intercropped with cassava covered many of the slopes around the village. The road leading into the village was still the same muddy track as it had been in 1995, though, and most houses remained built from wood and palm leaves.

In contrast, Phuc could drive his motorbike to Ho So on a paved road. Once he entered the village, he found fences of barbed wire, concrete walls, and iron gates along both sides of the road. Most of the gates revealed abandoned home gardens, deserted tea plantations, and chest-high grass and weeds. However, some gates offered the startling sight of wealthy "villas" built at the most eye-catching locations of the village. The other houses in the village were no longer simple structures made from wood and palm leaves, but most were now built from concrete, and proudly donned a second floor similar to the style of houses that had become popular in *Kinh* (ethnic Vietnamese) villages in the Red River Delta. Trucks loaded with construction materials and bulldozers roared along the road to help construct new houses. Stores offered electric fans, rice cookers, color televisions, and hi-fi stereos for sale to the homeowners.

As we observed in the Albanian and Romanian villages in chapters 1 and 2, these landscapes reflected the new values that villagers attached to land. In Than Con, villagers valued their land as a productive resource for commercial agriculture. They increasingly used the land to cultivate cassava and tea to sell. In contrast, residents of the capital city of Hanoi arrived in Ho So to search for land on which to build weekend homes. This was possible since the capital was only seventy kilometers from the village, and road improvements had eased the commute between Hanoi and Ho So. The buoyant land market encouraged most villagers to sell their house plots and gardens within a single year, leading the landscape in Ho So to become a "landscape of consumption," valued as residential sites and for recreational purposes (see also, Williams 1973; Neumann 1998). It was radically different from Than Con's "landscape of production."

In this chapter, we pursue an in-depth exploration of the dynamics driving the revalorization of land and the consequent changes in property relations in the two villages. We examine how the villagers of Than Con and Ho So repositioned their land in wider matrices of value, with a particular interest in the interactions between property and people's ideas about their own personhood and identity. To understand the latter we employ Henrietta Moore's notion of "fantasies of identity" understood as "ideas about the kind of person one would like to be and the sort of person one would like to be seen to be by others" (Moore 1994: 66). Moore's concept is relevant because the reference to fantasies "emphasizes the often affective and subconscious nature of investment in various subject positions, and in the social strategies necessary to maintain that investment" (ibid.). She suggests that the formation of identities requires investment by people—investment that takes the form of emotional commitments as well as the expense of material resources (see also, Berry 1989). People's fantasies and desires involve some degree of agency as they choose between different subject positions, but they also reflect the power of dominant and hegemonic discourses.

Commercializing Agriculture in Than Con

In 2004, village elders told Phuc that cassava had been around for several decades. Villagers planted the edible root, also called yuca or manioc, for the first time in the late 1960s, when they established Than Con at its current location. They experimented with cassava as a substitute crop for rice on their shifting cultivation (or swidden) fields in the uplands with the encouragement of extension staff sent by the Agricultural Office of Thanh Son district.[2] However, villagers did not like the cassava, the elders said, and focused on the cultivation of rice swiddens on the slopes of Luoi Hai Mountain.[3] Villagers also formed an agricultural cooperative, built terraces and cultivated wet-rice (or 'paddy' as it is commonly called) as instructed by the extension officers. They only returned to cassava in the 1980s when rice yields declined. Cassava became a convenient crop because it grew on the degraded soils, could be harvested virtually at any time, and provided nutritious animal feed. In addition, it served villagers as a buffer crop against unexpected rice shortages, since they could leave cassava in the fields for up to three years.

Villagers recounted that the cultivation of cassava underwent a radical transformation around the year 2000 as they began to produce it for sale. New varieties promised a doubling of yields if producers applied chemical inputs and short rotations (Ngo The Dan 2000). In reaction, a growing number of villagers harvested all plants at once at the end of the growing season. By 2004, when Phuc spent extended periods in Than Con, a few households even purchased chemical fertilizer for their cassava fields in order to raise yields. This practice had been unimaginable to them just a few years earlier when cassava was popular as a low-maintenance crop. Cassava was attractive to villagers because they could easily sell the crop to outside traders. Vietnam's rapidly growing food processing and animal feed industries demanded increasing supplies of starch, for which cassava was a cheap source.

In contrast to cassava, tea was a new crop to villagers. Villagers told Phuc how, in 1993, the first households decided to plant a few bushes of tea out of sheer curiosity. The first small tea plantations were merely one among the experiments that households commonly undertook in Than Con, just like other farmers across the world. In subsequent years, others followed after they saw their fellow villagers succeed. They purchased seedlings from the Phu Da Company located four kilometers from the village, sought advice from its workers, and established small plantations next to their houses. Once they harvested the first tea, they actively sought out market outlets, carrying the fresh leaves to the purchase points operated by processing companies along the main road. Toward the late 1990s the

Agricultural Office in the district center offered new varieties, free training, chemical fertilizer, and subsidized credit to farmers who wanted to plant tea. The state support allowed villagers to raise the productivity of their plantations and to reduce the number of years between the point of planting and the first harvest from three to two years. The increases in yield caused many households to invest significantly in production by applying increased amounts of chemical fertilizer, pesticides, and insecticides. By the time Phuc stayed in the village there was plenty of demand for their fresh tea leaves, from within Vietnam and abroad. Two large processing companies, one a joint venture between Vietnam and Iraq and the other owned by a Belgian company, were located in the same province of Phu Tho as Than Con. In addition, the companies competed with two more factories owned by the provincial People's Committee and forty-five small, private workshops for the purchase of tea.

The changes in farming practices in the 1990s were antecedents to much larger social and economic transformations in the 2000s, in particular the commercialization of agriculture. In the second half of the 1990s, villagers undertook limited efforts to produce a marketable surplus in agriculture in addition to covering their own subsistence requirements. By 2004 many villagers were no longer emphasizing their own subsistence needs but focusing on generating monetary returns from agriculture. Tea and cassava had become major cash crops. In 2004, nine out of ten households in Than Con grew tea, managing an average plantation of nine *sao*.[4] Nearly every household grew cassava for sale, thus making the cassava sales, the second largest source of income in the village, surpassed only by tea. Tea and cassava were as popular in Than Con as they were with villagers across other parts of Vietnam's northern midlands, the hilly region extending around the Red River Delta. Small-scale tea producers, such as the villagers of Than Con, made Phu Tho province one of the centers of tea production in the country, and helped Vietnam become one of the leading producers of cassava in the world.[5]

Consequently, Than Con experienced a broad transformation from subsistence cultivation to commercial agriculture in the decade between 1995 and 2005. Villagers changed the way they grew cassava and turned to tea as a new cash crop. The changes in cultivation practices were connected with improvements in villagers' access to agricultural product markets, crop varieties, information, inputs, and credit. In addition, they were made possible by the allocation of wet-rice land from the previous agricultural cooperative to individual village households in the late 1980s, and the transfer of upland fields to households implemented by the district-level Forest Protection Unit in the mid-1990s. Nevertheless, the changes in the larger political economic environment were only part of the unfolding dynamics. The transformation from subsistence cultivation to commercial agriculture occurred because villagers embraced the new opportunities available to them as the following story will illustrate.

"I save every single Dong to invest"

When Phuc first visited Than Con in 2001, he met an enterprising young couple, Trieu Van Thu and Nguyen Thi Tin. They impressed him with their ability to make a good living even though they had to take care of two small children aged four and seven. To his surprise, the couple had even decided not to work any paddy fields. This was rather uncommon in rural Vietnam, especially in remote areas such as Than Con, because villagers generally grew rice so they could eat it rather than anh Thu and chi Tin who were purchasing it for consumption and not growing it at all.[6] Furthermore, the couple had not taken up off-farm jobs in contrast to their peers in Albania and Romania (see chapters 1 and 2). Instead, anh Thu and chi Tin spent their time and energy on their tea plantation and on several plots in which they intercropped cassava with trees. Anh Thu told Phuc: "I save every single Dong to invest."

In previous years, the couple had skillfully acquired new land to grow tea and cassava, and they continued to do so. Anh Thu purchased seven *sao* of land from a fellow villager after the district People's Committee had distributed agricultural land to households in Than Con at the end of the 1980s. He successfully requested the allocation of two additional plots, totaling 3.5 hectares (ha), when the district Forest Protection Unit distributed forestland in 1996. After their marriage in 1997, anh Thu and his wife began planting tea on the purchased land and some of the allocated forestland. By 2004, their tea plantation had grown to a little more than 1 ha. The couple intercropped cassava with trees on some 8 ha of forestland, consisting of three parcels. They leased two of the parcels from fellow villagers and had permission from anh Thu's brother to use the third temporarily.

Anh Thu and chi Tin stood out among their fellow villagers because they actively pursued opportunities to generate profit in agriculture and invest it back into production. They wanted to make a financial profit on the labor they expended on production, which was a concept they learned on the training courses offered by the Agricultural Office. They tried to avoid wasting their scarce labor on activities that did not yield sufficient profit. They also sought to use as much of the profit as possible for productive reinvestment. For chi Tin and anh Thu it was no longer important to produce enough food to eat at home. They had never bothered to work paddy, even though the land purchased from fellow villagers included a small paddy field, and even though anh Thu's father had given them another small paddy field in 2001. Stretched for labor, they leased the two fields to other households in the village. "Rice is always available in the market nowadays," anh Thu commented to Phuc; "as long as you have money, you can buy as much as you want."

Talking with Phuc, anh Thu strongly identified with their emphasis on profit and investment. They were "doing a good job nowadays," he confided. Mirroring the message conveyed in the information brochures distributed by the Agricultural Office, anh Thu saw himself as a good farmer, and wanted Phuc to see him as such. He explained: "I have tried, [but] realize that paddy cultivation is labor intensive. Livestock production is not profitable. Raising pigs needs labor and feed. Raising cattle needs labor to tend." These activities could not compare with their tea and cassava plantations, for which chi Tin and anh Thu saved every single Dong. They did not want to spend any profit on unproductive activities. Anh Thu emphasized to Phuc that it was their choice to live in a simple wooden house, even though they made a profit of about 400 euros each year. The only other activity besides tea and cassava that generated comparable returns from their labor was the large fish pond next to their house, "because a fish only eats grass and drinks water."

The conversation with anh Thu demonstrates that the two young people saw themselves, and wanted to be seen, as commercial farmers. They not only lived their particular "fantasy of identity" (Moore 1994), but they also invested significant material and symbolic resources into acquiring it. They invested their earnings into production and lived a frugal life. They worked hard as they sought to maximize the profit made in agricultural production. Their focus on profit and investment made them stand out in Than Con, where such a strategy had been unthinkable just a decade earlier. Their dream of becoming commercial farmers would have been equally groundbreaking in other upland villages of Vietnam, as the production of subsistence remained a primary concern to many households (Le Trong Cuc and Rambo 2001). Yet it matched the image of the commercial farmer propagated in government publications and the media. It was no coincidence that anh Thu described his success in the same terms as the numerous newspaper columns and television reports on people "doing a good job." The discourse of commercial farming was hegemonic in rural Vietnam.

Tin, Thu, and other villagers felt proud of their achievements because they had long experienced economic and cultural disadvantages. In the early 1990s, villagers barely managed to produce enough food and income to ensure their subsistence. Their economic situation was similar to that in many other upland villages, where the level of economic activity was far lower than that in lowland villages and urban areas (Rambo 2005). Many Dao, in particular, lived at high elevations and experienced material difficulties, with more than 70 percent of them living below the national poverty line (Asian Development Bank et al. 2003). In addition, the villagers faced cultural stereotypes because they belonged to an ethnic minority group. The Kinh majority and central government generally stigmatized ethnic minorities. They blamed the low levels of economic activity among ethnic minorities on their supposed backwardness and resistance to change (Jamieson, Cuc Le Trong, and Rambo 1998; Michaud and Turner 2000; Rambo 2005). Dao were considered particularly backward because they employed a primitive form of production in the 1990s: swidden cultivation (Trinh 1995; Be Viet Dang 1996). Therefore it was of great importance that many villagers in Than Con were leaving swidden and subsistence cultivation behind to become commercial farmers.

"We have to work hard but still do not have enough to eat"

Some villagers were in less favorable positions than anh Thu and chi Tin to realize their fantasies of commercializing agriculture. Ban Van Thon and Duong Thi Con were in a precarious condition when Phuc met them the day he first arrived in Than Con in 2001. Phuc visited their house because the couple were hosting a small ceremony in their simple hut. Their newborn baby had fallen seriously ill but miraculously recovered after a few days. The parents organized the customary ceremony to thank the gods for saving their baby, and, as was expected from them, they invited their fellow villagers to a meal and drinks. Phuc learned only later that anh Thon and chi Con had had to borrow twenty-five euros from his uncle to be able to entertain their guests. In fact, they had still not repaid the loan when Phuc visited them again at the end of 2004. Life was becoming "more and more difficult" for them, anh Thon told Phuc; "we have to work hard but still do not have enough to eat."

The problem for chi Con and anh Thon was not that they did not have enough land but that they were unable to make a profit. When the Forest Protection Unit distributed forestland in 1996, the couple obtained two parcels totaling 5.5 ha. They had also received 1.7 *sao* from his grandparents and her parents when they built their own hut in 1999. They fared well in terms of land, and did better than anh Thu and chi Tin, who were of similar age and had two young children as well. The problem was that anh Thon and chi Con never managed to generate a profit from their land to reinvest into production. They planted some tea around their house, but because it was a small area, with low productivity, they barely managed to sell any.

They planted some cassava, but again the size of their plantation was small, while a large part of their forestland lay idle.

Chi Con and anh Thon could not make the transition from subsistence production to commercial agriculture. They continued to work their own paddy fields because they wanted to have rice to feed their own family. In a typical year, the paddy only produced enough rice for the family to last eight months, and yet it demanded a lot of work and absorbed much of their own labor, which was then not available for tea and cassava. In addition, anh Thon and chi Con also worked for other households (frequently for anh Thu and chi Tin). It was easy to find work in the village because nearly all well-off households needed additional labor on their tea and cassava plantations. Since this earned around 1.50 euros a day, the work also provided chi Con and anh Thon with a source of quick cash to pay for the purchase of additional food and other necessities. However, it prevented them from working on their own tea and cassava plantations during critical periods, thereby restricting their ability to expand their plantations. The couple became locked into activities that generated relatively low returns from their own labor.

Anh Thon and chi Con wanted to become commercial farmers just as much as chi Tin and anh Thu. In a conversation with Phuc, anh Thon expressed his desire to become a commercial farmer. "If we had money," he said, "we would buy fertilizer to apply on our tea and would clear our first plot to plant acacia and cassava." Yet they did not have the required money, and other villagers did not trust them to possess the required commercial skills. Their fellow villagers saw them as a couple who had problems making ends meet and were unable to generate a profit in agriculture. The latter became very clear when anh Thon and chi Con applied to the Agribank for a loan to expand their tea and cassava plantations. The village chairman refused to provide the required signature in support of the loan application because he did not have confidence in their ability to use the credit wisely and to eventually repay it.

Chi Con and anh Thon's failure to generate a profit was in part due to the greater skill and resourcefulness of some of the other villagers. For example, the couple leased an upland field to anh Thu and chi Tin, who agreed to pay a lease fee of twenty euros for the field of 2.1 ha over a period of ten years. The deal helped anh Thon and chi Con to generate some cash income, but it was much more profitable to the other couple. Speaking to Phuc, anh Thu estimated that he and his wife ended up with a profit of 120 euros a year, whereas the lease payment was next to nothing in comparison, being less than what anh Thon and chi Con made for a day's work. The failure of the one couple and the success of the other were two sides of the same coin; the meager lease payment and low daily wages transferred all profits from one couple to the other.

The example of these two couples reveals how some villagers were able to transition from subsistence cultivation to commercial agriculture, whereas others could not. Some households became commercial farmers and were seen as such because they generated sufficient profit to invest it back into production. This also lured others, even though they were unable to become commercial farmers. They were at a disadvantage because they did not have an alternative idea or plan that would fit their circumstances and possibilities. Moreover, they were at a double disadvantage because the ability of some villagers to transition to commercial farming directly impinged on others' chances of attaining the dream. The profits made by commercial farmers were tied to the losses incurred by others through unequal terms in land leases and labor hires.

Land allocation enabled this process of social differentiation by individualizing rights to land in Than Con. The transfer of land certificates to individual households not only prepared the ground for agricultural commercialization but also created the conditions for the emergence of new kinds of socioeconomic differences among villagers. Enterprising households, such as that of anh Thu and chi Tin, were able to generate profit because they could gain access to additional land through leases. Others, such chi Con and anh Thon, sought refuge in land leases because the new land legislation granted them the unprecedented possibility to lease out land. In the past in Than Con, villagers had only been able to claim rights to land if they put it to productive use. In this way, the right to land had been intimately tied to the obligation of good land husbandry. However, the 1993 Land Law did away with this link between "right" and "obligation" in villagers' customary dealings with land. Land allocation allowed households to retain rights to agricultural land even if they could not use it productively and leased it out to others against payment. Some villagers used these new rights in their efforts to make ends meet. Nonetheless, no household sold their agricultural land since it remained a critical productive resource. Villagers transferred land through land rentals and not sales, in stark contrast with Ho So, the village to which we turn now.

The Peri-urban Land Market Arrives in Ho So

Vietnam's capital Hanoi virtually exploded in the 1990s and 2000s.[7] Until the late 1980s, zoning regulations and the absence of transferable property titles had effectively contained urban growth (Leaf 2002). Starting in the early 1990s, residential houses and industrial plants rapidly expanded outward. House constructors and industrial investors switched large areas of agricultural land to non-agricultural purposes, purchasing the land from villagers and local People's Committees (Leaf 2002; Nguyen and Kammeier 2002; Kerkvliet 2006). By the end of the 1990s, many villages on the city outskirts were no longer characterized by small houses, dirt roads, and agricultural fields, but displayed long rows of new villas equipped with modern amenities.

For the first decade, the village of Ho So remained unaffected by the general land frenzy. Urban buyers were not interested in the village because it was located in the remote parts of Ha Tay, the province adjacent to Hanoi. A simple dirt road was the only way to access the village, which held some five hundred people living in one hundred households. Its inhabitants continued to make a living from agriculture, cultivating wet-rice fields at the village center, working cassava fields on the slopes above the village, and using the gardens around their houses to plant cassava, tea, medicinal plants, fruit trees, and vegetables. Many households also raised livestock for sale, which was the only other significant source of cash income besides cassava. Life was not easy for them because they could barely make ends meet due to the small size of their paddy fields.

The adjacent Ba Vi National Park significantly restricted villagers' options for making a living from the surrounding land. After the park was established in 1991, the park administration banned all agricultural activity—cultivation and livestock husbandry—above the 100-meter contour line. The ban forced many people to resettle at a lower location, which led to the foundation of Ho So village next to the original village of Ho Nha. Although the government had guaranteed initial support to all resettled households, and access to productive land, many villagers experienced food shortages and lived in poor conditions. They were forced to continue cultivating upland fields, collecting medicinal plants and grazing livestock inside the park. However, the ban on agricultural activities meant that their customary practices were now deemed illegal, which meant they always faced a risk of detection, punishment, and loss of their products (Sowerwine 2004). Land allocation, implemented in 2000, had given them land certificates, but only for their house plots, paddy fields, and gardens.

Ho So's location next to Ba Vi National Park became an advantage when Hanoians developed a taste for recreational tourism and weekend homes due to rising living standards, exposure to Western ideas about nature, and road improvements. Around the year 2000 high-ranking government officials and other well-off people from Hanoi began to purchase land and construct weekend homes in nearby villages that offered great scenery between Ba Vi Mountain and the Da River. Even a former president of the country constructed a posh villa in the village next to Ho So. Rumor ran rampant that the officials would bring development and infrastructure projects to the area; indeed two tourist companies bought large areas of nearby land and invested significant amounts of capital in two ecotourism projects in early 2003. This investment convinced villagers and potential buyers alike that Ho So offered an attractive location for Hanoians' weekend homes, unleashing a land rush that swept through Ho So.

Hanoians, many of whom were government officials, started arriving in late 2003 to inquire about the possibility of purchasing land. Some of them bought land for recreational purposes, with the conviction that the village offered a "better quality of life," as one land buyer explained to Phuc. Village life benefited from beautiful landscapes, trees, mountain ranges, clean air, quietness, and privacy—none of which could be found in the city. Some of the buyers constructed luxury villas equipped with modern amenities such as swimming pools, satellite receivers, and air-conditioning. Others built wooden houses on stilts, imitating the housing style of Thai and Tay ethnic minority people, and grew corn and fruit trees to make the village landscape look more "natural." Most of the buyers had speculative purposes in mind and subsequently left the land idle in the hope that land prices would rise. One buyer told Phuc: "If the land fetches a good price I will sell it, if not I will leave it here. It will not run away."

Part of the reason for the dramatically increased land market in Ho So was the brokers, who did their best to get villagers to sell land. Seven out of ten land sales involved four villagers with excellent relations to well-placed outsiders. One of these villagers was on the staff of the communal People's Committee and became a successful broker through his cooperation with a well-known real estate agent in Ha Tay province. Once they finished a deal, the brokers received a commission of between 5 and 8 percent of the total transaction. The lure of lucrative commissions made the brokers promote land sales among their fellow villagers, who lacked the necessary experience to match the wit of the broker and buyers.

The lure of quick money and the brokers' persuasive tactics caused many villagers to abandon their initial hesitation to sell land. This phenomenon is articulated in the following story that Duong Trung Thong told Phuc in 2004 about his land sale:

> I have no idea about it [the land market] … Ong Bi [a land broker] brought a man from Hanoi to my house and said this man is interested in our land … The man told me that he would pay me 5 million [250 euros] per *sao*. I never imagined we could have 120 million [6,000 euros] from selling our twenty-four *sao*. Our annual savings hardly reached 5 million … I then told the man that I needed to talk to my wife and would give him my answer the next day. In the evening, Ong Bi came over and told me that

5 million per *sao* was good enough, and that it was not easy to find a buyer. Afraid of not being able to sell the land, I decided to sell the land to the man the next day.

The rapid change in the land market transformed property relations in Ho So. By the end of 2004, just a year after the first transaction, eight out of ten village households had sold off all or parts of their gardens or house plots to outside buyers. The price paid for suitable land had risen rapidly over the course of the year, reaching five times the initial level. The land market not only modified the monetary value of land but also transformed the kinds of value attached to land. Until late 2003, villagers valued their land for its use as a productive resource in agriculture. A year later land had acquired new kinds of value as a site for recreation and an object of speculation.

Our emphasis on the powerful forces of the land rush does not imply that villagers did not play an active role in the events. As rapidly as the land rush swept through Ho So, as forceful as the buyers and brokers were to convince villagers to sell, and as powerful as the larger-scale forces of land markets were, many villagers were nonetheless complicit in the rush for lucrative deals and monetary income. Their reasons for eagerly embracing the land market are the subject of the following section.

Selling Land to Buy Modernity

One of the households that sold land belonged to Duong Trung Heu and Ban Thi Hoan. Phuc visited anh Heu, a young man born in 1978, on a hot summer day in August 2004 during lunchtime. Chi Hoan was not home; she had gone to another village to harvest tea for some households as a hired laborer. Anh Heu had just returned home from tending the small cow that he had purchased two months before. His three-year-old child was with him. The courtyard was covered with grass he had collected in the morning. Wearing only shorts, he was sat on the sofa, using a fan made from palm leaves. When Phuc entered his new house, anh Heu immediately stopped using the simple hand-held fan, instead turning on the electric fan. He also put on a T-shirt with a Star Wars image, and turned on foreign-made music videos on a shiny new Oasis amplifier and Samsung television set.

Over a cup of tea, pop music, and a water pipe, anh Heu told Phuc about their lives. He recalled how little land he and his wife had had when they built their own house in 2002. They did not receive any wet-rice fields from the cooperative, since all paddy land had been distributed earlier. His mother could transfer only two *sao* of paddy land and eleven *sao* of housing and garden land. Life was very difficult for them because the paddy fields did not produce enough rice, and their tea plantation yielded a mere twenty-five euros a year. It seemed like a stroke of good fortune to anh Heu and chi Hoan when, in late 2003, a land buyer offered them 3,000 euros for eight *sao* of their garden. Until then, it had been unimaginable that they could ever possess this much money. Overwhelmed by the sheer sum, they agreed to the sale and gave half of the payment to anh Heu's mother for her to live off as she aged.

Chi Hoan and anh Heu spent the remaining money replacing their simple wooden hut with a modern house. They hired a contractor from outside Ho So to build a nice "modern" house with a floor of flowery tiles. Their money ran out before the house was completed. To raise additional funds they sold another *sao* of their garden in 2004, receiving 1,500 euros for it: four times as much as the price per *sao* paid in the first transaction. The new money had allowed them to complete their house, purchase a new motorbike, acquire furniture, and buy electronic goods such as the Oasis amplifier and Samsung television set that played the music videos during Phuc's conversation with anh Heu.

The story of chi Hoan and anh Heu is emblematic of many households in Ho So who sold their gardens or house plots to construct new homes and purchase consumer goods. They hired outside contractors to build these new houses in a fashion that resembled the houses that were being built in villages throughout the Red River Delta. Cemented flat roofs replaced the tiled roofs of their old houses. Wooden walls gave way to brick walls painted in blue or yellow. Electric pumps lifted water from deep wells, saving households the work of manually fetching it. Some homeowners even prided themselves on building a second story. All of the homes possessed floors decorated with flowered enameled tiles made in China. Visitors were now expected to remove their shoes or sandals outside in order not to dirty the tile floor, as was common practice in urban and affluent rural houses. Even before entering a new house, visitors would notice new, Chinese-made motorbikes parked in the cemented courtyard or in a small shed next to the house. Once inside, their eyes would be caught by shiny new consumer goods. Many houses had a Toshiba, Samsung or Goldstar color television placed on top of a central cupboard, surrounded by new sofas and tables.

The land transactions generated a massive inflow of cash for the village. Villagers made a total of around 600,000 euros within a single year, equivalent to more than six times the total derived from all other sources. If one only includes the households that actually sold land, then the average annual income from land sales was 6,000 euros, eight times that from other sources. "Prior to the land market," a villager mentioned to Phuc, "I never dreamed of having ten million Dong [500 euros]. Now I have a hundred million Dong." Half of all households that sold land subsequently built new houses within a year. More than two-thirds of all land sellers bought a new motorbike, something virtually no villager had been able to afford before the onset of the land market.

The villagers sold land because of a desire for material wealth and a modern lifestyle. To them, modern life was intimately tied to their sense of Vietnamese cultural identity and lifestyle. As scholars have shown, their own ethnic group, the Dao, had long been associated with negative stereotypes in mainstream society (Jamieson, Cuc Le Trong, and Rambo 1998; Michaud and Turner 2000). The Vietnamese government's adoption of an evolutionary approach to ethnicity and human development resulted in the attribution of negative images and cultural stigmas to most ethnic minority groups. The evolutionary approach placed all ethnic groups at different stages of a linear development trajectory. It gave the ethnic Vietnamese majority, or *Kinh* as they are commonly referred to in Vietnam, a place at the highest stage of development.[8] The approach relegated most ethnic minorities to lower stages, deeming them inferior and backward. It readily blamed the low level of economic activity among many ethnic people on their cultural backwardness and resistance to modernization. The Dao, in particular, were kept at the bottom of the human development ladder in the ethnic classification projects commissioned by the government due to their residence in remote areas, low literacy rates, absence of a formalized social organization, and the use of agricultural practices considered outdated and unproductive.

When potential buyers arrived at their doorsteps, villagers considered the sale of land a unique opportunity to satisfy their long-harbored desire to adopt a modern—*Kinh*—lifestyle. Since the 1960s, when several resettlement projects brought an influx of *Kinh* migrants to the area, they had interacted with *Kinh* people. They had also been exposed increasingly to *Kinh* culture via the media. As a result, villagers had become aware of the cultural stigmas attached to Dao, and differences—real or perceived—with *Kinh* culture. *Kinh* culture and lifestyles had gradually infiltrated Ho So, influencing villagers' perceptions of what an appropriate way of life and a respectable culture could be. By 2000, casual visitors were no longer able to distinguish the villagers from *Kinh* people. The villagers dressed in the same clothes as *Kinh* and spoke Vietnamese perfectly. Furthermore, the land market offered an unprecedented opportunity for villagers to catch up fully with the *Kinh*: to construct modern houses and to use newly available consumer products. Many villagers were proud to point out that "We are the *Kinh* Dao," as they saw themselves transforming to achieve *Kinh* levels of economic and cultural advancement.

Villagers were strongly influenced by a particular "fantasy of identity" associated with modernity and mainstream culture. By aspiring to be *Kinh* they contested the cultural stigmas attributed to them on their identity card by government policy and the media. They invested heavily in their fantasy of identity, not only in an emotional sense but also materially. Houses in *Kinh* style, motorbikes, and color televisions became the most desirable assets for villagers because they served to signal household status and identity. They judged the most beautiful houses according to the number of stories, type of roof, and shapes of the doors and windows, just as they thought *Kinh* people would do. They appreciated glass tables, faux-leather sofas and colonial-style cupboards—the items commonly associated with affluent *Kinh* households. The new material assets and goods strongly evoked images of advancement and modernity to villagers and visitors alike. This fantasy was so powerful that it caused many of them to sell off their key productive resource: land.

"I will never sell my land"

Some households were not ready to give up agricultural land. A few did not want to sell any land at all, while others used part of the money made from selling their own house plots or gardens to purchase new land. Approximately a quarter of all households in Ho So who sold their gardens and house plots used some of the income to reinvest in agriculture by buying wet-rice fields or acquiring cattle to take up livestock husbandry. For all of these households, agricultural land remained a key productive resource that they wanted to retain for the future. They witnessed their fellow villagers' actions with great concern. One of the villagers said to Phuc, "Many households do not have cultivation land... I don't know how they will live in the future. I will never sell my land."

Duong Thi Bin and Trieu Van Trun were one of the couples who purchased wet-rice fields and cattle with the money made from selling land. Although they sold their large home garden for a low price very early in the land frenzy, they made sure they invested some of the money into expanding agricultural production. Together they decided to construct a fairly simple house, which only required expenditures of around a quarter of the 5,500 euros generated through the land sale. Instead of an expensive house, they spent more than a third of the money on the purchase of a small piece of garden land and a small wet-rice field. They also bought four small cows in order to start raising cattle. These investments still left them with significant savings. As chi Bin happily shared with Phuc: "I put all the remaining money in the bank. I will use it for my children's education."

The investments subsequently allowed chi Bin and anh Trun to make a living from agriculture. Together with their first, grown-up child, the couple tended a nice tea plantation around their new house. They grew cassava, bamboo plants, and acacia trees in a field on the slope above Ho So. Their wet-rice fields, which they had doubled in area thanks to the purchase in 2004, yielded sufficient rice for the whole household year round. Their younger children, aged between eleven and fourteen, took turns looking after the cows. In this way, the household generated a cash income of some 600 euros a year, which was enough to purchase reproductive necessities, agricultural inputs, and their children's schooling. They did not have to take up paid work with other households—unlike anh Hieu and chi Hoa, the couple described in the preceding section.

Another couple, Duong Trun Din and Duong Thu Hu, never sold any land. When Phuc was in Ho So in 2004, he often went over to the wealthy couple's house or their store to have a chat with anh Din. Anh Din told him how he had learned to make money. When he served in the army, he was responsible for supplies. When he came back to his village in the early 1990s, he started a small trading business, buying up cassava and other crops from fellow villagers and selling the produce in a nearby town. More recently, anh Din had signed a contract with the administration of Ba Vi National Park for the protection of some forest. He also lent money to fellow villagers, charging interest at a rate significantly above the bank rate. Alternatively, when villagers were in need of cash, he would provide them with fertilizer on credit or purchase their cassava pre-harvest, both activities yielding a decent profit.

The couple had used their income to build one of the most beautiful houses in the village. Located near the village road, no visitor to Ho So could miss chi Hu and anh Din's two-story house. Anh Din estimated that its construction had cost them 3,000 euros in 2000. In addition, they had furnished their house with an expensive sofa and a fancy cupboard, and purchased a shiny Toshiba television set. A Chinese motorbike was not good enough; they bought a more expensive Angel motorbike manufactured in Taiwan for double the price. Their house was also surrounded by a large plot of 20 *sao* containing a tea plantation, longan and litchi trees, soybean and peanut fields, and a vegetable garden. Anh Din and chi Hu worked five *sao* of paddy fields, which they had bought in the 1990s, and had dug out a large fish pond. They had invested a significant part of the money made through their trading activities in agriculture—and resisted the temptation to sell some of their large garden.

Prompted by Phuc, anh Din made it clear that he did not intend to sell any land. When Phuc asked him, partly seriously, why he did not sell his garden "to get a billion," he replied, quite seriously, that he would never sell his land. Din explained: "You are there, I am here, let's wait to see what happens to them [the ones who sell the land] in the future after their money is gone. Surely, they will have many difficulties." According to his own calculations, he and his wife earned about 1,000 euros a year. About three-quarters came from agriculture, which they considered their primary activity despite their successful trading and money-lending business. Agriculture was important to them even though both of their children received a good education and expected to find jobs outside the village. Moreover, despite the importance of capital and labor in production, land remained the primary productive resource for chi Huong and anh Din.

These two stories demonstrate that people did not stay in agriculture due to a rejection of the modernity so desirable to their fellow villagers. They remained in agriculture because they could afford to do so; they were able to shoulder the costs of a modern life without selling any land, or without using up all the money earned from land sales for a new house and other consumptive expenditures. The stories also indicate that villagers were not eager to abandon agriculture, even those who sold off all or large parts of their gardens. Instead, they wanted to retain their land as a productive resource and to continue cultivating the land and raising livestock. They may have found commercial agriculture as attractive as anh Dinh and chi Huong and their peers in Than Con. Yet, only the better-off could afford to live their dream of becoming modern citizens of Vietnam *and* retain their productive base. For most, it remained just a fantasy, and left scarce finances for productive investments.

Dynamics and Conflicts of Commodification

The land sales brought a group of newcomers to Ho So; by the end of 2004, some seventy people from Hanoi held almost 10 ha in total. The urbanites eventually occupied most of the land located along the village road, taking in more than half of the total garden land in the village. When Phuc walked down the village road, villagers would commonly make observations such as, "this plot belongs to Ong Sao from Doi Can street in Hanoi," "the plot on the left is Ba Yen's from the Ministry of Agriculture and Rural Development in Hanoi," and "the big plot behind hers is owned by Ong Sen, a journalist working for a Hanoi newspaper." In contrast, the houses of the large majority of villagers had moved farther away from the road and were much less visible.

The land transactions not only introduced newcomers with new conceptions of land to Ho So but also transformed how villagers looked at land. They increasingly saw land as a financial asset to be managed for profit. Consequently, some villagers hired workers, bulldozers, and excavators to convert paddy fields and fish ponds—once highly prized productive assets—into residential plots, which yielded a much higher profit if sold on the land market.

In addition to selling land to newcomers, villagers started to trade land amongst each other for profit. Nearly a third of all village households acquired new land from fellow villagers after they had sold off their entire gardens and house plots, as Chi Bin and Anh Tru discussed in the preceding section. They had to purchase the land from fellow villagers, like any outsider coming to the village. As a result, almost a third of all income made from land sales went back into the purchase of new house plots that had been bought from fellow villagers.

The land transactions brought about a hardening of boundaries around individual plots; boundaries that had once been permeable and flexible became impenetrable and fixed in space and time. Many new owners used barbed wire, concrete walls, and iron gates to demarcate their plots, and hired guards to keep trespassers out. Additionally, this hardening took place in less visible but equally significant ways. For example, village leaders faced mounting problems in their attempts to enforce the village collective's rights to some sixteen hundred pine trees, which the villagers together had acquired from Ba Vi Forest Enterprise in the early 1990s. The trees were not concentrated in a single stand but grew on land that had been allocated to thirteen households in 2000. That was not a problem in itself because these households made sure to protect the trees. The location of the collective trees on land allocated to individual households became a problem only in 2004 when some of the households wanted to remove trees in order to make space for house construction, and when six newcomers purchased some of the land with trees. Households and village leaders became embroiled in a conflict over who had the right to decide about the trees: the individual households possessing land certificates or the village collective. The village leaders tried to stop the households by asserting the village's collective ownership, pointing to the outstanding debt with the Forest Enterprise, and arguing that households had a duty to protect the pine trees. The affected households, in turn, rejected the village leaders' demands by contending that national land legislation granted them the rights to dispose of their land and associated resources as they wished.

Villagers came to attribute more significance to land certificates. Throughout the 1990s, villagers had not been troubled by the absence of land certificates, although the 1993 Land Law entitled them to such. They exchanged land amongst each other and occupied new land without seeking to complete the legally required paperwork. Yet by 2004, land titles had become a primary concern of crucial importance because urban buyers insisted on them, either to enhance the security of their land claim or to be able to sell the land again easily. The sudden importance of the titles created massive tensions between some households and the local officials in charge of land administration. The local officials found themselves overwhelmed by the sudden rise in demand for their services, including the demarcation of boundaries, the certification of the legal status of parcels, and the issuance of land titles. Some households wanting to sell land, in turn, became frustrated with the slow pace of their work, and with the officials' tendency to accept bribes to accelerate the process. The issue became the topic of heated debates at commune and village meetings, and eventually forced the communal People's Committee to dismiss its land administration officer.

As land titles, land officers, and land legislation gained significance, landowners paid less attention to the expectations of fellow villagers. In the past, all villagers had been expected to make good use of the land allocated to them, whether it was paddy, a garden, or an upland field. It was not acceptable for anyone to leave valuable productive land uncultivated. If people considered themselves unable to work land, they were expected to pass it on to another household in the village. However, villagers saw that a significant share of the best land lay idle from 2004 onward. Plots that had previously been used to grow vegetables, food crops, and tea were no longer in production because the new owners were waiting for land prices to rise before selling or beginning the construction of new homes. The plots were covered with chest-high grass and wild weeds growing between tea plants that were no longer tended and fruit trees no longer harvested—a state of affairs that was in direct contradiction to the villagers' ideas about good land husbandry.

Another effect of the weakening social ties was that it became more difficult for the village leaders to organize collective work. In previous years, villagers had joined forces to fix village paths after the rainy season. Most villagers participated in the required work, even though there were always some who opted to make a monetary contribution instead. In 2004, however, villagers were less willing to contribute labor than in previous years; a large number instead preferred to pay the required fee. The chairman of the village youth union complained to Phuc: "It is very difficult for me to mobilize villagers to work on upgrading the village road. They don't want to work now!"

Thus, the villagers changed the way they looked at land. It became an abstract entity to be traded on markets for financial profit. Land turned into a commodity, as people increasingly emphasized "its exchangeability … for some other thing [as] its socially relevant feature" (Appadurai 1986: 13). Commodification transformed not only how people exchanged land but also the kinds of property claims considered legitimate. The social relations regarding land changed radically: land rights became individualized; land certificates, officers, and legislation gained significance; and landowners rejected the obligations customarily tied to their land rights.

The commodification of land did not occur smoothly, but involved significant politics and conflicts. As discussed above, village leaders clashed with some households over the pine trees. The clash involved forest protection officers and threats of legal action. Villagers and communal officers repeatedly found themselves at odds over the conduct of land administration, culminating in the dismissal of the land administration officer. Other conflicts erupted between village households, husbands and wives, children and parents, and brothers and sisters, as Phuc has discussed elsewhere (To Xuan Phuc 2011).

The primary conflict was between villagers and newcomers. The severity of the tensions between the groups became apparent through a story of an incident that circulated in the village. Villagers commonly referred to the incident to vent their anger about the newcomers' perceived attitude, and to demonstrate their determination to stand up to them. The incident occurred when a village woman visited her new neighbor, a man from Hanoi, to ask for a small cash contribution to a collective project. The neighbor not only rejected her request outright but was also extremely rude to her, as she recounted to Phuc later. Apparently he told her that he did not give "a damn about contributing any money." He saw no reason to chip in as he had just arrived in Ho So. Feeling offended, the woman snapped back angrily: "You shit city people are very impolite. I thought well-educated people don't use foul language. But now I know that I was totally wrong."

The woman's angry reaction reflected the loss of a sense of belonging that was so important to villagers. They were afraid that they were becoming strangers in their own village. The luxury villas, iron gates, and concrete walls lining the village road demonstrated to them that the newcomers might take over their village. In addition, these items were so expensive that villagers felt they could not obtain them and thus never achieve a modern lifestyle. Their fear of loss fuelled a series of conflicts with urbanites, whose rising presence was causing resentment, and this was reflected in how villagers talked about the newcomers. They commonly observed that "the city people" were "very rich" but also "very mean," that they "passed by villagers without a greeting," and "looked down on villagers."

On one occasion, villagers' resentments even turned violent. At the end of 2004, the newly built vacation house of a Hanoi resident burned down one night due to arson. A villager or a few villagers had apparently turned their anger directly against what mattered most to the newcomers: their houses. If the newcomers did not want to fit in and comply with their social obligations as village members, the message seemed to be that they had no right to reside in the village.

Fantasies and the Politics of Value in Than Con and Ho So

The people of Than Con and Ho So welcomed the land certificates issued to them by their respective district People's Committee, just as their peers in Albania and Romania had done. They valued the land for its productive purposes, particularly the ability to produce food for their own subsistence. Yet, within a few years, land had undergone radical changes in value, referring not just to the monetary value of individual plots but also the kinds of value attributed to land. Agriculture was being commercialized in Than Con, turning land into a productive resource that was expected to yield monetary returns. In Ho So, a process of peri-urbanization enhanced the consumptive value of land to levels far above its productive value.

The changes in the value of land were intimately tied to broader shifts in value regimes in the two villages, as we have highlighted in the preceding two chapters. A central dynamic in the Vietnamese villages originated from people's negotiations over various "fantasies of identity." The changes in value regimes involved questions about the kind of persons villagers wanted to be, and how they wanted to be recognized by others. People in Than Con found it increasingly attractive to become commercial farmers, and they wanted to be seen as such. They thought about how to make a monetary profit in agricultural production, and how to invest the profit back into production to maximize the return to the expended labor. In Ho So, villagers increasingly held the fantasy of becoming modern citizens of an urbanizing Vietnam. Eager to build new houses and to purchase flashy consumer goods as a demonstration of their modernity, they sold their land for financial profit.

Vietnam's larger political economy conditioned villagers' fantasies of identity and their possibilities for realizing these fantasies. The dominant discourses of agricultural commercialization and modernization proved too powerful for villagers to resist.[9] Changes in agricultural product markets, access to productive resources and consumer goods, and peri-urban land markets determined the possibilities for villagers' to pursue commercialization and modernization. Villagers' chances to resist these institutionalized discourses and to benefit from market changes were severely limited due to their disadvantaged position in Vietnam's larger political economy. Despite the rapid growth that was achieved countrywide since economic liberalization in the late 1980s, people in both villages were still experiencing tremendous difficulties in making ends meet in the 1990s. Moreover, the Vietnamese government's approach to ethnic classification produced popular discourses about Dao as backward and at a low stage of development. It was out of this disadvantaged position, rooted in the structural inequality of economic and cultural production in Vietnam, that villagers embraced new fantasies of identity and engaged in corresponding material practices to overcome their economic and cultural marginalization. Moreover, the possibilities available to the two villages were unequal because only Ho So was attractive to the highly capitalized peri-urban land market.

Not all villagers were able to live these dreams equally, as the revalorization constituted new relations of privilege and social control (see also Appadurai 1986; Berry 1989). In Than Con, some villagers quickly took advantage of the new market opportunities to grow large tea plantations and cassava fields. Others remained caught in an enduring subsistence crisis as they struggled to produce sufficient rice for their own consumption under the new conditions. In Ho So, virtually all villagers built new houses and purchased expensive consumer goods in their eagerness to have a modern life. Yet, in the end, only a portion of them could actually afford to do so, and the others quickly ran into trouble making ends meet. In both villages, the less privileged ended up working for the privileged on terms that made it difficult for them to move out of their disadvantaged positions. In Than Con, land leases were another mechanism tying the disadvantaged to the privileged, thereby establishing new forms of social control.

These politics of value affected property relations in the two villages. In Than Con, some households began to rent upland fields from fellow villagers to plant tea and cassava. Land rentals were a new phenomenon in the village; the practice had not been considered legitimate in the past. In Ho So, land sales quickly spread as a legitimate way of transferring land rights, creating a new group of landowners with distinctively different backgrounds and interests: the urbanites. In addition, they were part of a broader process of commodification, involving changes in the way land was exchanged, and in what kinds of claims were considered legitimate. Property relations in Ho So increasingly resembled the ideal of exclusive individual ownership informing property reforms worldwide (see Introduction).

Changes in property were also intimately tied to changes in authority, as indicated by the growing tendency of people in Ho So to justify their claims on land in reference to state law, courts, and officials. Villagers and newcomers alike increasingly refused to comply with obligations towards the village collective, which had previously gone unquestioned. These developments reflected a shift in authority away from the village collective to the state. Such changes in authority were an important element in negotiations over property, and they will be the focus of the next part of this book.

Notes

1. The Dao are one of the fifty-three ethnic minority groups officially recognized in Vietnam. Most of them reside in separate villages sprinkled across Vietnam's northern mountains. The 1999 Population Census reported the Dao group to number some 621,000. All fifty-three ethnic minority groups accounted for 10.5 million people, or roughly 14 percent of Vietnam's population (General Statistics Office 2010).
2. The district is the second-lowest level of administration in Vietnam, the commune being the one at the bottom. At each level, there is a People's Committee with different branch offices or officers, such as the Agricultural Office at the district level.
3. Rice swiddening was a common practice in many villages throughout the uplands of Vietnam and Southeast Asia (Fox et al. 2009).
4. *Sao* is a common area measure equivalent to 360 m² in northern Vietnam.
5. See http://fsiu.mard.gov.vn/News.asp?act=XemChiTiet&Cat_ID=47&News_ID=4145&LinksFrom=http://fsiu.mard.gov.vn/News.aspx (accessed 13 March 2006).
6. "Anh Thu" is the colloquial way most adult villagers' and Phuc would address Trieu Van Thu. Chi Tin is the corresponding way for Nguyen Thi Tin. In conjunction with the given name (which comes last in Vietnamese names), the personal pronouns "anh" and "chi" are used for men and women to signify respect.
7. The following sections build on To Xuan Phuc (2011).
8. The term *Kinh* comes from *kinh do*, which signifies capital city. This distinction between "people from the capital" and others fits our case very nicely.
9. See also Harms (2012) for an insightful account of how urban residents in Ho Chi Minh City progressively look at land in terms of monetary value due to the influence of a dominant modernization discourse.

References

Appadurai, Arjun. 1986. "Introduction: Commodities and the Politics of Value." In *The Social Life of Things: Commodities in Cultural Perspective*, ed. Arjun Appadurai. Cambridge: Cambridge University Press, 3–63.

Asian Development Bank et al. 2003. "Vietnam Development Report 2004: Poverty." Joint Donor Report to the Vietnam Consultative Group Meeting, 2–3 December. Hanoi.

Berry, Sara. 1989. "Social Institutions and Access to Resources." *Africa* 59(1): 41–55.

Be Viet Dang. 1996. *Cac Dan Toc Thieu So Trong Su Phat Trien Kinh Te-Xa Hoi O Mien Nui*. Hanoi: National Politics Publishing House and People's Culture Publishing House.

Fox, Jefferson, et al. 2009. "Policies, Political-Economy, and Swidden in Southeast Asia." *Human Ecology* 37(3): 305–22.

General Statistics Office. 2010. "Vietnam Population Census 1999." www.gso.gov.vn (accessed 10 October 2010).

Harms, Erik. 2012. "Beauty as Control in the New Saigon: Eviction, New Urban Zones, and Atomized Dissent in a Southeast Asian City." *American Ethnologist* 39(4): 735–50.

Jamieson, Neil L., Cuc Le Trong, and A. Terry Rambo. 1998. "The Development Crisis in Vietnam's Mountains." *East–West Center Special Reports* 6. Honolulu: East–West Center Publications Program.

Kerkvliet, Benedict J.T. 2006. "Agricultural Land in Vietnam: Markets Tempered by Family, Community and Socialist Practice." *Journal of Agrarian Change* 6(3): 285–305.

Leaf, Michael. 2002. "A Tale of Two Villages: Globalization and Peri-urban Change in China and Vietnam." *Cities* 19(1): 23–31.

Le Trong Cuc and Terry Rambo (eds). 2001. *Bright Peaks, Dark Valleys: A Comparative Analysis of Environment and Social Conditions and Development Trends in Five Communities in Vietnam's Northern Mountain Regions.* Hanoi: The National Political Publishing House.

Michaud, Jean, and Sarah Turner. 2000. "The Sa Pa Marketplace, Lao Cai Province, Vietnam." *Asia Pacific Viewpoint* 41(1): 85–100.

Moore, Henrietta L. 1994. *A Passion for Difference: Essays in Anthropology and Gender.* Cambridge: Polity Press.

Neumann, Roderick P. 1998. *Imposing Wilderness: Struggles over Livelihood and Nature Preservation in Africa.* Berkeley: University of California Press.

Ngo The Dan. 2000. "Strengthening International Cooperation in Cassava Research and Development Programs." Paper presented at the Sixth Regional Workshop on Cassava's Potential in Asia in the 21st Century: Present Situation and Future Research and Development Needs, Ho Chi Minh City, 21–25 February 2000.

Nguyen Quang, D., and H.D. Kammeier. 2002. "Changes in the Political Economy of Vietnam and Their Impacts on the Built Environment of Hanoi." *Cities* 19(6): 373–88.

Rambo, A. Terry. 2005. *Searching for Vietnam: Selected Writings on Vietnamese Culture and Society.* Kyoto: Kyoto University Press.

Sowerwine, Jennifer. 2004. "Territorialisation and the Politics of Highland Landscapes in Vietnam: Negotiating Property Relations in Policy, Meaning and Practice." *Conservation and Society* 2(1): 97–136.

To Xuan Phuc. 2011. "The Development of a Land Market in the Uplands of Vietnam." In *Upland Transformations in Vietnam*, ed. Thomas Sikor et al. Singapore: Singapore University Press, 208–27.

Trinh Ba Bao. 1995. "Kinh Te Xa Hoi Nguoi Dao Thoi Ky 1970–1997" [Socioeconomic Development of the Dao 1970–1997]. Paper presented at the International Workshop on the Dao. Thai Nguyen, Vietnam.

Williams, Raymond. 1973. *The Country and the City.* London: Hogarth Press.

PART II
FORESTS

Contesting Property and Authority

Introduction

In Part I, we explored how property reforms played out in agriculture. In Part II, we return to the villages in Albania, Romania, and Vietnam to examine property dynamics in forestry. Forests not only covered significant areas of each country's surface but also provided important sources of income and wealth in all three. In Part I, we found that people redefined value in their negotiations over property, which lends credence to the idea that changes in property and value influenced each other. As property changed, so did the material and symbolic values people attributed to agricultural land and, more generally, their valuations of agriculture and rural life. In Part II, we again inquire about the political and economic dynamics connected to property reforms regarding land in the Albanian, Romanian, and Vietnamese villages, but now we turn our attention to forests.

A reiteration from the Introduction may be helpful. We started with the observation that governments and their international advisors expected property reforms to serve as vehicles for the state to distribute objects of known value. In Part I, we showed how this expectation was faulty when applied to agriculture, since value could not be known at the onset of the reforms. Now we want to see how, if at all, the expectations driving the propertizing projects relate to actual events in forestry. Property reforms in forestry unfolded in the context of state management under socialism, just as they did in agriculture. The reforms applicable to forests redefined the rights given to landholders, and initiated a broad shift away from the state; in fact, they were often contained in the same piece of legislation as agricultural reforms. Despite obvious differences—such as the near-complete absence of cooperatives in socialist forest management and a less radical shift from state to private in forestry—the intention to propertize was the same: that is, to bring about desirable economic, political, and cultural outcomes through property reforms.

A brief look at the three countries helps to substantiate this point. Albania's socialist regime nationalized all forests in the 1950s. Before nationalization, only 8 percent of the country's forests had been in private or communal ownership formally, although local people used many forests in customary ways (de Waal 2004: 33). Therefore, nationalization did not have any significant effect on the structure of formal ownership, but it did have a drastic effect on forest management and use. The regime established the Directorate General of Forests to manage forests and run logging operations. Local people lost their customary rights to forests, and found it increasingly difficult to continue their customary uses of forests over time (de Waal 2004).

The limited extent of private and communal ownership before nationalization implied that the restitution of forests legislated by Albania's first postsocialist government in the 1991 "Law Concerning Land" did not have much effect on the ownership structure. Virtually all forest, a little more than 1 million ha (hectares), remained in state ownership and under the management of the General Directorate of Forests and Pastures (Ministry of Agriculture and Food 2002). A major task of the directorate was to enforce forest regulations. The 1992 "Law Concerning Forests and the Forest Service Police" provided the basis for the directorate's involvement in law enforcement, complemented two years later by another law that updated forest guards' powers and detailed applicable fines. Another change was the introduction of auctions to allow for private sector participation in logging. The 1992 law established rules for private individuals to acquire business licenses and bid for harvest quotas.

Romania's socialist regime nationalized forests in 1948. At that time, nearly three-quarters of Romania's forests were in private ownership or belonged to towns, villages, communities, or organizations such as the church (Ioras and Abrudan 2006: 362). The government established the National Forest Administration, Romsilva, to manage the country's forests and set up three large enterprises to undertake logging nationwide. Romanian forest management became known around the world for "producing some of Europe's best silviculture and technical specialists" (Stewart 1999: 8).

Romania's restitution laws transformed forest ownership and management structures. Various postsocialist governments transferred approximately a third of the country's forests back into private ownership up until 2004, and were preparing to restitute another third in subsequent years. Restitution had originally been relatively small scale, as the first restitution law (Law 18 in 1991) led to a mere 350,000 ha being returned to former owners or their heirs. However, restitution achieved significant scale after the Romanian parliament passed Law 1 in 2000, when another 1.8 million ha were passed back to former owners. The restituted land was finally expected to surpass the land retained in public ownership with Law 247, which was passed by Romania's parliament in 2005 (Ioras and Abrudan 2006: 362). Romsilva continued to manage the shrinking state forests and began to offer its services to the owners of non-state forests. Private logging companies entered the sector, as auctions became mandatory for all timber sales from state forests in 1991, and from forests owned by local councils in 1998. In addition, the government set up a separate Forest Inspectorate in 1999, giving it significant law enforcement powers under the 1996 Forestry Code.

In Vietnam in 1954, the country's newly independent government declared all forest to be under national ownership. To oversee the management of forests the government created the General Department of Forestry, which later became the Ministry of Forestry. Day-to-day management rested with State Forest Enterprises (SFEs), which were under the control of the ministry, provincial governments, and district administrations. By the late 1980s there were 413 such enterprises, in charge of nearly two-thirds of the country's total land surface (Nguyen Van Dang 2001). Many of them were in formal control of forests that local people had used under customary arrangements historically.

The property reforms enacted by Vietnam's government around 1990 modified the legal and policy framework for forest management in radical ways. The 1993 Land Law caused local government to allocate a quarter of the total forestland to households and groups until the end of 2003 (Forest Protection Department 2012). Allocation granted fifty-year land use rights to forestland holders, even though forests remained in the ownership of "the people" according to Vietnam's constitution. At the same time, the government increasingly strengthened the law enforcement powers given to the Forest Protection Department and its branch offices at provincial and district levels (Sikor and To 2011). It also zoned nearly two-thirds of the forestland for protection based on the 1991 Forest Protection and Development Law (Forest Protection Department 2012). To support forest conservation, Vietnam's government started up large financial programs, which paid local people annually to protect forests in the continuing possession of SFEs or other state entities. The stated goal was to reforest 5 million ha, thereby bringing nationwide forest coverage back up to where it had presumably been in 1943.

This short overview reveals differences in the specific policies guiding property reforms and their implications for forest ownership in these three countries. One key difference that emerged was in the approaches employed to implement property reforms. The Albanian and Romanian governments opted for a responsive mode, which meant that it was up to historical owners to submit their claims to local restitution commissions. In Vietnam, provincial and district governments identified areas for allocation and then distributed the available land among local people in a bureaucratic fashion. Another difference was the relative emphasis given to forest exploitation versus conservation. Whereas Vietnam's government put two-thirds of the country's forests under protection status and paid villagers for their protection, Albania and Romania gave higher priority to establishing regulatory oversight of forest exploitation. A third difference was the extent to which the balance between state entities and non-state actors shifted as a result of property reforms. Romania's restitution laws moved one-third of the country's forests out of state possession, and Vietnam's land allocation moved one-quarter of theirs; in comparison, little changed in the ownership structure of Albania's forests.

Nonetheless, there were striking similarities between the reforms enacted in the three countries. The governments of all three sought to define property rights and obligations regarding forest in new but similar ways. Even though Vietnam's legislation did not grant ownership to forest holders, the long-term land-use rights resembled the legal rights accruing to forest owners in Albania and Romania. In all three countries, property reforms accorded private actors significant rights to forest, limiting the powers of the state to interfere. The focus on the extension of private rights cannot obscure another equally important similarity among the countries. In Albania, comparable to Romania and Vietnam, governments put police-like forest services in place to enforce forest regulations. Law enforcement became the primary *raison d'être* for powerful state agencies: the General Directorate of Forests and Pastures in Albania, the Forest Inspectorate in Romania, and the Forest Protection Department in Vietnam.

Another similarity—this one unintended by national lawmakers—lay in the difficulties encountered when government officials sought to implement property reforms. Despite the build-up of the new enforcement apparatus, in many places property relations regarding forests did not take the course prescribed in national legislation. The discrepancies between local dynamics and national law were not lost on governments, which was perhaps best illustrated by the concerns about "illegal logging" that arose around 2000. The governments of all three countries came to realize that a significant share of total logging did not comply with the new legal frameworks. A survey sponsored by the World Bank found that 40 percent of all logging in Albania was illegal (ACER 2001). Vietnam's government estimated that illegal harvests accounted for over half of the national roundwood supply (Government of Vietnam 2005). It was only Romania's government that put the incidence of illegal logging as low as 1 percent of total harvests in official figures, but that was a stark underestimation of its actual extent (Bouriaud and Niskanen 2003).

The apparent discrepancies between national property reforms and local dynamics discussed here establish the groundwork for our ethnographic investigations in the following three chapters. How did these reforms play out in the villages of Albania, Romania, and Vietnam? We begin with Albania.

References

Albanian Center for Economic Research (ACER). 2001. "Illegal Logging Independent Study: Final Report." Tirana: World Bank.

Bouriaud, Laura, and A. Niskanen. 2003. "Illegal Removals in the Context of the Sound Use of Wood." In *International Symposium on Strategies for the Sound Use of Wood*. Poiana, Brasov, Romania: United Nations Economic Committee for Europe.

Forest Protection Department. 2012. "Annual Forestry Statistics." Hanoi, Vietnam.

Government of Vietnam, Department of Forestry. 2005. "National Report to the Fifth Session of the United Nations Forum on Forests." Hanoi.

Ioras, Florin, and Ioan Abrudan. 2006. "The Romanian Forestry Sector: Privatisation Facts." *International Forestry Review* 8(3): 361–67.

Ministry of Agriculture and Food, Government of Albania. 2002. Annual Report. Tirana.

Nguyen Van Dang. 2001. *Lam Nghiep Viet Nam (1945–2000)*. Hanoi: Nha xuat ban Nong nghiep.

Sikor, Thomas, and To Xuan Phuc. 2011. "Illegal Logging in Vietnam: *Lam Tac* [Forest Hijackers] in Practice and Talk." *Society and Natural Resources* 24(7): 688–701.

Stewart, John Fraser. 1999. "Romania Forestry Sector: Status, Values, and the Need for Reform." *Environmentally and Socially Sustainable Development*. Washington, DC: World Bank.

Waal, Clarissa de. 2004. "Post-Socialist Property Rights and Wrongs in Albania: An Ethnography of Agrarian Change." *Conservation and Society* 2(1): 19–50.

4

Forests, State, and Custom in Albania

In 2004, when Johannes visited Dardha, he asked villagers where they obtained their wood. They pointed him in the direction of a degraded forest beyond the large agricultural plain described in Chapter 1. However, when he explored that specific area he did not find much more than shrub and coppice. There were a few small oak and beech trees, but otherwise he only saw bushes. Asked about the lack of mature trees, villagers explained to Johannes that there had been mature forest until 1997. In that year loggers had descended on the forest and cut all of the valuable timber and firewood. Even though the forest had ostensibly been under state ownership, and the District Forest Service had the legal mandate to preserve it, loggers had depleted most of the firewood and the timber entirely. State ownership and forest protection were ineffective back then. The villagers said that in the 1990s, there was no state and there was no law.

In contrast to Dardha, when Johannes arrived in Bagëtia in the summer of 2004, mature forest was very visible above the village and around the uncultivated land. He found plenty of oak, beech, and fir trees scattered across the slopes of the Gorë Mountains. Moreover, when Johannes hiked up the mountain slopes, he noticed warnings that people had sprayed on rocks and trees, such as "Don't touch Bagëtia's forest!"[1] His host explained to him that villagers had written them in an effort to keep out loggers from elsewhere. The forests formally remained in state ownership, they admitted, but they felt that they were the true owners and held customary rights to the forest because it had been in their possession until collectivization.

Custom was also at the fore of people's minds in Kodra, as already indicated by the contestations of agricultural land distribution (see Chapter 1). Villagers told Johannes in 2004 that they managed the chestnut forests above their village according to long-held customs. The forests had been in the possession of families from Kodra until collectivization, when the state had assumed ownership of them; but in 1991 and 1992 they successfully regained possession of the forests, and distributed the village's forest back to the families in whose possession it had been in the past. They felt that it was the right thing to do. People in Kodra respected custom, as did the people living in surrounding villages. There was no reason why chestnut management needed the state.

Though state and custom were important topics in people's general conversations about their lives, these subjects figured most prominently when discussing forests. Villagers knew that forests formally remained in state ownership but they also questioned whether the state should be involved in forest management. They also asked why the state did not keep the loggers out of the forests near their villages. In reaction, many turned to customary rights and customary regulations, asserting their significance at a time when the state seemed irrelevant. They argued that forests should be given back to those villages and families who held customary rights to them, mirroring the calls for the restitution of agricultural land in Bagëtia and echoing the contestations of state-sanctioned agricultural land distribution in Kodra (see Chapter 1). They also demanded that disputes over forests should be resolved through customary methods.

When people discussed the state in relation to forest management, they often referred to their very conceptions of what the state was about. They not only deplored the activities undertaken by particular state officials—or, most frequently, their lack of action—they also questioned the notion of the state as an institution governing forests. They discussed "the idea of the state" (Abrams 1988). Abrams notes that "[t]here is, too, a state-idea, projected, purveyed and variously believed in, in different societies at different times" (ibid.: 82). He distinguishes this idea from the concrete practices employed by state officials, particular political regimes, central governments, and so on. We find the distinction helpful even though we may not agree with Abrams' conclusion that the state is a "collective misrepresentation" (ibid.: 75). Nevertheless, the concept of the state as an idea is relevant to our purposes since it calls attention to practices and processes of representation that render some forms of power as legitimate, and distances these from others considered illegitimate.[2] Thus, Abrams equips us with an effective concept to begin our empirical inquiry into the property dynamics of forests in the three Albanian villages.[3]

Kodra: Cutting "Communist Trees"

When Albania's socialist regime collapsed in 1991, some villagers in Kodra reacted aggressively; they went on a rampage. Alone and in small groups, villagers sneaked out at night to loot the infrastructure that was in the possession of the agricultural cooperative. Within a few months, they had plundered the cooperative's irrigation system. The concrete plates used to cover small irrigation canals attracted particular attention because villagers could use them to lay the ground in their home gardens and on their terraces. Likewise, villagers looted the cooperative's five livestock shelters, carrying off the bricks for use in private construction projects. They also cut down most of the fruit trees that villagers had planted under the cooperative, and sold off the valuable wood.

Some villagers set their eyes on the chestnut forests above Kodra, cutting down significant portions of them. The hills around Kodra had long included blocks of planted chestnut forest (*Castanea sativa*) towering above the wheat fields and fruit orchards. Chestnuts were a prized specialty throughout Albania, and Kodra and other surrounding villages were known to be their primary producers. Until collectivization in the late 1940s, villagers had considered the chestnut forests as their own. After the initial collectivization, the forests had fallen into state ownership and were then managed by the cooperative. That made the cooperative chestnut forest a prime target of the looting in 1991.

People in many other villages of Albania reacted similarly (Vickers and Pettifer 1997). In the aftermath of the collapse of the social regime in 1991, rural Albanians took things into their own hands, destroying physical structures associated with the socialist state: the buildings of agricultural cooperatives, schools, and most of the rail and rural telephone systems. Cooperative buildings, in particular, were common targets of looting and destruction, since they were the key centers of state presence and signifiers of state power in the countryside. For villagers, they embodied everything that had been wrong about the socialist regime: the isolation from the rest of the world (Sjöberg 1991), the severe food shortages throughout the 1980s (de Waal 1995), and the gulags, arbitrary imprisonments, and psychiatric confinements (Woodcock 2007).

When Johannes talked to villagers in 2004, many of them readily defended the looting. Of course, the looters had profited personally from it, as illustrated by the concrete plates that continued to adorn people's gardens and terraces. But people felt there was nothing negative or antisocial about their actions. Instead, many saw the looting as a conscious effort to destabilize the cooperative's assets. Dismantling socialist infrastructure and cutting down "Communist trees" were deeply political acts to them, acts aimed at eliminating any possibility that this kind of cooperative could once again exist to assert control over production and their lives.

By cutting "Communist trees," we suggest, villagers sought to do away with the socialist regime. For them, the rampage of 1991 was more than a mere attempt by individual villagers to take cooperative and state assets into their personal possession. It did not simply arise from random acts of violence caused by villagers' frustration with the socialist regime. Instead, the actions reflected a conscious desire to "unmake" socialist property. By cutting down "Communist trees" and destroying cooperative buildings, they wanted to bring down the pillars upon which the regime's control over their lives had rested. In a way, the fruit trees and chestnuts were no longer assets but liabilities because they were "Communist"—and as long as they existed, some people feared, the socialist regime could always return.

Custom in Common

There was another type of reaction to the collapse of the socialist regime in Kodra: some villagers started to patrol patches of chestnut forest. A few of them even camped out among the chestnuts at night as a way to keep loggers away. They focused on the patches that they or their parents had owned prior to collectivization. They felt that they continued to possess rights to the forest, and that now was the time to assert their rights before others cut down the forest.

More than a decade later, villagers still remembered with pride their efforts and eventual success when they spoke to Johannes in 2004. They also told him how they had engaged in collective efforts to assert their claims to chestnut forests. In 1991, the men making up the village council went to the neighboring village of Arrat to press Kodra's claims on a block of chestnut forest located between the two villages. They felt prompted to assert their claims because people from Arrat had started to log the forest. The men eventually convinced the council of Arrat that Kodra held exclusive rights to the chestnuts because it had been in the possession of families from Kodra prior to collectivization. A year later, Kodra's people took possession of three more patches of chestnut forest located in the immediate vicinity of the village.

Historical rights also became the defining criterion for the distribution of chestnut forests within Kodra. When the villagers divided the chestnut forests, they did so in reference to the distribution that had existed prior to collectivization. The village elders still remembered the old borders and they had no problem pointing out which family was entitled to what parcel of forest based on the historical pattern. Additionally, it was not a problem that, after more than thirty years of collectivization, many households had grown into extended families (*fis*). In such cases, the extended families divided the parcels among all member households in an egalitarian manner. As a result, about 60 percent of Kodra's approximately three hundred households received some chestnut forest—the size of the parcels ranged from tiny patches to a hectare (ha)—and for those that did not receive any, it was not an issue. Nearly everyone Johannes spoke to in 2004, with or without chestnuts, said that it was the right way to distribute the forest.

In Kodra, villagers did not bother to seek endorsement of their customary rights from the District Forest Service (DFS). After all, the forests formally remained in state ownership under the 1991 Land Law, and according to the 1992 Forest Law, the DFS had the mandate to manage the forest. Villagers were aware that the DFS did not initiate any action in opposition to Kodra's repossession of the chestnuts, as it was busy concentrating its limited law enforcement capacities on the protection of other, more valuable forest.

Nonetheless, we suggest that there was another reason why villagers did not seek DFS approval: they had a more powerful justification for their claims on the chestnuts. Historical rights mattered more to Kodra's people than statutory rights, and they could count on other people—including the very people working in state offices—to respect them. This was how they understood an appeal launched by the district government in 1992. The government called upon villages to protect "their" forests against logging. Kodra's people seized the opportunity not only to protect the chestnut trees against outsiders but also to claim possession.

There was widespread recognition of customary rights to forests not only in and around Kodra but across Albania. In reference to "custom" (*sipas zakonit*), villagers around the country restituted forests back to historical holders (and discussed if they should do the same with agricultural land—see Chapter 1). In many villages, people asserted customary rights to forest or agricultural land on the basis of historical possession. Particularly in the northern part of the country, villagers claimed possession of land and forests based on historical rights in the aftermath of the socialist regime's collapse. Asserting their customary rights, they sought to keep out woodcutters from other areas, even loggers licensed by the General Directorate of Forests and Pastures (de Waal 2004).

References to customary regulations, or "the Kanun" (*sipas kanunit*), made a dramatic reappearance in Albania after the suppression of these regulations ceased with the collapse of the socialist regime (Voell 2003; de Waal 2004). This was especially true of the people from Northern Albania, who referred to the Kanun in many facets of personal life and economic production. They not only justified the distribution of land and the resolution of land disputes on the basis of the Kanun, but also asserted its relevance in varying contexts: from the prosecution of killings and rules of inheritance to rituals for childbirth, marriage, and death (Lastarria-Cornhiel and Wheeler 1998; de Waal 2004). The influence of the Kanun was also evident in squatter settlements in the capital Tirana (Voell 2003).[4]

What happened in Kodra, we argue, was that custom emerged as an alternative institution to the state for governing chestnut forests (see also Sikor, Müller, and Stahl 2009). As people asserted customary rights to the chestnuts, they also attributed legitimacy to custom as an institution in control over forests. To them, customary rules provided alternative legitimizations to state law; they decided to refer to custom and not the state when backing up their claims on forest.[5] We are speaking here of "custom in the singular," despite the "many forms of expression" custom takes in practice (Thompson 1993: 2). People valued the idea of custom itself, not just particular customs. The idea of custom emerged as an alternative to "the idea of the state" (Abrams 1988). Through customary claims on forests in Kodra, people did not just want to dismantle the socialist regime, as we noted in the previous section, but they also wanted to establish custom as an alternative institution to the state.

To further illustrate this significance of custom as an institution governing forests we now turn to Bagëtia, the second village. We tell the following story in relatively extensive detail to demonstrate how villagers were accustomed to setting out into local forests, and felt entitled to consider them their own. Additionally, the story reveals how villagers persuaded other people to recognize their claims to local forests on the basis of customary notions of proper practices and decent behavior. In the words of Thompson, custom served them as "rhetoric of legitimation" (Thompson 1993: 6).

Bagëtia: The Story of Gjergji

Early one morning in the late summer of 2004, Johannes accompanied Gjergji Hoxha on his trip to the Gorë Mountains. Riding Gjergji's mules, they crossed the thick coppice and underbrush surrounding the village of Bagëtia, and headed north until they reached the vast stretch of deciduous forest that extends from the Qafë Panje Pass to far beyond the Shkumbin River. They rode for several hours through the woods, making sure to stay on barely visible paths and never leaving the cover of the forest. Gjergji had taken the trip many times before. His pursuit of high value timber from old-growth oaks and fir trees had led him all over the Gorë and Mokra mountains.

Gjergji regularly traveled to the mountains above Bagëtia to cut fir stanchions. He, his brother, and their parents had not been able to migrate to Greece permanently, unlike most other villagers (see Chapter 1). They could not obtain the usual three-year visas for Greece because they had a Muslim family name. Nevertheless, the Hoxhas learned how to make a living in

Bagëtia. The father, Agim, became director of an elementary school in a nearby village. More importantly, both sons went into the timber business.

After nearly three hours, Gjergji and Johannes reached the place that Gjergji had in mind. Until then, the ride had felt like a Sunday excursion, but now Gjergji was determined to get some work done quickly. As Johannes hobbled the mules, Gjergji prepared the chainsaw. He then felled an impressive mountain fir about twelve meters tall, removed the branches, cut three two-meter pieces from the log, and halved them into six stanchions. The entire chainsaw operation did not take more than twenty minutes. Afterwards, when the heavy stanchions were being loaded onto the mules, Johannes realized how Gjergji had come to acquire his impressive muscles.

Gjergji felt entitled to take the fir, just like the other villagers who cut mainly firewood for subsistence consumption in the forests above Bagëtia. They said that they held historical rights to the forests surrounding their village. They marked their claims by spraying warnings over trees and rocks. "Property of Bagëtia," the signs read, or similar warnings.[6] When Johannes asked about the historical roots of their assertions, they referred to Bagëtia's glorious history as a settlement along the Via Egnatia, a major trade route connecting Western and Eastern Europe, from Roman times until the eighteenth century. Back then, people said, the village had been much larger and they had owned land and forest all around it. This was the reason they now felt they deserved to repossess local forests for themselves.

The guards sent by the District Forest Service did not present a problem; Gjergji recounted one of the rare encounters he had with one. Just as he had done on the day he spent with Johannes earlier in the year, Gjergji traveled up the mountain to cut fir stanchions with his chainsaw. But the noise gave away his location to a forest guard on patrol nearby, and made it impossible for him to hear the guard approaching. Since Gjergji had been caught in the act, he could neither run nor talk himself out of the predicament. All he could do was to cautiously offer a bribe. "Come on," Gjergji said to the forest guard, "let's find a common language!" The guard clearly understood the intention, but initially declined. Gjergji reacted by insisting: "Come on, you are not a Serb, you are an Albanian. It must be possible to find a common language!"

That was a strong way of putting things. For many Albanians, Serbs were considered as enemies. Historical animosities between Serbs and Albanians had come to a peak during the Kosovo War in 1998–99. Albanians living in Albania had openly declared their support for their ethnic compatriots living in Kosovo, then a province of the Federal Republic of Yugoslavia. Many had supported the armed struggle of ethnic Albanian forces for an independent Kosovo against the Serbian security forces and Yugoslav army. Many had personally experienced the suffering of their compatriots when thousands of ethnic Albanians fled to Albania during the war. Thus, virtually all Albanians felt sympathetic toward their ethnic compatriots in Kosovo, and harbored deep resentments against anyone they identified as being affiliated with the Serbian domination of what was Yugoslavia back then, and the Serb-led war against ethnic Albanians (Pettifer and Vickers 2007).

Indeed, Gjergji's stern words helped. The guard settled on a bribe of eight euros, and Gjergji thereby avoided paying a fine of several hundred euros. The forest guard averted the accusation of being unreasonable and indecent— besides pocketing a small monetary reward for looking away. When Gjergji raised doubts about whether the guard would honor their agreement, the guard reassured him: "Are we men [of honor], or what are we?"[7]

Gjergji and Johannes did not encounter a forest guard on their trip. Johannes heard later that the outing had paid off for Gjergji. The following week he sold the stanchions to a timber trader from the lowlands, along with others he and his brother had cut in the weeks before. They received eight euros for each, in addition to the money they had made from previous sales. Over the entire year, Agim, Gjergji's father, estimated they had made about 6,000 euros from the two sons' logging activities—almost half the Hoxhas' income of 13,000 euros in 2004.

At the Frontiers of Property, Custom, and State

Gjergji and the other woodcutters from Bagëtia were not the only ones logging timber and cutting firewood in the rich forests of the Gorë and Mokra mountains. There were also people like Fatos and Tomorr Shkurtaj, who ran a wood business. Johannes visited them one day at their newly built house in the lowland village of Çerekja. They described how they used three IFA trucks and a Mercedes truck to haul firewood from the mountains and deliver it to households and retailers in the lowlands. The IFA truck was the "work horse" in the Gorë and Mokra mountains. Produced in East Germany until 1990, it remained a frequent sight in the Albanian countryside. Yet, Fatos and Tomorr's pride was the Mercedes. Fatos had purchased it himself in Germany and driven it to Albania.

Fatos and Tomorr were serious businessmen. They had acquired a license for the wood business back in 1993, for which they had to pay a fee and prove that they did not have any criminal record. Most recently, they had participated in the tendering process organized by the District Forest Service and placed the highest bid. That won them a harvest quota of 15 ha for a six-month period, together with another five companies. At the time, the six of them were the only ones holding harvest quotas for the Qafë Panje and Guri Nikes forest sector near Bagëtia.

Similar to the villagers, people in the licensed wood business asserted that they, and no one else, had the right to extract timber and firewood from the forests. They based their claims on the fact that they had followed the legal stipulations for forest exploitation, as laid out in Albania's forest regulations. The District Forest Service had marked the areas that they could harvest. In contrast, everyone else acted in violation of the law. Fatos and Tomorr did not mention, though, that licensed wood businesses circumvented the forest regulations whenever they could. For example, they habitually cut trees other than the ones permitted by the DFS, and took out higher volumes of wood than permitted.

Besides villagers and licensed wood businesses, an ever-growing number of people in the region had become involved in logging the forests from 1997 onward. Every summer, when the dirt roads dried up, large numbers of woodcutters went up the mountain to cut timber, but mainly firewood. This included individual woodcutters from surrounding villages working on their own behalf. They could number at least a hundred over the course of a summer, but possibly up to two or even three hundred. These woodcutters would cut down trees with their own chainsaws and transport the logs to the roads using horses or mules, where they would split them into firewood. They would sell the wood on to firewood traders without harvest quotas, who would then sell it to households in the lowlands.

The woodcutters asserted the legitimacy of their activities, similar to how the villagers and licensed wood businesses did. The most common argument was that they had problems making ends meet and relied on the income gained from woodcutting for their subsistence. It was this reasoning that was behind an angry exchange between an elderly man and a forest guard. The elderly man told Johannes that the guard had asked him to stop extracting wood. In reaction, the man yelled at the guard: "Do you think we came here for fun? We came here because we have to eat!" To emphasize his point, and to make clear that he felt entitled to extract wood, the elderly man added: "Okay, fine me if you want! I have five children who cut trees; fine them too, if you want to! Start the prosecution! We will all go to jail and the state will have to feed us."

It was not only the elderly man who felt this way; many woodcutters claimed they had the right to ensure they had enough to eat, even if it meant breaking the law. Moreover, they could expect forest guards to ignore the violation, the very people holding a mandate to enforce the law.

Finally, there were the logging crews who worked with unlicensed wood traders. They accounted for most of the logging in terms of the volume of timber and firewood cut. Johannes estimated that in 2004 the traders' trucks may have brought approximately five hundred woodcutters up the mountain. The crews typically consisted of four to six young men from the lowlands. They worked under their own auspices, similar to the individual woodcutters. They also sold to the same truck drivers. In contrast to the woodcutters from the surrounding villages, however, they did not make any property claims on the forests of Qafë Panje or Guri Nikes. They just wanted to earn money as quickly as possible, and maybe with no intention of traveling up the mountain again.

It was not mere coincidence that unlicensed loggers began to cut the forests above Bagëtia in 1997. That year, people across the country again went on a rampage reminiscent of the chaos in the aftermath of the socialist regime's collapse. Across the country people ransacked banks, town halls, courthouses, land registries, police stations, and even military barracks (de Waal 1998). The turmoil came to a head when military depots were looted and arms stolen, including some 600,000 Kalashnikov AK-47s. The European Union eventually felt compelled to send in an international intervention force and support new elections (Saltmarshe 2001). Nationwide, the situation had calmed down by the end of 1997. On the slopes above Bagëtia, however, loggers continued to exploit forests for many years.

The forests above Bagëtia represented a frontier, not only because they offered plentiful opportunities for personal enrichment but also because of the ongoing negotiations over property, state, and custom. Many of the people seeking a share in the benefits that could be derived from the forests also asserted property rights to them, which were customary as well as referring to state law. Villagers' and individual woodcutters' customary claims existed side by side with the statutory rights claimed by the licensed wood businesses on the basis of Albania's forest law. Moreover, villagers and woodcutters adhered to different notions of customary rights: villagers asserted customary rights based on historical possession, whereas woodcutters upheld their right to make a living. Custom offered people a dynamic point of reference for making claims on forests, since it was malleable, contested, and subject to ongoing negotiations. "[C]ustom was a field of change and of contest, an arena in which opposing interests made conflicting claims" (Thompson 1993: 6). Due to this malleability, custom held significant appeal to both villagers and woodcutters, as suitably illustrated by the latter referring to customary subsistence rights when they came to exploit forest around Bagëtia. Moreover, the appeal to custom as a basis for property rights was similar to the ways in which the appeal to the state functioned for licensed wood businesses.

The contestations had profound implications for the forests on the Gorë and Mokra mountains, similar to many other frontier situations.[8] Total wood extraction, the former Director of the District Forest Service in Pogradec estimated, increased by more than 50 percent between 1990 and 2004. Dense forest turned into open-canopy forest, rapidly diminishing mature forest throughout the Qafë Panje and Guri Nikes forest sector. Participatory land use maps prepared by a few villagers under Johannes's facilitation suggested that closed-canopy forest coverage declined from 59 percent of the total village area to 44 percent. The degradation of the forests around Bagëtia was not unusual in Albania, however. Nationwide, forests shrunk by some 20 percent between 1991 and 2001 (Jansen et al. 2006; Stahl 2010b).

Conflicts at the Frontier

The struggles over property, state, and custom not only caused the degradation of the forests around Bagëtia, but also led to conflicts between people. The people involved in these conflicts commonly appealed to custom and state, even though the conflicts were not simply a clash between state and customary regulations. The problem was not that people found the idea of the state as the institution governing forests incompatible with the idea of customary forest management. Rather, the conflicts arose because people could not agree on a set of practical procedures on how to deal with competing property claims in a peaceful manner.

One of the most violent conflicts Johannes became aware of in 2004 resulted in the hospitalization of a young shepherd. The twenty-year-old man from Bagëtia lay on the brink of death in the military hospital of Tirana for several days due to severe injuries sustained in a confrontation with a logging crew. His family had had to arrange for him to be transported to the capital. The woodcutters, with their substantial physical strength, had nearly beaten the shepherd to death in a dispute over forest access.

The dispute involved the damage that was being done by logging trucks to pastures in Bagëtia. The trucks often drove across them for the most direct access routes to the forests. Villagers had long been upset about this, in the same way they were upset about the wanton exploitation of forest that they considered theirs. In this particular case, the shepherd and his father had watched the truck trespass over the family's pasture for a few days, and noticed how the truck's wheels were destroying the grass cover.

Violence erupted when the family decided that they would no longer accept the intrusion. In addition, Johannes learned, they wanted to teach the loggers a lesson. The next morning they placed a camouflaged nail board across the IFA's path and waited in a blind until the truck drove across the board. When the driver and his crew got out of the cabin and saw two flat tires, they started cursing and shouting insults. Rather than remain hidden, the young shepherd felt provoked to leave his hiding spot. The ensuing angry exchange of insults soon turned violent, leaving the young man close to death.

The conflict, it appears, turned violent for two reasons. First, the logging crew did not want to stay away from the family's pasture; this was no different than when they ignored the signs requesting them to stay away from Bagëtia's forests. Second, loggers and villagers did not possess any peaceful means by which they could resolve their disputes in a manner acceptable to both sides. Villagers' reference to custom as the institution that governed rights to forests and held sway over dispute resolution did not hold appeal to the loggers. Neither were they inclined to respect state law or invoke state officials for the resolution of their disputes. Consequently, there was no one to turn to for conflict resolution, and their dispute descended into direct confrontation and physical violence.

The District Forest Service considered the unlicensed wood trade and logging to be "organized crime," and the trees cut to be "contraband." As such, the traders and loggers became the primary target of law enforcement. To bolster its enforcement powers the DFS sought cooperation with the police. For example, it requested the police to send them a list of all (approximately one hundred) truck owners in the district, with their places of residence and license plate numbers. The list was important, as they regarded all truck owners as potential forest poachers even though only some people on the list had registered a wood business.

The District Forest Service sought to employ a strategy of deterrence against unlicensed loggers. The director explained to Johannes, "Fear guards the graveyard," implying that the loggers would only stay away if they were too afraid of potential drastic consequences to engage in unlicensed logging, even if no forest guard was visible. To demonstrate DFS intent, they occasionally organized concerted actions in addition to the regular patrols. One day in August, for example, Johannes found truck drivers, logging crews, and individual woodcutters alike in a panic. Nine guards from the DFS, plus its director, had come up to the Qafë Panje mountain pass and confiscated all wood they detected that did not have an accompanying license, and amassed a huge pile.

The problem for the District Forest Service was that they lacked the capacity to "guard the graveyard" effectively. This became clear on that same day in August when they could not transport the confiscated wood back to Pogradec with the means available to them, and so had to call in the military and request military trucks for the transport of the confiscated wood. The means available to the DFS for law enforcement were extremely limited. The entire office in Pogradec commanded only two off-road cars, one of them being in permanent use by the director. The nine guards had no way of patrolling the sectors assigned to them, particularly in remote areas such as the Qafë Panje and Guri Nikes forest sector. Moreover, their monthly salaries amounted to a meager one hundred euros, which was not enough to feed a family.

The District Forest Service's strategy to instill sufficient "fear" in the logging crews was also not as effective as the director had hoped. The lack of fear, or even basic respect, became apparent in another event in early 2004 that left a forest guard physically injured and emotionally upset. He had stopped an IFA carrying unlicensed wood near Qafë Panje. When the driver opened the door, he saw that the guard had already begun to fill out the slip for the fine. The driver became so furious that, yelling profanities, he jumped out of the truck, beat up the guard, and left him in the ditch next to the road.

The lack of respect for the forest guards reflected the widespread decline in the legitimacy Albanians attributed to the state. The decline gained momentum in the years before 1997 and culminated in the nationwide rampage of that year—and it did not dissipate. Many Albanians felt betrayed by the state. They saw political leaders engage in personal feuds, perpetrate violence, and enrich themselves in office. Many people resented the state for not being able to guarantee their personal security. They felt that it had done little to stop the cross-border trafficking of people, arms, and drugs by Mafia-style gangs, which openly challenged state monopoly over the means of law enforcement (Saltmarshe 2001). The frustrations came to a head in 1997 when people implicated political leaders in the collapse of pyramid investment schemes, which wiped out approximately 60 percent of Albania's private savings (Abdul-Hamid 2003). It was not mere coincidence that the rush on the forest in Bagëtia started in the same year. The decline in the legitimacy of the state lingered long after 1997, in Bagëtia as elsewhere.

Thus conflicts erupted in the forests above Bagëtia when some actors tried to exclude others. Whether it was villagers asserting customary rights or forest guards seeking to enforce state regulations, their attempts met fierce opposition from those they wanted to keep away. The unlicensed woodcutters did not want to recognize their exclusion on either customary or statutory grounds. Nor did they accept customary or state procedures for the resolution of disputes. The problem was that the different actors could not agree on a set of practical procedures on how to deal with competing property claims (see also Sturgeon and Sikor 2004). They had not developed "routinized rules [or] crystallized practices of exclusion and inclusion" (Verdery 1999: 55). Conflicts did not arise due to a straightforward clash between state and custom.

Routinizing New Rules: The Frontier Closes

Despite the conflicts, the incident involving the forest guard and the IFA driver recounted above also indicated to Johannes how guards and unlicensed traders were developing a more peaceful arrangement. To his surprise, he learned that the driver had not stopped for the forest guard in order to obey state law. Quite the contrary—he could have easily driven by. Instead, despite driving a truck carrying unlicensed wood, he stopped to give the forest guard a ride. That was common practice, Johannes heard; guards often hitched rides on trucks if they needed to get up to Qafë Panje. Since they rarely had their own vehicle, they went on trucks to avoid walking for several hours. It was no contradiction to them that many of these trucks operated without a license.

In 2004, the District Forest Service and unlicensed loggers were in the process of routinizing new rules of engagement, a fact Johannes discovered through another experience in that year. One day, a high-ranking official from the DFS saw a young man from Kodra on his way home. The 25-year-old Dani Sherifi had been cutting trees at Qafë Panje all day and his truck was fully loaded with firewood. When Dani refused to stop, the official began to chase the truck in his off-road vehicle. The wild chase ended in the center of Kodra where Dani stopped his truck and ran off.

Dani had become involved in the firewood business after his family had bought him a truck for 3,200 euros the previous year. They were able to afford the truck only after his father had saved up from income he had earned working for ten years as a taxi driver. The father had also taken out a small loan from the Kodra farmers' association. Like so many others, Dani had not obtained the required business license or harvest quota. As soon as the dirt road leading up the mountain from Kodra had dried up, Dani drove his truck there on a regular basis. Usually he took along three or four other young men from the village to cut firewood together, and return at night. Occasionally he also purchased firewood from woodcutters who had set up camp in the mountains for the summer.

During his narrow escape, Dani asked a village elder, Bashkim Zela, to intervene on his behalf before he ran off to hide. Bashkim was sitting at a small bar in the center of Kodra drinking with other village elders. Bashkim knew the forest guard from high school and promised to help. When the official arrived shortly after, Bashkim began a conversation with him. He continued to distract the official, even though it was clear that the guard wanted to pursue the chase as quickly as possible. Bashkim's intention was to persuade the guard to disregard the offender.

After a long discussion and a lot of *raki* (locally distilled liquor), Bashkim succeeded. The official eventually agreed to let Dani off the hook. He gave the young man until midnight to get rid of the firewood—by which he meant that Dani could sell it, as long as he found a buyer immediately. If not, he emphasized, he would come back to fine Dani 4,000 euros, the sum equivalent to the approximate value of the truck and its load.

This incident demonstrates how the District Forest Service and unlicensed loggers were developing new rules to govern access to the forests of Qafë Panje and Guri Nikes. The new rules had taken firm hold by 2008, when Johannes visited Bagëtia to follow up on his earlier fieldwork (see also Stahl 2010b). Traders admitted to tacit agreements with the DFS, to their mutual advantage. The forest guards now ignored their activities, even though they did not hold licenses. In return, they paid 400 to 500 euros per truck to the DFS director each season. He then redistributed the money internally within the DFS, making sure that all guards received some of the money. In fact, they had entirely stopped issuing harvest quotas. Obviously, this had not prevented the exploitation of the forests, but there were no longer open conflicts over the forests of Qafë Panje and Guri Nikes. Moreover, the forest guards had a safer and a somewhat wealthier life than before.

Similarly, forest guards and villagers continued to leave each other alone. During his entire time in Bagëtia, Johannes never heard about a violent conflict between the two sides. As indicated by Gjergji's story above, forest guards and villagers developed an arrangement that was mutually beneficial. Neither state officials (or licensed wood businesses) nor villagers contested each other's claims on the forest. The subsistence argument carried weight with forest officials. The DFS director, for example, frankly admitted that "the directorate has been a bit lax with loggers around Bagëtia." He justified the lack of law enforcement against them with the following words, "We know that they are poor and need the forest as a livelihood source." The subsistence argument had much traction with the forest guards because they originated from local villages, possessed strong allegiances to the rest of rural society, and felt the pull of local loyalties.

The actors involved in the extraction of wood thus developed new rules to govern the forests of Qafë Panje and Guri Nikes. A key rule was that no actor would try to exclude another. The new rules instead kept access and claims to the forests inclusive of all actors, since no "practices of exclusion" had crystallized (Verdery 1999: 55). A second, equally critical element in the new rules was that forest guards and wood traders agreed on new routines to define and enforce the rules and resolve possible disputes. They routinized new rules via direct, personal contacts, often helped by mutual friends who brokered specific deals. The new rules reflected the influence of the District Forest Service's statutory powers and the legitimacy accorded to customary regulations. They were not simply customary, as the DFS's involvement rested on the mandate it received in national legislation. Nor did they simply reflect the powers and procedures defined in the Forest Law, because an additional characteristic of the new routines was that in practice they were only loosely interpreted and applied.

Unlicensed wood extraction was a common phenomenon in Albania. A survey conducted by the Albanian Center for Economic Research found that unlicensed extraction of timber and firewood amounted to 40 percent of the total harvest (ACER 2001). In some parts of the country, forestry experts estimated that up to 95 percent of the wood cut annually was felled without a license (Legisi 2001, cited in de Waal 2004: 35).

Dardha: Efforts of State Comeback

Wood extraction peaked in Dardha in 1997. Loggers discovered the mature forest nearby the village as the entire country descended into turmoil. The logging mirrored the events in Bagëtia, not only in terms of timing but also by villagers' recollection of the circumstances surrounding it: their feeble attempts to keep outsiders away; the rush on the timber and firewood; villagers' inability to secure a significant share of the profit for themselves; the conflicts and occasional flares of violence. One critical difference was that Dardha's forest was much smaller than the forests above Bagëtia, a mere 260 ha. The loggers quickly depleted the available timber and firewood and went on to other areas in early 1998. By the time they left, the mature forest had been reduced to shrub and coppice.

From 1998 on, Dardha's forest might have followed the fate of Kodra's chestnut trees if it had not been the target of two international donor initiatives. Villagers may have resorted to customary ways of managing the forestland, which remained a source of firewood and an area to graze livestock, yet the two initiatives executed by Albania's Directorate General of Forests and Pastures (DGFP) effectively closed down space for customary management by giving the state a visible presence. The perplexing element in this was that both initiatives sought to accommodate customary forest management.

One initiative was the Communal Forests and Pastures Management Program funded by the World Bank and USAID. Designed according to international standards in participatory forest management, the program aimed to facilitate devolved management of forests based on their customary use by local people. Its key rationale was that devolution to local associations would allow villagers to satisfy their firewood and fodder needs from adjacent forests, and simultaneously enlist them for the protection of these forests. It was an ambitious national program, seeking to facilitate local management for 40 percent of all forest in the country. To create a supportive policy framework, Albania's Ministry of Agriculture and Food passed Regulation 308, which set out procedures for the transfer of use and management rights regarding forest and pastures to so-called Forest User Associations (DGFP et al. 2002).

When Johannes was in Dardha in 2004, the program had facilitated the establishment of a Forest User Association to manage Dardha's degraded forest. The association managed not only this forest, but also another 3,500 ha of forest in the commune, most of it low-value coppice. The association held use and management rights to the forests under a ten-year contract with the District Forest Service. The contract allowed villagers to cut firewood and fodder, and to use the forest for grazing livestock. In return, villagers had to purchase permits from the association for modest fees— the annual fee for cutting firewood, for example, was only four euros (CFPM/SNV 2003). An essential part of the contract between the association and the District Forest Service was a management plan, which a private consultancy had prepared and the DFS approved. The association's board had little influence on the management plan, which was also the case for the village committees, even though the villagers had elected the board.

The second initiative was a conservation and development project supported by the German Agency for Technical Cooperation (GTZ) in conjunction with Prespa National Park.[9] Dardha became a part of the park when Albania's government founded it in 2000 to contribute to the development of the first transboundary protected area in the Balkans. On the Albanian side, the park not only included the Prespa Lakes but also forests, meadows, and agricultural land under intensive use by the local population. GTZ committed technical assistance in an effort to ease the looming conflict between biodiversity conservation and local development.

The management plan granted customary wood cutting a "temporary exemption" from the general prohibition imposed on many kinds of natural resource use within the park's boundaries. Nonetheless, villagers resented the heavy-handed manner in which the park restricted customary land uses. For example, the management plan did not simply exempt woodcutting from the long list of prohibitions but tied the exemption to the condition that the woodcutting be done in ways "that allow the restoration of the forest" (Parku Kombëtar "Prespa" 1999: 5). Moreover, the park's staff concentrated their efforts on enforcing the rules and regulations pertaining to wood extraction.

Ultimately both state initiatives had limited effects on villagers' forest use practices (see also Stahl, Sikor, and Dorondel 2009). On the one hand, people did pay the obligatory fees for the collection of firewood. The association hired two elderly women, who took their task of guarding Dardha's forest seriously and, during Johannes's time in the village, typically sat by the main path leading into the forest. They reported that they rarely caught anyone carrying firewood or oak twigs who had not paid the fee. On the other hand, the forest was no longer worth much since loggers had depleted the timber in 1997. It hardly needed to be guarded against firewood poaching because it was of little interest to outsiders or to wealthier villagers, who typically purchased the needed firewood. As for grazing livestock, goat herders continued to take their animals to the forest to feed on the leaves and young branches of deciduous trees. The ubiquitous signs set up by the park administration prohibiting these practices did not deter them.

The two initiatives, we argue, made the state's presence clear to the villagers. By 2004, seven years after the logging frenzy, the state was very much on people's minds due to the practices of representation used by officials to implement the two initiatives. There was one vexing element to this: the initiatives promoted the idea of the state even though they ostensibly followed the declared intention to facilitate customary forest management. This apparently contradictory outcome occurred because the initiatives put state officials in charge of promoting customary uses, which was not the same as recognizing custom as an independent institution governing forests. This did not mean, however, that the District Forest Service and park administration had actual control over villagers' forest use practices. The initiatives had no real effect on villagers' lives. On paper, however, in official meetings and on the billboards (the concrete means available to officials), it looked like the state was in charge of forest management.

Property, State and Custom in Kodra, Bagëtia, and Dardha

We find that there was nothing less than a mad scramble for timber and firewood in the aftermath of the socialist regime's collapse in the three villages. To villagers and outsiders alike, forests represented one of the few assets remaining in the countryside that were valuable to them for various reasons.[10] Many rushed on the forest whenever they could, because they were afraid to lose out if others made the first move. Many also asserted their own property claims on forests, that they were legitimate users of the forest, or that the forests should be in their possession. However, not all of those extracting wood made this assertion. Some, such as the unlicensed logging crews cutting trees in Bagëtia's and Dardha's forests, did not care to claim possession. As all of these actors struggled over access and asserted claims, they made and unmade property relations regarding the forest.

Forest property relations remained in a peculiar "postsocialist limbo" (de Waal 2004: 47), in contrast to agriculture where property relations had become more settled (see Chapter 1). In none of the three villages did the involved actors come to a shared understanding of which claims on the forest were legitimate and which were not, whereas they did so regarding agricultural land in Bagëtia and Dardha. Negotiations over property were ongoing because of a general lack of routinized rules governing access to and control over forests. Underlying this lack of clarity was also an ambiguity about which institutions of authority people wanted to govern forests, and which they considered to exercise legitimate control over forests. The involved actors made claims that related to a variety of institutions, including national law, the actual practices employed by the District Forest Service, village customs, widely shared norms of entitlements, and so on. Just as the relationship between these politico-legal institutions remained unclear, so property relations were similarly ambiguous (see also Sturgeon and Sikor 2004).

The "postsocialist limbo" found reflection in significant variation between villages with regard to the specific forms of negotiations over property and authority. In Kodra, forest property became defined in customary ways, custom becoming the primary institution governing the forests. In villagers' views, chestnut management did not require the state, although most accepted the distribution of agricultural land by the state (see Chapter 1). Bagëtia, in contrast, long remained at the frontiers of property, state, and custom, as the involved actors did not agree on what kinds of forest claims were legitimate, if there was a need to legitimatize some claims at all, and if so, what sort of institution should sanction the claims as legitimate. The negotiations over forests came after the restitution of agricultural land, but did not take the same customary course due to the intervention of powerful outsiders. Yet, over time the people of Bagëtia developed new rules for dealing with claims on forests, rules that fitted both their notions of the state as well as custom. Not unlike Bagëtia, Dardha experienced a dramatic collapse of state control over nearby forest. However, the state staged an unexpected comeback a few years later, asserting itself once again as the proper institution to hold control over forests, just as the state had done in agriculture by way of land distribution. Comparing the three villages, and looking at agricultural land and forest, negotiations over property and authority thus accorded the state the most central role in Dardha. We notice that negotiations over property were intimately linked with contestations over the idea of the state, as conceptually distinct from struggles involving concrete political regimes, policies, agencies, or officials (see also Abrams 1988; Nuijten 2003). The very notion of the state itself, as an institution holding authority over people's affairs, was at stake in villagers' negotiations over property. Villagers were not sure whether they should attribute authority over property regarding forest to the state, or to other institutions. This does not mean that they did not see ruptures within the state, such as between national law and local officials' actual practices, or between the actions of different agencies. Nor does it imply that social actors did not contest particular state practices. However, we do wish to suggest that people believed there were alternatives to the state. Other institutions offered social actors alternative authorizations for claims on forests, and at times, there was no need for the state to govern forests.

Custom emerged as an alternative to the state, "custom in the singular" (Thompson 1993: 2). Just as people questioned the very idea of the state, they explored how useful the idea of custom was as an institution to authorize claims as legitimate and offer them the required backing. Of course, they understood that custom, like the state, was a somewhat ambiguous institution that supported multiple and often competing claims on forests. They also saw that all the claims made in the name of custom did not come together into a single coherent set of customary rights to forest or customary ways of dispute resolution. Nevertheless, custom, in its varied incarnations, emerged as an alternative to the state. In a certain way, custom even competed with the state over authority, in the sense that social actors had a choice of whether they wanted to reference their claims to the state or to custom. However, in other ways, state and custom coexisted quite happily because people developed concrete rules that related to both of them.

The linkage between property and authority will remain relevant for our inquiries in the following chapters. Struggles over property may not put the idea of the state up for negotiation, and contestations over authority may take other forms. However, struggles over property in the forests of Romania and Vietnam are just as likely to raise contestations over authority as the struggles in Albania documented here.

Notes

1. *"Mos prek pyllin e Bagëties!"* in Albanian.
2. Monique Nuijten (2003) provides a wonderful illustration of how negotiations over property feed into everyday processes of state formation in Mexico. Her account shows how the state, as an idea or conception, gets constituted through people's experiences in their concrete struggles for the recognition of land claims.
3. The following account draws on Stahl (2010b).
4. Looking for further insights on "the Kanun," the literature points first to a booklet written in 1933, in which a Catholic priest tried to systematically codify the customary rules that had previously been transmitted orally from generation to generation in Albania over many centuries (Gjeçov [1933] 1989). Yet it also makes very clear that it is not helpful to understand the Kanun as a clearly identifiable,

consistent set of rules, as we will argue in the course of this chapter. It is more useful to see the Kanun as a constantly evolving set of rules and practices that take on highly varied expressions across space and time (cf. Voell 2003; de Waal 2004).

5. See Lastarria-Cornhiel and Wheeler (1998) on inheritance, and Lemel (2000) on agricultural land rights, for how custom and state emerged as alternative legitimizations in other fields.
6. *"Prona e Bagëties!"* in Albanian.
7. *"Jemi burra o ç'farë jemi?"* in Albanian.
8. See also Stahl (2010b) on the distribution of overall benefits among the different actors involved in the logging.
9. The organization changed its name to German Agency for International Cooperation (GIZ) subsequently.
10. See Stahl (2010a) for a wider discussion of how forests were valuable assets to various kinds of social actors.

References

Abdul-Hamid, Yara. 2003. "A Fair Deal for Albanian Farmers." Oxfam Briefing Paper 45. Oxford: Oxfam.

Abrams, Philip. 1988. "Notes on the Difficulty of Studying the State (1977)." *Journal of Historical Sociology* 1(1): 58–89.

Albanian Center for Economic Research (ACER). 2001. Illegal Logging Independent Study: Final Report. Tirana: World Bank.

Communal Forests and Pastures Management Program and SNV Netherlands Development Organisation. 2003. "Communal Forests and Pastures Management: Case Studies." Peshkopi, Albania.

Directorate General of Forests and Pastures (DGFP), Food and Agriculture Organisation (FAO), World Food Programme (WFP), and SNV Netherlands Development Organisation. 2002. "Effects of the Albania Forestry Project on Poverty Reduction." Tirana.

Gjeçov, Shtjefën. (1933) 1989. *Kanuni I Leke Dukagjini* [The Code of Leke Dukagjini]. Translated with an Introduction by L. Fox. New York: Gjonlekaj Publishing Company.

Jansen, Louisa J.M., et al. 2006. "Analysis of the Spatio-Temporal and Semantic Aspects of Land-Cover/Use Change Dynamics 1991–2001 in Albania at National and District Levels." *Environmental Monitoring and Assessment* 119: 107–36.

Lastarria-Cornhiel, Susana, and Rachel Wheeler. 1998. "Gender, Ethnicity, and Landed Property in Albania." Working Paper No. 18: Albania Series. Madison, WI: University of Wisconsin-Madison Land Tenure Center.

Lemel, Harold. 2000. *Rural Property and Economy in Post-Communist Albania*. New York: Berghahn Books.

Nuijten, Monique. 2003. *Power, Community and the State: The Political Anthropology of Organisation in Mexico*. London: Pluto Press.

Parku Kombëtar "Prespa." 1999. "Plani Për Ruajtjen Dhe Menaxhimin E Parkut Kombëtar Të Prespës" [Plan for the protection and management of the Prespa National Park]. Prespa, Greece: Prespa National Park.

Pettifer, James, and Miranda Vickers. 2007. *The Albanian Question: Reshaping the Balkans*. London: I.B. Tauris.

Saltmarshe, Douglas. 2001. *Identity in a Post-Communist Balkan State: An Albanian Village Study*. Aldershot: Ashgate.

Sikor, Thomas, Daniel Müller, and Johannes Stahl. 2009. "Land Fragmentation and Cropland Abandonment in Albania: Implications for the Roles of State and Community in Postsocialist Land Consolidation." *World Development* 37(8) (*The Limits of State-Led Land Reform*): 1411–23.

Sjöberg, Örjan. 1991. *Rural Change and Development in Albania*. Oxford and San Francisco: Westview Press.

Stahl, Johannes. 2010a. "The Rents of Illegal Logging: The Mechanisms Behind the Rush on Forest Resources in Southeast Albania." *Conservation and Society* 8(2): 140–50.

———. 2010b. *Rent from the Land: A Political Ecology of Postsocialist Rural Transformation*. London: Anthem Press.

Stahl, Johannes, Thomas Sikor, and Stefan Dorondel. 2009. "The Institutionalization of Property Rights in Albanian and Romanian Biodiversity Conservation." *International Journal of Agricultural Resources, Governance and Ecology* 8(1): 57–73.

Sturgeon, Janet, and Thomas Sikor. 2004. "Postsocialist Property in Asia and Europe— Variations on 'Fuzziness.'" *Conservation and Society* 2(1): 1–17.

Thompson, E.P. 1993. *Customs in Common*. New York: The New Press.

Verdery, Katherine. 1999. "Fuzzy Property: Rights, Power, and Identity in Transylvania's Decollectivization." In *Uncertain Transition: Ethnographies of Change in the Postsocialist World*, ed. Michael Burawoy and Katherine Verdery. Lanham, MD: Rowman & Littlefield, 53–81.

Vickers, Miranda, and James Pettifer. 1997. *Albania: From Anarchy to a Balkan Identity*. London: C. Hurst and Co.

Voell, Stephane. 2003. "The Kanun in the City: Albanian Customary Law as a Habitus and Its Persistence in the Suburb of Tirana, Bathore." *Anthropos* 98: 85–101.

Waal, Clarissa de. 1995. "Decollectivisation and Total Scarcity in High Albania." *Cambridge Anthropology* 18(1): 1–22.

———. 1998. "From Laissez-Faire to Anarchy in Post-Communist Albania." *Cambridge Anthropology* 20(3): 21–44.

———. 2004. "Post-Socialist Property Rights and Wrongs in Albania: An Ethnography of Agrarian Change." *Conservation and Society* 2(1): 19–50.

Woodcock, Shannon. 2007. "The Absence of Albanian Jokes about Socialism, or Why Some Dictatorships Are Not Funny." In *The Politics and Aesthetics of Refusal*, ed. Caroline Hamilton et al. Cambridge: Cambridge Scholars Press, 51–66.

5

Property, Predators, and Patrons in Romania

In 2004, when Stefan walked into the beech, oak, and fir forests surrounding the agricultural fields of Dragomireşti, he could not help but be impressed. One row of solid trees lined up against another. Ordered in neat stands of homogeneous age classes, the trees indicated the sound silvicultural practice applied by the *Ocolul Silvic* (Forest District) Mihăeşti during socialism. Stefan also discovered clearings that dissected the forests. Ranging from a single hectare (ha) to several dozen, the clearings attested to recent logging. The loggers also left tree trunks of approximately one meter in height in many clearings, which was perplexing. Why had the loggers left valuable wood behind? When Stefan asked villagers about this, he received a unanimous reply: the Rudari had done the logging, and they left stumps because, as they told him, "Rudari are too lazy to bend down to cut a tree near the ground." Moreover, villagers explained, the Rudari were not only lazy but also thieves; they had logged in villagers' forest without their permission.

While he was in Dragova, Stefan did not find any stumps of similar height in the oak or fir forests. There were clearings, but the loggers had made certain to remove every possible centimeter of wood from the forest. Talking to villagers, Stefan learned that a single firm, the local Beaver Company, was responsible for most of the logging. The firm had been eager to make as much profit as possible. This was revealed by the missing stumps and indicated by villagers' resentments against the firm. The firm may not have stolen the wood like the Rudari in Dragomireşti, but forest owners in Dragova felt just as robbed of their entitlements. Many new owners felt that the firm had taken unfair advantage of them, by paying an unreasonably low price for timber or putting undue pressure on them to sell.

In both Dragomireşti and Dragova, villagers had lost much of the euphoria that had prevailed when many of them first became owners of agricultural land (see Chapter 2) and forest a few years earlier. The joy and elation that many villagers experienced when receiving forest in 1993 and again in 2001 had given way to disappointment and frustration. The majority of the new owners felt that they had never received a fair share of the financial benefits flowing from the forests that belonged to them individually (in both communes), as members of a certain social group (in the form of collective forest in Dragova), or through their residence in a commune (as communal forest in Dragova). They also felt cheated as much by the promises of private ownership as by the exploitative practices of the Rudari and the logging firm.

This chapter examines the causes underlying the new forest owners' frustrations in Dragomireşti and Dragova. Our inquiry leads us to look at the predatory practices of police officers, forest guards, and mayors, because they enabled Rudari and the logging firm to take advantage of the new forest owners. Local officials targeted new owners as easy prey as they developed relations of patronage with the new owners and other villagers. Thus, our account draws upon insights from earlier research on patron–client relationships.[1] The concept of patron–client relationships may have dropped out of favor in the more recent literature, but we find certain useful insights from it that help make sense of forest dynamics in Dragomireşti and Dragova. The insights include the observation that relationships between patrons and clients develop based on unequal power relations. They tend to involve exchanges of economic and political resources generating benefits for all involved parties, even if only nominal in some cases. Additionally, patronage relations are intimately interwoven with the role of the state. Our interest in forest property connects with another debate about the nature of the Romanian state, in particular the notion that powerful actors "capture" the local state (Mungiu-Pippidi and Althabe 2002; Mungiu-Pippidi 2010).

How were the Rudari able to exploit forests in Dragomireşti even though the government had transferred them to villagers, and forest guards and police officers were in place to protect private ownership? What allowed the logging firm to take advantage of the new owners in Dragova even though the mayor and Forest Inspectorate had the mandate to protect the new owners against exploitation by such firms?

Forest Restitution in Dragomireşti: The Seductiveness of Individual Private Ownership

"It is my forest. Why does the state regulate how the forest should be used when the forest belongs to *me*?" This is a complaint that Stefan heard frequently from villagers in Dragomireşti. They had received forest for the first time in 1993, the Romanian Parliament having passed Law 18 two years earlier. This law entitled historical owners or their heirs to a maximum of 1 ha of individual private forest each, regardless of how much they had owned prior to the nationalization of forests by the socialist regime. In Dragomireşti, people responded enthusiastically to the law, just as they had embraced the chance to claim agricultural land in the previous year (see Chapter 2). Many filed claims with the Restitution Commission in the commune, and 172 households convinced the commission of the validity of their claims. As a result, the local Ocolul Silvic Mihăeşti, a local division of the National Forest Administration, had a meeting with the commune council in 1993 to sign a protocol about the transfer of 172 ha—that is, 1 ha for each of the households whose claim the commission had recognized. Like these households in Dragomireşti who received forest, so did some other 350,000 households elsewhere in Romania (Ioras and Abrudan 2006). However, before passing forest on to the commune, the Ocolul Silvic extracted valuable, mature trees from the forest—so the forest given to the commune was either young or degraded forest, which did not contain any valuable timber but only firewood.

In 2000, Law 1 expanded the maximum forest area that could be restituted to an individual private owner from 1 to 10 ha. In Dragomireşti 152 people could prove they had owned more than 1 ha in the past and so received forest from the Ocolul Silvic that was in addition to the single hectare restituted to them earlier. Taken together they received another 428 ha, tripling the total area of forest restituted to people in Dragomireşti to 600 ha. Looking beyond Dragomireşti, hundreds of thousands of Romanians filed similar claims in reaction to Law 1. In the process, Romania's National Forest Administration passed close to 2 million ha of forest to non-state actors, decreasing the percentage of total forest under its management to 65 percent.[2]

The language of private ownership proved convincing to villagers in Dragomireşti, not only to the new owners but even to villagers who did not receive any forest. For villagers, restitution meant a significant departure from the exclusive state forest management under socialism. They generally embraced the ideas of private ownership and private enterprise, even though only a fraction actually received titles to forest. People cherished the notion of individual ownership. From their perspective, the move away from socialism was only complete if private owners could exercise their new rights individually, without any restrictions imposed by the state or the collective. Those who felt that they were entitled to forest gathered the required documents to file a claim with the Restitution Commission after Law 18/1991 and again after Law 1/2000.

The lure of individual ownership became clear after the Ocolul Silvic handed the forest over to villagers in 1993, not in individual parcels but in a large tract, without designating the boundaries of individual holdings. Overwhelmed by the task of subdividing the forest tract into 172 individual holdings, the commune council decided to manage the tract collectively, regulate the extraction of timber and firewood from the forest, and hire a guard to enforce the regulation. The regulations required the new owners to seek permission from the guard if they wanted to exploit their forest. Many new owners resented the regulations and the guard because it smacked of intrusiveness similar to the socialist state of the past. To the villagers, private ownership meant that they could exploit their own forest at will, whenever and however they wanted. In short, they did not feel like owners despite their titles. Some owners lobbied the council to abandon the communal management. They eventually succeeded, causing the council to dismiss the guard, delineate individual parcels, and pass those parcels on to individual management by the entitled households.

Even after the guard was dismissed, there were a number of local state officials with a legal mandate related to the management, exploitation, transport, and trade of forest products. They were in charge of exercising state oversight of forestry as defined in Law 26/1996, which is known as the "Forestry Code" in Romania. One of the officials in Dragomirești included the local forest guard, Marian Popovici, who reported to the chief of the Forest Inspectorate who was located in Mihăești, approximately thirty kilometers from Dragomirești. Marian enjoyed police-like powers, and continually demonstrated this by carrying a firearm. Another important official was a police officer named George Ionescu, who was stationed in Dragomirești. In addition, the mayor's office administered local records on forest ownership.

New forest owners quickly learned how important the officials were, even after they had acquired individual ownership titles. In order to harvest timber or firewood, they first had to send a written request to the mayor's office for verification of forest ownership. Then they had to hire the Ocolul Silvic to prepare an assessment of their forest and to determine the harvest potential. Once the study was complete, the Ocolul Silvic would notify the owner and the forest guard, Marian, so they could mark the trees to be felled. Only then were owners allowed to harvest. The procedures proved cumbersome and expensive, a fact that was deeply resented by new owners. There were often prolonged delays in the process, which could mean that a request for firewood submitted to the mayor's office in June might not have generated the required permits until the end of October. Moreover, the procedures were clearly more cumbersome for some than for others who were on good terms with the involved officials or "lubricated" the process through additional payments. Marian, in particular, displayed little eagerness to do the required marking if there was no bribe.

When Stefan conducted his fieldwork in Dragomireşti in 2004, virtually every forest owner he met complained about the restrictions on their ownership rights. As Stefan has highlighted elsewhere, owners perceived a stark discrepancy between the idea of private ownership and their limited ability to harness the significant value of the forest (Dorondel 2009). The forest was one of their most valuable local assets. It covered some 60 percent of the commune's territory, including many stands with higher timber volume. Wood was important for heating, helping owners save valuable cash for other expenditures. Moreover, the potential sale of timber was a significant source of cash income, especially when timber prices rose in the late 1990s and 2000s. Timber and wood sales offered a welcome complement to their wages, pensions, and social assistance payments. Many new owners felt that state regulations threatened to turn the presumable asset into a liability, a condition that Thomas has observed in other settings (Sikor 2006).

Nonetheless, people's commitment to private ownership went beyond an interest in financial returns. New owners were not ready to give up the idea of private ownership as they understood it. Forest restitution signified a move away from state management, just as the restitution of agricultural land encapsulated the dissolution of the collective farm and a move towards individual farming for them (see Chapter 2). They had become owners and managers of forest, breaking into the monopoly held by the Ocolul Silvic in the past. In people's views, this promise of restitution to restore private ownership (seen in opposition to state ownership) was in direct contradiction to the regulations defined in the law and implemented by local officials. People rejected the legitimacy of state regulation, which is exemplified by the quote cited at the beginning of this section. Moreover, many asserted the primacy of individual ownership, because it meant a departure from collective ownership and the collective organization of work during socialism. Even though they had problems exercising their new ownership rights individually, they did not want to consider cooperative approaches to management. This set Dragomireşti's new owners apart from those in Bulgaria discussed by Cellarius, who embraced cooperative management for its technical and economic superiority (Cellarius 2004a and b). In addition, Cellarius's villagers invoked social memory on pre-socialist forest cooperatives, a historical experience that villagers in Dragomireşti did not possess.

The Rudari: Out of the Woods and Back into the Woods

"The forest guards are as bad as dogs" was a Rudari saying in the 1930s (Chelcea 1940: 120). Logging became a more frequent phenomenon in the forests in the commune from 2003 onward. When Stefan stayed in Dragomireşti in 2004, he often heard the sound of chainsaws from the forest. He also noted clearings in the forest indicating recent logging. Much of the logging did not involve new owners and took place without their consent. When Stefan asked villagers about the logging, he received the unanimous reply that "the Rudari cut our forest."

"The Rudari" referred to the people who lived in a small settlement on the outskirts of Dragomireşti. Its inhabitants were part of a relatively small ethnic group in Romania considered to belong to the Roma. The Roma are most likely descendents of slaves in the Romanian-speaking lands north of the Danube River and are different from the Balkan and West European Roma (Chaix et al. 2004). The number of Rudari in Romania is unknown because the Romanian state does not recognize them as a separate ethnic group. They are instead lumped together with other Roma groups in the official population census, which shows the Roma comprising only 2 percent of the population in Romania—but other counts put it as high as 15 percent (Csepeli and Simon 2004).[3]

Neither Romanian nor foreign anthropologists have given much attention to the Rudari. One of the few exceptions is Ion Chelcea, whose books render the lives and history of the Rudari in the1930s (Chelcea 1940, 1944). In spite of some racist interpretations made by Chelcea, he provides us with an ethnographic account of how the Rudari eked out a living at the margins of Romanian society. We learn that the Rudari lived in or next to the forest, because they did not possess any land and did not have another way to make ends meet. A Rudar told Chelcea, "We have no country of our own; we settle wherever we find forest" (Chelcea 1940: 76). His account matches the stories that Stefan heard in the Rudari settlement. "We used to live in the wood," an elderly Rudar told Stefan. They lived not only in the wood, but also partly underground in holes they dug and covered with roofs. They did not possess any land or forest, and many of them worked as laborers in a local nobleman's forest. The Rudari collected branches from nut trees to weave baskets, used small pieces of wood to make handles for knives and agricultural implements, and gathered wild strawberries, bilberries, apples, raspberries, and mushrooms to sell at weekly markets. The Rudari told Stefan that they referred to themselves as "worms of the wood."

According to Chelcea's account, the relations between the Rudari and the guards employed by forest owners were filled with tension. The Rudari cut wood and timber in forests even though that was deemed illegal by state regulations. They demanded access to forests, arguing that it provided them with resources vital for their livelihood. According to the Rudari's own regulations, access to forest was open to everyone, and the idea of "theft" from the forest was non-existent in their value system. The Rudari also opposed the efforts of forest guards and police officers to enforce their exclusion from the forest. An informant complained to Chelcea, "You can't go in the forest because they [the forest guards] would catch you" (Chelcea 1944: 124). He continued, "If you go to the market to trade your wooden stuff they [the police] ask you for the permit." To avoid detection, the Rudari resorted to clandestine practices. They would enter the forest after midnight and wrap old blankets or clothes around the trunk of a tree to minimize the noise of their axes. At other times, they bribed forest guards because "for half a kilo of liquor the forest guards would turn a blind eye" (ibid.: 120). Overall, the Rudari were at constant risk of being caught by the forest guards. It was critical to the Rudari that the guards overlook their activities.

The Rudari told Stefan that their living conditions had improved under socialism, which resonated with broader accounts of rising Roma living standards during that time (Brearley 2001). The Rudari of Dragomireşti continued to make brooms, baskets, pitchforks, and other wooden implements. They also helped the forest guards employed by the Ocolul Silvic Mihăeşti to plant trees, weed between newly planted seedlings, and conduct thinning. The guards called upon their help and, in return, overlooked their collection of dry branches and firewood in the state-managed forest. At the same time, Rudari men found work in Dragomireşti's agricultural cooperative or in those of other communes because cooperatives were chronically short of labor. A few, both women and men, even found formal employment at the nearby Dacia plant as janitors or in other low-skill positions. In this way, the 1970s and 1980s brought improvements to the livelihoods of the Rudari in Dragomireşti.

Although the Rudari emerged from the woods during socialism, they were forced back into the woods after 1990.[4] Above all, the government's decision to restitute agricultural land and forest to historical owners meant a familiar hardship for the Rudari. In 1991, they were compelled to return the small parcels of agricultural land that they had just received a year before. In line with national policy, the mayor's office had given each household 4,000 m² in 1990, but withdrew that when Law 18/1991 mandated the return to historical landholdings. More importantly, they were not entitled to any of the agricultural land or forest restituted to villagers in the 1990s and 2000s. Furthermore, the Rudari who found employment in the Dacia plant were the first to be laid off when the plant trimmed its labor force. Like Roma in many other places, the Rudari in

Dragomireşti experienced the most radical declines in living conditions and the highest rates of unemployment after 1990 (Brearley 2001).

Once again, the Rudari had no choice but to make a living from the woods. They entered the forest and cut wood clandestinely. Men banded in small groups, which typically consisted of one person with a horse cart and chainsaw, and one or two additional woodcutters. They filled up the horse cart with firewood from the forest and returned to their settlement. The cart owner then sold the wood to other Rudari engaged in the firewood trade. The traders, in turn, sold the firewood in southern Romania where people were in desperate need of cheap fuel. Firewood became the key source of income for the Rudari of Dragomireşti, even though its collection and trade was deemed illegal by Romania's laws.

Restitution re-created pre-socialist patterns of inequality and injustice. The institution of private ownership, enthusiastically embraced by new owners and ethnic Romanian villagers more generally, resulted in the utter dispossession of the Rudari. Since restitution was based on historical ownership patterns in 1948, no Rudari received a single hectare of forest. The Rudari's dispossession went beyond matters of asset distribution. As noted by Kaneff, the turn to private ownership reconstituted historical divisions between ethnic groups (Kaneff 1998). Just as land became ethnic territory in the village studied by Kaneff, private forest ownership was essentially an ethnic Romanian institution in Dragomireşti. In other words, restitution ethnicized private ownership by re-creating pre-socialist inequalities. The ideology of private ownership devalued social norms and ways of life important to the Rudari. It also threw the Rudari loggers back into dependence on the forest guards, as we show in the following section.

Predatory Practices and Relations of Patronage

"The forest guards are *worse* than dogs"[5] is a Rudari saying from the 2000s. In addition to the new owners and the Rudari, a third group was keen on benefiting from the private forest: local state officials. In Dragomireşti, these included the forest guard Marian, the police officer George, and the staff of the mayor's office. As discussed above, new owners had to deal with them when they sought to comply with legal procedures that regulated forest exploitation. It turned out that these officials also assumed an important role in the Rudari's illegal logging activities.

The Rudari were only able to extract firewood from Dragomireşti's private forests because Marian and George actively encouraged the practice. The horse carts returned from the forest at regular intervals and Marian rarely failed to confront them. Every time he encountered a cart, he fined the owner a small amount of money (approximately fourteen euros). Although this was not enough to stop them from exploiting the forest, it served as a reminder of Marian's importance. He wanted the Rudari to know that they risked a fine or even a prison sentence if he reported them to his superiors or to the Prosecutor's Office. However, Marian seldom reported anyone. Instead, he expected the Rudari to return his favor by delivering logs to his house. His father ran a small sawmill at the house they shared, where they produced fence posts and wooden elements used in the interior design of houses. The highest cost to his business was the raw material. By manipulating conditions in his favor and obtaining the logs for free, Marian made his father's business exceptionally profitable.[6]

While spending time with him, Stefan learned just how confident Marian was about the relations of patronage he had developed with Rudari loggers. When they heard the noise of a chainsaw emanate from a nearby forest, it seemed of little concern to Marian. "They [Rudari] won't dare to cut trees in the state forest," he said after some prodding by Stefan. His confidence rested on the fact that, as of that time, no logging had occurred in state forest (i.e., the forest that had not been transferred to villagers).[7] This was astonishing given Marian's own admission that he possessed limited means to enforce his control. He was responsible for approximately 600 ha, but had no off-road vehicles available. His limited powers became that much more evident because the Ocolul Silvic Mihăești held him financially liable for unlicensed logging. He had to pay for each tree missing from the forest that was managed by the Ocolul Silvic. Marian was sure that the Rudari would not go into state forest since there was plenty of private forest. It was clear to the Rudari that they would have endangered the protection from law enforcement that Marian offered to them if they would have entered state forest. The deal was explicit to both sides: Marian overlooked Rudari activities in the private forest as long as they helped him protect the state forest.

Like Marian, George enacted his role as a local patron with confidence. As a police officer, he was able to assert certain powers only to abuse them. When presented with the opportunity, he reminded Rudari loggers of his undeniable importance. Nearly every other week, George demanded a bribe from one of the horse-cart drivers returning from the forest with firewood. Occasionally, he also levied a fine or initiated legal prosecution procedures against some of them. In one case, for example, his report led to the arrest of a young Rudar caught in the forest. It did not matter that the Rudar had only a small cart and was amongst the poorest in the settlement. Sadly, he received a prison sentence of six months. His wife, who had just given birth, had to sell the cart in order to survive. In contrast, George never pursued the wealthier and more powerful Rudari engaged in the firewood trade. He ignored the trucks parked directly in front of their houses, even though half of them did not possess the mandatory registration. For a fee of roughly forty euros per truck, George sometimes accompanied them for part of their trip to southern Romania to protect them against checks by the highway patrol.

Neither Marian nor George could have developed these relations of patronage with Rudari loggers without protection from and collusion with their superiors. Not only had they enrolled Rudari loggers as their clients, they had become clients to their superiors and relied on their patronage. The chief of the regional Forest Inspectorate ignored the practices of local forest guards. In return, the guards ignored the chief's manipulations of timber auctions and logging in the state forest. The guards also campaigned for the chief's political party in local elections. The head of the county police not only ignored the practices of local police officers but also benefited from them financially. The bribes paid in illegal logging operations raised the amount of money he could extract from anyone who wanted to become a local police officer. Lucrative opportunities, such as the presence of local wood trade, raised the amount that job applicants had to pay to become a local police officer to 5,600 euros.

As a result, the new forest owners in Dragomirești ended up with nothing when the Rudari, sanctioned by local officials, descended on the forest. All profits accrued went to the woodcutters, cart owners, firewood traders, and officials. Comparing gross margins for an average truck, we find that the firewood traders secured almost two-thirds (190 euros).[8] The cart owners received sixty euros, and state officials forty-eight euros. Woodcutters only reaped a meager twelve euros from their involvement. Moreover, cutting trees was a dangerous activity, and many of them sustained serious injuries. The local medical worker told Stefan that she had treated fourteen woodcutters for serious injuries in 2004: broken arms and legs, crushed thumbs, and cuts turning into nasty infections. Two years later a woodcutter even died after being struck by a falling tree.

Marian and George were not the only local officials who profited from the Rudari's actions in the forest. The staff at the mayor's office easily convinced some of the new owners to sell their forest for a low price. A reference to the Rudari's activities was enough to persuade some new owners, especially those living outside Dragomirești, to sell the standing trees in their forest at a price much below their market value. Moreover, the duplicitous staff convinced the owners to sell the trees to them while pretending to help the owners in their predicament. Once the transaction was complete, the staff immediately sold the trees to logging firms in neighboring villages. In this way, they often achieved unimaginable profits within a matter of a few days or weeks. It was not unusual for them to sell the trees for ten times the price they had paid to the owner.

Many of the deals involved the agricultural officer of Dragomireşti, a woman we call Iuliana Negru. She was in an excellent position to offer the new owners protection and privileges because she was in charge of restitution procedures. She received the written requests and issued the documents certifying restitution. In one case, Vasile Mantescu filed a restitution claim to 5 ha of forest, because he was the heir of a historical owner. Vasile did not live in Dragomireşti and had long ago moved to Bucharest. At a meeting about restitution procedures, Iuliana pointed out the "Rudari problem." She offered to purchase the trees from Vasile, ostensibly so he would not take a loss on the value of his new forest. Furthermore, she indicated that if they made the deal, she would locate Vasile's forest at a safe distance from the Rudari settlement as a way to ensure future harvests. She said she would also find a way to arrange the deal so that he paid no taxes or fees. Vasile immediately decided to sell the trees on his 5 ha of forest to her for less than 3,000 euros. In the following few days, Iuliana sold the trees to a logging firm for 28,000 euros, making a profit of just over 25,000 euros.

Consequently, new owners were unable to gain tangible benefits from their titles. As much as they valued the symbolic significance of the titles, they quickly became frustrated with the low financial returns due to illicit Rudari activity and official corruption. They were exploited in both directions. If the Rudari stole from their forest, they came away empty-handed because of the losses sustained. If they held on to their trees, they were constantly worried about the possibility that the Rudari would cut them down. If they sold the standing trees, they received a low price. The owners were painfully aware that officials would directly undermine them through price manipulation, malfeasance, and flagrant neglect of their professional duties. Indeed, it was obvious that Marian and George showed little or no interest in the Rudari's activities in private forest, even if they occasionally fined a Rudar. Nevertheless, the owners also understood that they depended on Marian's and George's goodwill and protection.

The titles that were enthusiastically embraced by new owners did not translate into "effective ownership" (Verdery 2003). Verdery finds that agricultural producers in Transylvania are unable to attach tangible benefits to agricultural land titles, and we observed a similar phenomenon among new forest owners. Nevertheless, there was a fundamental difference in the processes producing ineffective ownership. Verdery, and our own account in Chapter 2, emphasize the workings of relatively abstract economic and political forces, symbolized by the decline (and occasional rise) of agricultural product prices. In Dragomireşti's forests, in contrast, there was nothing abstract about the activities of Rudari and local state officials. The predatory individuals responsible for the new owners' predicament were obvious, as was their dependence on the patronage offered by local state officials.

Villagers React: "The Law Should Be Enforced!"

How did ethnic Romanian villagers react to the situation? Above all, they blamed the Rudari and called for drastic action against them. Stefan repeatedly heard in 2004: "The Rudari should be killed since they are not good for anything else but stealing our forest." Although villagers acknowledged that Romanians cut forest as well, they readily blamed Rudari and continually portrayed them as thieves. Moreover, it was not only new owners who blamed Rudari for the loss of financial value. Nearly all ethnic Romanian villagers, regardless of whether they owned forest or not, shared the resentment against Rudari's "immoral" behavior in the new world of private ownership and private enterprise.

Perhaps the best illustration of the resentment against Rudari logging comes from the remarks villagers' made about the tree stumps alluded to earlier in this chapter. Rudari tended to leave stumps of approximately one meter in height when they illegally logged forests. For people in Dragomireşti, this was not only theft but also a clear waste of resources because the loggers had not taken all of the potential wood. Efficient logging cuts trees as low as possible. Villagers explained the apparent waste as Rudari "laziness." Stefan often heard villagers claim that the Rudari loggers did not want to bend down when cutting a tree because they were "lazy people." In other words, villagers concluded that the Rudari were not up to the new economic order because of an inherent flaw in their character. Villagers did not consider another interpretation: because the logging was clandestine, and mostly occurred at night, the loggers may have wanted to finish their job as quickly as possible; it was faster to cut trees at one meter height because the diameter tended to be smaller and because there was no need to bend down.

Villagers made Rudari the scapegoat for everything amiss in the new world of private ownership. That Rudari loggers exploited forest inefficiently was the best evidence that they were not fit for the new economic order. Villagers' comments about Rudari mirrored the racist discourse against Roma commonly found in Romania. As Tileagă notes, this discourse views certain undesirable practices undertaken by some Roma as reflective of the character and way of being of all Roma taken together (Tileagă 2005, 2006). It finds its expression in prejudiced and discriminatory statements against Roma found across the entire political and civil spectrum in Romania. For example, in a 2003 Gallup poll, four out of five respondents believed that the vast majority of Roma break the law, and more than one-third believed that Roma should be forced to live separately from the rest of society because they cannot integrate (Ahmed, Feliciano, and Emigh 2007). C.V. Tudor, a right-wing politician who achieved a 30 percent share in the 2000 presidential ballot, called for isolating "Roma criminals in special colonies." This racist discourse ignores the political economic context in which Roma act—a reality that became clear in Dragomirești. Ethnic Romanian villagers readily ignored the fact that the restitution of agricultural land and forest had left Rudari with nothing, and that Rudari had been the first to lose jobs in the downturn of the 1990s.

Villagers reacted by calling for law enforcement. They appealed to the state to protect private ownership and to prosecute infringements on private ownership—with mixed success. Some owners with large forests reported tree theft to the county police on several occasions. Their reports caused special police forces to come to Dragomirești repeatedly, sometimes in the middle of the night, but they were unable to make any arrests. The owners concluded that an insider had warned the Rudari loggers to stay home when a police raid was imminent. That insider, they suggested, could only be George or Marian. However, Stefan heard in 2006 that justice finally caught up with George. Special police forces arrested him on corruption charges, and he was forced to retire.

Villagers called for law enforcement even though they knew of local officials' complicity in, and active support for, illegal extraction. They were aware that Marian's father ran a wood-processing company out of the forest guard's house, despite a regulation banning forest guards from engaging in the wood business. They were sure that the timber stacked around their house had originated from Rudari logging. Moreover, villagers noticed that the candidates who participated in a televised public debate in the 2004 elections for a new mayor circumvented making any clear statement against Rudari logging. Three days before the final ballot, neither of the leading two contenders acknowledged that there was any deforestation or that Rudari may have illegally extracted wood. Since the race was very close, neither candidate wanted to risk losing Rudari votes, as Stefan discusses elsewhere (Dorondel 2016).

Nevertheless, a few owners initiated actions against local state officials to enforce their compliance with the rules of private ownership. The level of difficulty that new owners encountered in their attempts to get local officials to comply with the law became clear in a legal case brought by Dr. Andrei Popescu against Radu Pivniceru, the bookkeeper for Dragomirești's communal administration. Dr. Popescu lived in Bucharest, where he worked at the Romanian Academy of Sciences. In 2003, he received 10 ha of forest in the village, because his uncle once owned a large tract of forest there. When he heard that Rudari had been logging illegally in the area, he decided to harvest the forest before they could get access. He inquired at the mayor's office regarding applicable procedures. While there he spoke with Radu, who offered to help Dr. Popescu and connected him with a logging firm. Radu arranged with the firm to pay a certain amount of money to Dr. Popescu in advance. However, soon after logging started, Radu instigated Rudari to chase away the workers sent by the firm. He suggested to the Rudari that they exploit the forest before the firm hired by Dr. Popescu could finish logging. Radu was in a powerful position since he was responsible for distributing social assistance payments. He had also become a godfather to several Rudari children, which indicated the close relationships Radu had developed, and his ubiquity in the intricate activities of the community. Some Rudari, out of obligation to the bookkeeper intertwined with a need for livelihood, did not hesitate to cut trees in Dr. Popescu's forest. They threatened the workers from the logging firm that Dr. Popescu had hired, and forced them to abandon the job after only one-fifth of it had been completed. The Rudari then finished the job within a short time. The doctor's original intention to prevent the Rudari from logging his forest by acting first had thereby been thwarted.

Unlike many other owners, Dr. Popescu did not accept the *fait accompli*. As soon as he heard from the logging firm that they had withdrawn from the job he went to Dragomirești. When he inspected his forest he discovered that not a single tree was left standing. In reaction, he filed a complaint with the police in Dragomirești. When he saw that George had little inclination to act on his complaint, Dr. Popescu reported the incident to the national police headquarters and the National Department of Anti-corruption in Bucharest. By the time Stefan finished his fieldwork in 2004 the national-level police units had nearly completed their investigation. They had uncovered Radu's complicity in the logging and expected to try him in court. Other staff in the mayor's office commented that the case was an unfortunate combination of excessive spite on Radu's side and an unusually assertive owner. If Radu had been more careful, or if it had been an owner who did not pursue official recourse, the two would likely have cut a deal.

Three years later, Stefan heard that it never went to court. Even more surprisingly, Radu was now the new mayor. In the end, Dr. Popescu and Radu did cut a deal: Dr. Popescu dropped his case against Radu, who then made certain that Dr. Popescu's request for the restitution of an additional 990 ha was successful. That request became possible after Law 247/2005 removed the previous limits on the maximum area of forest that could be restituted to individual owners. It saved Radu's political career and personal fortune. Dr. Popescu explained to Stefan that he was glad to avoid the hassles of court proceedings and, above all, wanted to make sure to get all of his uncle's forest restituted. He allegedly sold the harvest on the restituted forest for 1 million euros.

These events indicate how villagers called upon the state to protect private ownership by enforcing the law. When Rudari loggers did not comply with the rules of the new economic order, concerned villagers called for an enforcement of state regulations protecting private owners. When they saw local officials exploit their forests, they appealed to higher-level organs of the state to enforce the law. Their responses included repeated references to the rules and procedures instituted by the Romanian state after 1990. Villagers—owners and non-owners alike—called upon law enforcement even though new owners loathed the restrictions imposed on their own forest management.

To expand and reinforce our argument, we now want to turn our attention to Dragova, the second case study in Romania. New owners in Dragova, we will show, also faced problems in exercising their newly acquired forest titles, but for different reasons.

Ion, Maria, and the New Owners in Dragova: Predators and Prey

Like Dragomireşti, a significant number of people in Dragova received titles to individual private forest in the process of restitution. Villagers filed their claims for the restitution of 1 ha with the local land commission after Law 18/1991 passed. Many returned to the commission in the early 2000s, after Law 1/2000 expanded the maximum allowable area to 10 ha. Ninety-two people received forest titles for a total of 879 ha. In contrast to Dragomireşti, they acquired individual titles from the beginning. Similar to the other commune, much of the "forest" conferred to villagers in the first round was young forest that the Ocolul Silvic Rucăr had logged over and replanted just a few years before.[9] This situation changed dramatically, however, in the second round when the Ocolul Silvic transferred not only a much larger area but also significantly richer forest to villagers.

Maria and Ion Dragomirescu, a middle-aged couple in Dragova, sensed that there was more to gain from forest privatization than titles. Under socialism, Ion had managed the cooperative guesthouse in a village next to Dragova. After the demise of the socialist state, not unlike other socialist managers turning into capitalist entrepreneurs (see Chapter 2), Ion and Maria opened a small store, selling locally produced smoked cheese to tourists. When they realized that the state was transferring forest to private owners, and creating opportunities for private involvement in wood processing and trade, they recognized a unique business opportunity. In 1993, Maria and Ion started a private logging firm, initially exporting only small numbers of logs. Over time, their business flourished and expanded, which eventually allowed them to purchase three trucks in addition to several they had already leased. Until 2004, when Stefan stayed in Dragova, their firm remained the only one in the commune. Thus, they were more successful than many of the other private logging firms in Romania that emerged in the 1990s, but which ceased operations a few years later.

Another reason their logging firm was exceptionally profitable was that Ion had decided to run for mayor in 1996, and won the election. He ran as a candidate of the Liberal Party, which was a calculated decision as it was one of Romania's political parties in favor of expanding the maximum area for restitution to 10 ha. In 2000, Ion successfully sought an extension of his term. His re-election put him in an advantageous position when Law 1/2000 was implemented, since he was then head of the commune-level restitution commission. Moreover, when he had first become mayor in 1996, it was of no consequence to him that he had to resign formally from his firm. Acting within the law's edict, and further exploiting her position, Maria took over sole responsibility. It was clear to villagers, however, that they continued to run the firm together.

Clearly, Maria and Ion seized the opportunity to influence the restitution of forest to their personal advantage. Even though Ion could not control the area that successful claimants were given, he had undue influence over the quality of forest they received, and in what location. Both forest quality and location made a considerable difference to an owner's ability to derive financial return from forest. Ion used his leverage to transfer much of the high-value forest to the older people in the commune—not for reasons of charity but because it was easier to convince them to sell the wood to Maria's firm.

In 2004, villagers in Dragova frequently told Stefan a story about a woman named Angela Paraschiv. Angela was 65 years old, lived alone, and was restricted in her ability to get around. Back in 2003, she was pleased when the restitution commission gave her an additional 4 ha to the 1 ha that she had received as individual private forest in the early 1990s. Living off a meager pension of approximately 100 euros a month, Angela became even more excited when Maria offered to buy the harvest on the 5 ha for nearly 4,000 euros. She happily took the money and let Maria's firm log over the forest, which was located along the main road, thus making it easy and cheap for Maria's woodcutters to remove the trees. Although Stefan never found out for how much Maria sold the timber harvest, she could easily have received 200,000 euros at the then current market prices, which was fifty times the price she had paid to Angela.[10]

Angela's story provides another illustration of how new owners fell prey to local state officials in the wake of restitution. Ion abused his office for his personal gains, just like George, Marian, and the staff at the mayor's office did in Dragomireşti. Nonetheless, the predatory dynamics in Dragova were different from those in Dragomireşti. In Dragomireşti, appointed local officials took advantage of their positions to derive personal benefits. In Dragova, a private entrepreneur ran for public office and then used his position as mayor to promote the interests of his private business. In this way, Maria and Ion sought to merge the public conduct of local affairs with their private business dealings. They achieved their goal by influencing restitution.

The Shrinking Collective Forest

In his position of power, Ion also found a way to manipulate the restitution of a collective forest in Dragova to his personal benefit. After Law 1/2000 expanded restitution to include not only individual forest holdings owned by single households prior to nationalization but also collective forest holdings owned by groups of households, communal councils or other organizations, villagers filed a claim with the restitution commission on behalf of a few families. They reported that the families had jointly owned forest on Dragova Mountain, a small mountain within the commune's borders. They wanted the commission to restitute what villagers commonly referred to as the "small collective forest."

The villagers even produced historical documents from the 1930s and 1940s that specified the total surface of the small collective forest as 52 *fârtare*. The problem was that nobody knew exactly how many hectares a *fârtar* measured, because people no longer applied the unit. In addition, the historical records accepted by the restitution commission indicated that the small collective forest was on Dragova Mountain, but they did not provide distinct boundaries. Some elderly villagers asserted that a *fârtar* was equivalent to 6 ha. An elderly man was even in the possession of a technical study from 1936 in which an engineer reported that Dragova Mountain measured 300 ha, which the report stated clearly was equivalent to 52 *fârtare*. The man had hidden the report during socialism, since it was illegal to keep old records. He had hoped that one day it would become useful as evidence of villagers' historical rights to the collective forest. Unfortunately, the restitution commission did not recognize the report as valid proof.

In 2004, the restitution commission ruled that a *fârtar* was equivalent to only 3 ha, and conferred rights to 156 ha of forest to the families. The commission maintained that there was no legally valid evidence that a *fârtar* was 6 ha. Its decision received the backing of the regional restitution commission in Pitești, to which the families had appealed. The regional commission stated that they did not know the size of a *fârtar* and referred the case back to the local commission. As a result, the small collective forest became even smaller, shrinking from 300 to 156 ha. The forest met the same fate as some of the agricultural land discussed by Verdery (1996). Land was surprisingly elastic during restitution, Verdery found, expanding and shrinking over time according to the varied accounts of different actors.

However, as noted by Verdery, the elasticity does not work in everybody's favor. It affords maneuvering space to the powerful, such as Maria and Ion in Dragova. The couple were in an influential position to exploit the ambiguity regarding the small collective forest on Dragova Mountain, as Ion was the head of the restitution commission. In addition, the restitution of the small collective forest had direct bearing on their interests. From an economic viewpoint they had compelling reasons to shrink the collective forest, thereby making forest available for restitution to individual villagers. It was much easier to convince the owners of small individual forest holdings than the managers of a sizable collective forest to sell the harvest to them. The owners of the collective forest would have been in a much stronger bargaining position and may have approached other firms. From a political perspective, Ion also had important reasons for reducing the size of the collective forest. The shrinking collective forest created space for political maneuvering. Since no one else could make a legally valid claim on this forest, he had 150 ha available to restitute according to his own preferences.

The mayor's maneuvers regarding the collective forests demonstrate how he aptly created possibilities for himself to offer patronage to villagers. He now had plenty of possibilities to use the non-restituted collective forest on Dragova Mountain for creating personal allegiances and favoring his allies. Similarly, he also found ways to use the adjacent National Park Piatra Craiului for personal gains, as we have discussed elsewhere (Stahl, Sikor, and Dorondel 2009). Ion persuaded the owners of forest located in the park's protection zone to sell their trees to Maria's firm before the park could ban any further exploitation. In return, he promised them that he would overlook violations of the strict logging ban that applied to the forests in the national park. Ion knew how to employ patronage, as we will discuss later in the chapter.

The Mayor's Manipulation of Timber Auctions

Law 1/2000 also led to the restitution of a communal forest in Dragova (i.e., forest owned by the commune as the local state entity). Its origins date back to the years after World War II, when the Romanian state rewarded some veterans in the commune with small forest parcels. In 1948, when the socialist regime was about to nationalize all forest in Romania, the veterans decided to jointly transfer their ownership rights to the commune. Their action did not prevent nationalization, yet it implied that the commune possessed a legally valid claim on the forest since then. As a result, the commune received 70 ha of forest in 2003, and in other parts of Romania communes received a total of 750,000 ha. The understanding within the commune council was that the forest should be used to supply firewood for Dragova to heat the schools, the church, and the houses of poor and elderly villagers. The council approved several sales of firewood from the forest to needy villagers at a price below market rates.

Even so, Ion was not satisfied with the subsistence use, and lobbied for the commercial exploitation of the communal forest. He manipulated circumstances to his benefit when the commune council approved his proposal to repair local roads and raise the required finances by logging over the communal forest. What looked like sensible public investment and effective use of the communal forest, however, worked heavily in favor of Ion and Maria. Their heavy logging trucks were a primary cause for the dilapidated state of the roads in Dragova. Indeed, the poor condition of the roads became the focus of villagers' ire. Disgruntled councilors introduced several motions to the commune council requesting that they collect the fee levied on all vehicles visiting Dragova, including Maria's trucks. In the end, the council upheld the fee exemption for their trucks. Not only were Maria and Ion pleased with this, they readily welcomed the decision to repair the roads since Maria's firm received the contract to log over the communal forest.

Auctions were another centerpiece in Romanian forestry legislation. In 1991, Ministerial Order 572 mandated that all timber sales from state forests to private enterprises must involve auctions. Four years later, Government Decision 342 created a consistent and comprehensive legal basis for the auction system. In 1998, another legal act expanded the auction system to include forest that was under the jurisdiction of local councils. The legislation mandated that auctions were to be announced at least thirty days in advance, and in at least two newspapers. They were also required to include at least two registered bidders. By means of the regulations, the central government sought to ensure that private enterprises participated in the auctions on an equal footing.

There was an expectation that auctions would prevent collusion among potential buyers and between firms and state officials, thereby minimizing predation on the revenues from state and communal forests—however, this was not the case. Ion was in charge of organizing auctions for the commune and, despite the regulations, he arranged for Maria's firm to win them all.

He tilted the odds in her favor by announcing an auction for the communal forest only a few days before the event, and by posting a small advertisement in a local newspaper with limited distribution. As a result, competing firms had only a few days to register their interest and assemble the necessary paperwork. Ion informed Maria before the other firms could act, giving her ample time to put together a bid. In addition, Ion and Maria took care to organize another bid for the auction in a way that satisfied the regulatory requirement. They asked a friend, who also owned a logging firm, to submit a pro forma bid so the auction could be held. Not surprisingly, this process worked, as it did in many other places in Romania.[11]

Thus, Ion made his position as mayor beneficial to their logging business in multiple ways. The benefits did not end with his influence over the restitution process and the auctions. His position also allowed his wife to employ impoverished fellow villagers for low pay. Maria did not give them regular contracts nor register them for social benefits. Furthermore, Ion's position protected him from the law enforcement efforts of the Forest Inspectorate. That was important because Maria's firm, like many others, often harvested forest without obtaining the required permits, or cut a larger volume than authorized through the permit. Whenever the inspectorate was about to send in an officer, Ion was among the first to find out. This afforded Maria enough time to send the workers home and hide the trucks. On one occasion, Stefan waited for hours in the commune center for a ride on one of the logging trucks but none passed by. Typically, he would have caught a ride within an hour. He later discovered that Ion and Maria had expected an inspection team and so had kept the trucks in the garage.

The Challenge of Staying in Office: The Mayor's Campaign in 2004

'The mayor has high-level connections. If you fight with him you fight with the state. You can't win when you fight with the state.'[12]

Ion's predatory actions presented him with an enormous challenge when his second term as mayor was ending. How could he convince the people of Dragova to give him another term in office? The situation differed from that in 2000, when he successfully ran for re-election. Since then, Ion's exploitation of the new owners' forest had been particularly egregious. He manipulated the restitution of individual forest, reduced the collective forest by half, and influenced the auctions for timber from the communal forest for his personal gain. He and his wife were clearly responsible for the meager financial returns many new owners derived from their forests. His electoral competitor announced that he would initiate investigations on the implementation of forest restitution and the contracts with Maria's firm. In addition, there was a great deal at stake for them because Maria had taken out a bank loan of over 130,000 euros to purchase additional trucks and to bid for forest concessions.

Ultimately, Ion attained his third term in office. He won the elections with the slightest margin possible; his party won only three of the nine seats on the council. He managed to win partially through the political maneuvers that are common to local elections in Romania. Ion portrayed himself as a hard working guy (*gospodar*) to the electorate. He cut a deal with the local head of the National Liberal Party (the main opposition party nationwide), getting him to withdraw from the race and instead support Ion's campaign. He also made a deal with a former vice-mayor, granting him the permission to turn the public bus stop into a private parking lot for his restaurant in return for political support. When the elections arrived, he was able to count on the additional support of two influential men and their extended families in Dragova. Furthermore, Maria and Ion spent some of their personal wealth on small presents for the elderly. Ion delivered packages containing flour, sugar, and other basic food items to them, engaging in the kind of "vote buying" that newspapers reported were a widespread phenomenon in the elections of 2004 (Mungiu-Pippidi 2010).

Ion took advantage of every opportunity to exert influence over forest restitution to enhance his political aims by enrolling villagers as clients of the patronage he offered. Villagers were certain he gave preferential treatment to people from Podu, the largest settlement in Dragova, where Ion and Maria lived. Many confided in Stefan that Ion, in both subtle and overt ways, intimidated them. That is, Ion let it be known that if they voted him out of office they would be placed at a further disadvantage. The message was clear: they needed him as their patron.

His ability to create possibilities for patronage and then utilize them for his own gain became even more evident in the case of Maria Nicolescu. Maria held a position in the mayor's office directly under Ion's supervision and was also member of the restitution commission. She worked diligently to support her father's claim for the restitution of 4 ha close to his house. In the early 1990s, Vasile Nicolescu, Maria's father, had received 1 ha nearby. The restitution commission had also validated his right to receive another 4 ha of forest after Law 1/2000. Vasile wanted all of his forest in a single location and close to his house so it would be easier for him to manage. He also argued to the commission that it was exactly this forest that his father had owned prior to nationalization in 1948. Despite the advocacy from Maria, the commission decided to allocate the additional 4 ha to Vasile at a different, more remote location. As Maria told Stefan, the forest near her father's home was too valuable: Ion could not resist the opportunity to abuse his authority. The father's forest contained mature trees and was very accessible. When she went on vacation for two weeks, Ion took advantage of her absence. He arranged for the restitution of the forest to a friend who had supported him during the electoral campaign in 2000. The friend lacked proof of historical ownership, but this was rendered irrelevant by Ion's self-interested machinations.

Finally, Ion made sure he built good relations with external actors, which revealed to villagers the backing he received from outside the community. He switched to the Social Democratic Party, which was one of the major parties in Romania in 2004. He also promised the villagers he would secure funding from the European Union to construct new roads—something that the hotel owners, guesthouse operators, and people living in more remote parts of Dragova were pleased to hear. He even arranged for a visit to Dragova by the president of Romania's national parliament, the second most important office in Romania. Furthermore, Ion proved to have outstanding diplomatic instincts in his dealings with Piatra Craiului National Park, as we have discussed elsewhere (Stahl, Sikor, and Dorondel 2009). He presented himself to villagers as a protector of their interests against the park. He also managed to appease the park management by maintaining a pretense of compliance with their demands.

These observations show how Ion was able to build and sustain relations of political patronage. He not only developed a powerful network of allies in Dragova, but also used his external contacts for political purposes. Many villagers harbored a feeling of helplessness. They noted his "high-level connections," and concluded that "if you fight with him you fight with the state." The state, in turn, was still a powerful institution in people's minds. It made little sense to contest the state: "You cannot win when you fight with the state." They were convinced that Ion enjoyed strong support from the central government, as observed by a middle-aged man: "All people from this village know that he is well known in the central government as well. We know his power." To many villagers, Ion was the state.

Predators, Patrons, and the State in Dragomireşti and Dragova

Many new owners embraced their forest titles in Dragomireşti and Dragova. To them, the titles meant the right to exploit an important economic asset. Moreover, owners and non-owners alike welcomed the titles as an indicator of the departure from the restrictions on their productive activities and personal lives under socialism. The language of private ownership was highly persuasive, since it promised unlimited freedom in the pursuit of prosperity. However, new owners quickly fell prey to the actions of powerful local predators. Despite holding ownership rights, many villagers did not derive any significant economic benefit from forests. Much of the value contained in their forests accrued to local state officials, wood traders, and logging firms.

The flaws of private ownership manifested themselves in the forest landscapes of the two communes. Logging drastically rose in 2003, when the forest area and quality under private ownership increased as a consequence of expanded restitution. By the end of 2004, forests had already vanished on nearly 130 ha (roughly 5 percent of the total forest area) in Dragomirești and another 130 ha (4 percent) in Dragova. This implied that the villages' forests would be depleted within twenty to twenty-five years if logging continued at the same rate. Private ownership affected people's visions of a desirable forest landscape. New owners and other, predatory actors combined forces in a detrimental coalition that used forests as a source of short-term financial returns. New owners wanted their forests to enhance their incomes and to allow the exercise of personal freedom in economic affairs. For the predators, forests became a financial asset to be exploited for maximum profit.

The unraveling of private ownership and short-term exploitation was partly due to powerful relations of patronage. The significance of local patronage set the forest dynamics apart from those observed in agriculture (see Chapter 2). In agriculture, as in forestry, many new owners were unable to translate their rights into tangible benefits. Underlying their inability to accomplish this in agriculture was the corrosive influence of more abstract processes of devaluation and revaluation. In forestry, the exploitation of new owners was much more concrete. New owners struggled against the predatory practices of local actors, who sought to appropriate the riches of the forest by various means. Local state officials, traders and logging firms accrued profits by way of influencing the restitution process, manipulating permits and auctions and controlling wood markets, even though they did not own any forest. Struggles over forests, therefore, were about the significance of private ownership as a means to secure tangible benefits from them. Private ownership experienced stiff competition from patronage as an alternative means by which various social actors derived benefits from forests.

The patronage relations assumed different forms in the two communes. In Dragomirești, local state officials took advantage of a highly unequal distribution of productive resources re-created by restitution. This inequity prepared the grounds for them to incite and exploit certain practices of the disempowered that were illegal under Romania's legislation. They were able to enroll Rudari loggers as clients since the latter depended on their protection. The situation was a fundamentally different one in Dragova. There was no marginalized group to abuse and not much space for illegal operations. In Dragova, the head of a local logging firm sought election as mayor. Once in office, he resorted to tactics that stretched the limits of his formal powers as sanctioned by the law. At the same time, the mayor never employed the illegal or violent practices used by state officials in Dragomireşti. He knew how to enlist villagers as his clients in other ways.

The involvement of local state officials and villagers in patron–client relations reveals how the negotiations about property were simultaneously contestations over the state. In contrast to the Albanian cases (see Chapter 4), property negotiations never challenged the authority of the state per se. Instead, people's struggles over property involved different forms of exercising state authority. From the perspective of people in Dragomireşti, the extension of forest titles served to reconstitute the authority of the Romanian state over forests on a new basis. This basis rested on the positive notions villagers attached to private ownership and the need for the state to enforce ownership rights. When Rudari and local officials encroached on their rights, villagers responded by calling for protection by the state and law enforcement. In this way, they separated the practices of the officials from the state. They called upon the state to enforce the law, even though the very agents of the state had abused the positions that the law had conferred on them. The paradoxical result was that both the institution of private ownership and its unraveling served to enhance the legitimacy of the Romanian state. Villagers wanted a state that exercised its authority over forests by way of abstract rules and procedures. Such a state was particularly important when local officials tried their best to ignore and undermine these rules, as Verdery notes in her discussion of land reform in Romania (Verdery 1996: 213–15).

In comparison, the new owners exerted little effort to rein in the mayor's practices in Dragova, even though many voted for his competitors in elections. Once the mayor was in office they felt helpless to act against his political manipulations and maneuvering. People's feeling of powerlessness indicated the extent to which the mayor was able to enact an intimidating, personalized style in managing communal affairs. He managed to "capture" not only the local state (Mungiu-Pippidi and Althabe 2002) but also the state as an idea in local people's minds. Many villagers in Dragova equated the mayor with the state, similar to the way in which the mayor Lupu was perceived in Verdery's account (Verdery 2002). As a result, the exercise of state authority over forests took on a different quality in the two communes. Dragova's mayor was much more successful than the officials in Dragomireşti in making his case for a personalized exercise.

The intimate connection between postsocialist struggles about property and contestations over the exercise of state authority is a theme that continues in the following chapter. Shifting our attention to Vietnam, we make a radical change in geographical setting. But as will soon become apparent, property dynamics regarding forests in Vietnam were as much about the conflict between rule-based and personalized forms of exercising state authority as they were in Romania.

Notes

1. For useful overviews, see Eisenstadt and Roniger (1980) and Littlewood (1980). As emphasized by the former, it is useful to consider patron–client relationships not as setting up simple dyadic relationships but as part of complex hosts of social relationships. See also Berry (1985) and Hart (1989) on political patronage.
2. Ioras and Abrudan (2006) estimate that the more recent Law 247/2005, which mandates the restitution of all forest to former private owners, will further lower the percentage under state management to 35 percent.
3. We recognize that the ethnic categories are problematic, and do not want our use of the terms "Rudari" and "Roma" to imply any judgment about their appropriateness.
4. This is also the reason why Chapter 2 does not mention the Rudari. They simply did not matter for agriculture in Dragomirești.
5. The emphasis is our own to highlight the difference between this quote and the quote ("*as bad* as dogs") at the beginning of the previous section.
6. Note the parallel with the practice under socialism that forest guards looked away from Rudari firewood collection in return for their help in forest management.
7. A participatory mapping exercise with villagers produced convincing evidence that no logging had taken place in state forest. See Dorondel (2016) for more details.
8. Gross margins are revenues minus variable costs, excluding labor. To get from gross margins to profits one needs to subtract the costs of capital depreciation and labor.
9. This was very apparent from a map on forest conditions and forest tenure that Stefan drew with the villagers. All the forest that the Ocolul Silvic had exploited in the 1980s went to villagers in the first round of restitution.
10. This is how we arrive at our estimate: (a) Maria purchased five ha; (b) Grodzińskca et al. (2004) estimate the average timber volume in Carpathian forests of Romania as between 300 and 400 m³; and (c) the price of timber was 200–380 euro/m³ for beech and 95–140 euro/m³ of spruce fir. This gives a range of potential revenues from 142,500 to 760,000 euros. One would need to subtract costs to arrive at profits.
11. Saphores, Vincent, and Marochko (2006) provide statistical evidence of collusion in two forest directorates of Romania.
12. This is a quote by a villager involved in a land dispute with the mayor.

References

Ahmed, Patricia, Cynthia Feliciano, and Rebecca Jean Emigh. 2007. "Internal and External Ethnic Assessement in Eastern Europe." *Social Forces* 86(1): 231–55.

Berry, Sara. 1985. *Fathers Work for Their Sons: Accumulation, Mobility, and Class Formation in an Extended Yoruba Community*. Berkeley: University of California Press.

Brearley, Margaret. 2001. "The Persecution of Gypsies in Europe." *American Behavioral Scientist* 45(4): 588–99.

Cellarius, Barbara A. 2004a. *In the Land of Orpheus: Rural Livelihoods and Nature Conservation in Postsocialist Bulgaria*. Wisconsin: The University of Wisconsin Press.

———. 2004b. "'Without Co-Ops There Would Be No Forests!': Historical Memory and the Restitution of Forest in Post-Socialist Bulgaria." *Conservation and Society* 2(1): 51–73.

Chaix, R., et al. 2004. "Vlax Roma History: What Do Coalescent-Based Methods Tell Us?". *European Journal of Human Genetics* 12: 285–92.

Chelcea, Ion. 1940. *Originea Rudarilor* [The origins of Rudari]. Bucharest: Atelierele "Imprimeria" S.A.

———. 1944. *Ţiganii din Romania. Monografie etnografică* [The Gypsies from Romania. Ethnographical monographs]. Bucharest: Editura Institutului Central de Statistică.

Csepeli, György, and Dávid Simon. 2004. "Construction of Roma Identity in Eastern and Central Europe: Perception and Self-Identification." *Journal of Ethnic and Migration Studies* 30(1): 129–50.

Dorondel, Stefan. 2009. "'They Should Be Killed': Forest Restitution, Ethnic Groups and Patronage in Post-Socialist Romania." In *The Rights and Wrongs of Land Restitution: "Restoring What Was Ours"*, ed. Derick Fay and Deborah James. Abingdon: Routledge-Cavendish, 43–66.

———. 2016. *State, Peasants and the Politics of Land in Postsocialist Romania*. Oxford and New York: Berghahn Books.

Eisenstadt, S.N., and Louis Roniger. 1980. "Patron–Client Relations as a Model of Structuring Social Exchange." *Comparative Studies in Society and History* 22(1): 22–47.

Grodzińskca, Krystyna, et al. 2004. "Vegetation of the Selected Forest Stands and Land Use in the Carpathian Mountains." *Environmental Pollution* 130: 17–32.

Hart, Gillian. 1989. "Agrarian Change in the Context of State Patronage." In *Agrarian Transformations: Local Processes and the State in Southeast Asia*, ed. Gillian Hart, Andrew Turton, and Ben White. Berkeley: University of California Press, 31–49.

Ioras, Florin, and Ioan Abrudan. 2006. "The Romanian Forestry Sector: Privatisation Facts." *International Forestry Review* 8(3): 361–67.

Kaneff, Deema. 1998. "When 'Land' Becomes 'Territory': Land Privatisation and Ethnicity in Rural Bulgaria." In *Surviving Post-Socialism: Local Strategies and Regional Responses in Eastern Europe and the Former Soviet Union*, ed. Sue Bridger and Frances Pine. London: Routledge, 16–32.

Littlewood, Peter. 1980. "Patronage, Ideology, and Reproduction." *Critique of Anthropology* 15: 29–45.

Mungiu-Pippidi, Alina. 2010. *A Tale of Two Villages: Coerced Modernization in the East European Countryside*. Budapest: Central European University Press.

Mungiu-Pippidi, Alina, and G. Althabe. 2002. *Secera și buldozerul. Scornicești și Nucșoara Mecanisme de aservire a țăranului român* [The sickle and the bulldozer. Scornicesti and Nucsoara. Mechanisms of Romanian peasant subjugation]. Iași: Polirom.

Saphores, Jean-Daniel, Jeffrey R. Vincent, and Valy Marochko. 2006. "Detecting Collusion in Timber Auctions: An Application to Romania." World Bank Policy Research Working Paper. Washington, DC: World Bank.

Sikor, Thomas. 2006. "Land as Asset, Land as Liability: Property Politics in Rural Central and Eastern Europe." In *Changing Properties of Property*, ed. Franz von Benda-Beckmann, Keebet von Benda-Beckmann, and Melanie G. Wiber. New York: Berghahn Books, 106–25.

Stahl, Johannes, Thomas Sikor, and Stefan Dorondel. 2009. "The Institutionalization of Property Rights in Albanian and Romanian Biodiversity Conservation." *International Journal of Agricultural Resources, Governance and Ecology* 8(1): 57–73.

Tileagă, Christian. 2005. "Accounting for Extreme Prejudice and Legitimating Blame in Talk about the Romanies." *Discourse & Society* 16(5): 603–24.

———. 2006. "Representing the 'Other': A Discursive Analysis of Prejudice and Moral Exclusion in Talk about Romanies." *Journal of Community & Applied Social Psychology* 16(1): 19–41.

Verdery, Katherine. 1996. *What Was Socialism? And What Comes Next?* Princeton, NJ: Princeton University Press.

———. 2002. "Seeing Like a Mayor. Or, How Local Officials Obstructed Romanian Land Restitution." *Ethnography* 3(1): 5–33.

———. 2003. *The Vanishing Hectare: Property and Value in Postsocialist Transylvania*. Ithaca, NY: Cornell University Press.

6

Land Allocation, Loggers, and Lawmakers in Vietnam

Tree stumps were a frequent sight in the forests around Than Con and Ba Ye when Phuc conducted his fieldwork in the villages in 2004. Logs had been cut extensively in the forests, just as we observed in the Albanian and Romanian villages. In Than Con, the village we discussed in Chapter 3, loggers had set their sights on the Luoi Hai area as it had once harbored mature forest and was easily accessible on a dirt track. In Ba Ye, another agricultural village in Vietnam's northern mountains, there were no roads leading into the forest. Yet, difficult access had apparently not stopped loggers from cutting trees, particularly the precious ironwood. Additionally, the allocation of forests to villagers—connected to the obligation to protect them—did not guarantee that the trees would actually be protected.

When Phuc last visited Ba Ye at the end of 2004, logging trucks were still running down the narrow road that connected the village with the Red River Delta. About once a week, a truck carried heavy loads of timber out of the village of Dao. The trucks no longer carried ironwood, because it had all but disappeared from the surrounding forests. Instead, they transported timber such as *khao* (*Nothophoebe sp.*) and *sang* (*Sapindus oocarpus Radlk*), which were of lower quality than ironwood but had attained commercial significance in the general processes of revalorization discussed in Chapter 3. The trucks traveled down the road into the Red River Delta even though Vietnam's forest regulations deemed the logging and transport illegal. Despite the illegality, the trucks easily passed a series of government checkpoints.

In contrast, logging had ceased in Than Con during the course of 2004. There were no more trucks leaving the village loaded with *sen* (*Fosree cochinchinensis Pierre*), *tau* (*Vatica thorelii Pierre*), or *gioi* (*Talauma A.Chev*), despite their continuing commercial importance. Loggers had disappeared from Luoi Hai by the end of 2004, having been a frequent sight earlier in the year. Logging had stopped not merely because it was illegal, but also because the provincial Forest Development Department had sent in an inspection team. Reports of illegal logging in Luoi Hai published in provincial and national newspapers had prompted the department to investigate the situation in Luoi Hai, particularly accusations of complicit behavior and corruption by local officials.

Timber was a significant source of income in both Than Con and Ba Ye, and although logging was illegal in both places according to Vietnam's forestry regulations, loggers stopped their activities in Than Con only. This observation motivates our inquiry in this chapter. We examine not only the political and economic dynamics driving illegal practices but also the ways in which some practices deemed illegal—based on Vietnam's national legislation—provoke reactions by state officials while other practices do not. Moreover, we explore different notions of illegality as they relate to multiple processes that define what is legal and what is illegal. In our inquiry, we find plural dynamics of lawmaking at work. Lawmaking occurs at the national level, by way of the central party-state enacting legislation and designing policy, and also takes the form of powerful actors developing and enforcing rules in particular contexts—rules which may or may not fit with national law.

We then examine the symbolic construction of the state, similar to what we did in Chapter 4. However, in this chapter we find it helpful to employ Gupta's take on the everyday processes of state formation (Gupta 1995). Gupta's framework helps us to connect actual state practices to the symbolic construction of the state. Moreover, Gupta reveals how certain state practices defined as undesirable or illegitimate (such as corruption or, in our case, illegal logging), can serve as a template against which public discourse defines the image of the state. Images of the state result both from the everyday practices of local state officials and the discursive construction of the state in law and policy, even if these appear contentious at first sight. This insight allows Gupta to conclude: "Instead of treating corruption as a dysfunctional aspect of state organizations, I see it as a mechanism through which 'the state' itself is discursively constituted" (ibid.: 376). In other words, illegal logging and local officials' complicity in it may not be a mere malfunction in state operations but may contribute to everyday processes of discursive state construction in Vietnam.

Than Con: The Village Head and the Forest Protection Contracts

The Luoi Hai forest experienced heavy logging in the 1980s—but not by villagers. The forest was under the control of Tam Dai Enterprise, one of the many State Forest Enterprises (SFEs) set up by Vietnam's government to manage the country's forests. Tam Dai constructed a logging road into Luoi

Hai, hired about fifty workers from the Red River Delta, and cut logs until, by 1992, virtually none of the previous ironwood remained. Years later, when Phuc visited Luoi Hai, people vividly recalled how heavy logging trucks would drive right through their village. Standing at the bottom of the valley with Phuc, Trieu Van Phu, an elderly villager, pointed to Luoi Hai, noting that, "dozens of trucks fully loaded with ironwood ran out of the forest each day."

As soon as the logging crews withdrew, villagers set out to glean timber from the forest. Villagers commonly used the term "glean" (*mot* in Vietnamese) when they talked to Phuc as a way to distinguish their harvesting from the more destructive practices employed by the logging crews. In addition, they wanted to emphasize that they extracted only the timber left over from the logging conducted by Tam Dai. Most men in Than Con set out to cut logs as a way to complement their meager household incomes derived from agriculture (see Chapter 3). They had no problem selling the logs, as private traders came directly to Than Con to buy them. Villagers could offer the harvested logs to them in the open, because forest protection officials never made their way up to the village.

The staff of Tam Dai Enterprise returned to Than Con in 1994 with the intention to stop the "gleaning" by way of protection contracts. The contracts, to be signed between State Forest Enterprises and villagers, were a new means by which Vietnam's central government wanted to connect forest protection to improvements in rural livelihoods (Sikor 2001). The rationale was that past attempts to exclude villagers from forests no longer made sense. Instead, SFEs would sign up villagers to assist with forest protection, helping the enterprises to do their job and simultaneously enhance their own livelihoods. The new policy did not expand villagers' rights to forests, however, because these rights remained restricted to the collection of dead branches for firewood and other minor products. The funding for the contracts came from the so-called 327 Program initiated by the central government in 1992 through Decree 327. One of the "327 projects" had gone to Tam Dai Enterprise. This is why enterprise staff returned to Than Con to sign protection contracts for part of the forest in Luoi Hai.

The contracts helped forest protection in Luoi Hai, but they did nothing to increase most villagers' livelihoods. The only villager to derive material benefits from the contracts was the village head, who earned decent pay, which was equivalent to 150 euros a year. Ban Van Ba, the village head at the time, made sure that he became the sole contractor for all of the 102 ha in Luoi Hai. He did not inform the other villagers that he had signed a protection contract with Tam Dai. He only told them that Tam Dai had assigned the protection of the Luoi Hai forest to him, since he was the only one in Than Con capable of protecting the forest. All of the other villagers lost out, not only on the payments, but also because anh Ba no longer allowed them to harvest timber or other forest products from Luoi Hai.[1] The staff of Tam Dai also took a significant cut in protection payments. They subtracted almost 40 percent from the national quota of the 2.60 euros allocated for the protection of each hectare included in the 327 Program. The People's Committee of Van Son commune, in turn, took another 5 percent. "The money spreads out at various levels," anh Ba commented to Phuc.

The village head managed to hold on to his privileges when the protected forest area in Luoi Hai increased to 321 ha in 1998. He even succeeded in channeling the additional payments to close kin and a friend. The increase in area and payment occurred when the Department of Forest Protection of Phu Tho province set up a Provincial Management Unit to implement a new national program. Nationally, the so-called 661 Program now replaced the previous 327 Program. In reaction, Phu Tho province terminated all "327 projects" and started new "661 projects." In Than Con, anh Ba managed to gain a new contract for the protection of 100 ha. Since the national quota had now increased to 2.80 euros per ha, he increased his annual earnings from forest protection by another 45 euros. In addition, the village head succeeded in assigning the protection of the remaining 221 ha to just three other people: his brother, his father-in-law, and a close friend.[2]

Villagers deeply resented anh Ba's predatory practices and sought ways to make him accountable. They used the tactics commonly employed by the disenfranchised—gossip and badmouthing—calling him *"can bo tham lam"* (greedy official). In addition, they voiced their frustration at village meetings, requesting the village head to enlarge the protection team as a way to share the protection payments more widely. Yet anh Ba always refused; he would argue that the team already had sufficient members. Villagers even sent a letter to the chairman of the commune People's Committee, Con Van Ha, reporting the manipulation of contracts and denouncing anh Ba's predatory practices. They directly asked the chairman to release anh Ba from his post, something anh Ha had the power to do in reaction to the village head's wrongdoings. The chairman never initiated any actions against the village head, however, most likely because the arrangement worked well for the commune People's Committee, which now received 8 percent of the budget allocated for forest protection.

Thus, local officials' maneuvers undermined the central government's intent to provide economic entitlements to villagers through forest protection contracts. The rules set in national policy were clear: villagers were entitled to receive contracts and compensation according to a fixed quota per hectare. The village head managed to circumvent the rules by signing the largest contract himself and distributing the remaining contracts to close kin and to friends. Villagers' reacted by calling him greedy, and requested corrective action from his superiors. When the latter did not materialize, the state itself faced the danger of appearing greedy and duplicitous, at least with regard to the forest in Luoi Hai, one of the most valuable remaining assets in Than Con.

To Allocate, or Not To Allocate, That is the Question

The forest policy reforms initiated by Vietnam's central government in the early 1990s went beyond the issuance of contracts. Similar to the process of transferring agricultural land from agricultural producer cooperatives to individual households, they mandated the allocation of forestland to households. To facilitate the transfer the central government required the once omnipotent State Forest Enterprises to make some of their land available for allocation. Thus, these forest policy reforms were in line with much broader and more radical transformation in the exercise of state power sought by the central party-state. The top echelons of the Communist Party and national government wanted to base the relations between state and citizens on a set of uniform rules (Balme and Sidel 2007). The 1993 Land Law encapsulated this desired transformation by mandating the transfer of long-term land use rights to households throughout the country (see also Chapter 3). It explicitly referred to forestland as well, giving the same bundle of rights to the holders of forestland as to the holders of agricultural land.

The Tam Dai Enterprise heeded the request they received from the government hierarchy. Enterprise staff met with the provincial Department of Forestry to decide about the amount of forestland they had to make available for allocation to households. Their negotiations resulted in the transfer of nearly three-quarters of the enterprise's forestland in Thanh Son district, which was the district that included Van Son commune and Than Con village. Tam Dai eventually signed the required paperwork for a transfer of nearly 1,000 ha with the Van Son People's Committee in 1996. The area included the forests around Than Con, together with some degraded slopes used by villagers, as well as the natural forest of Luoi Hai.

The mandate to allocate to households the forestland received from Tam Dai Enterprise created a dilemma for anh Ha, the chairman of the Van Son People's Committee: should he support the allocation, as national policy and provincial guidelines required him to do, or should he seek ways to retain the forestland under the direct control of the People's Committee? Allocation would have restricted his leverage over the land, because forestland use right certificates had a duration of fifty years. The certificates provided forestland holders with a significant bundle of use rights to the forest that effectively limited anh Ha's ability to dispose of the land and derive material benefits from it. Moreover, some of the forestland transferred from Tam Dai still contained timber of financial value, particularly in Luoi Hai.

The chairman decided to support the allocation of only barren forestland—that is, land that did not have any trees but was still zoned for forestry and legally classified as forestland. In 1996, anh Ha joined the allocation team established by the People's Committee of Thanh Son district. The team drew up a list of those they considered eligible to be recipients, and eventually proposed the allocation of 226 ha of production forestland to thirty-one people in twenty-six households of Than Con. In 1997, the district People's Committee issued the official land use right certificates. Then, in 1998, another three households left out in the initial allocation received 30 ha of forestland between them. Thus, by the end of 1998, twenty-nine households held land use right certificates to forestland in Than Con, and only three had none. Three households held more than one certificate in direct contradiction of the national rule that each household should receive one certificate only.[3]

More importantly, anh Ha successfully opposed the allocation of the forest of Luoi Hai, keeping it under the direct management of the commune People's Committee. Why was he so keen to retain the forestland? When Phuc stayed in Than Con in 2004, the only evidence he could gather were villagers' speculations. Some suspected that the forest in Luoi Hai had caught the leaders' attention because it was one of only two patches of mature forest remaining in the area, so it was a site of relative economic value. Others thought that the leadership wanted to set aside Luoi Hai for management under the People's Committee because of the protection payments (discussed in the previous section). Thus, rumors spread that the leadership were retaining the forest as a way to secure economic gains for themselves or for the commune People's Committee.

The land allocation team therefore soon felt compelled to allocate 256 ha of forestland in Luoi Hai to households after all, in order to comply with the orders sent down from the provincial and district levels. The team could now report to the district People's Committee that they had completed their task. At the same time, anh Ha made sure not to publicize the allocation in Than Con or the other villages of Van Son commune. He kept the land certificates locked in a cupboard in his office so that no one, not even the sixteen households named on the certificates, knew about allocation. The maneuvering allowed anh Ha to satisfy the expectations of the higher-level government agencies and simultaneously preserve the benefits for himself and his People's Committee.

In addition, anh Ha wisely picked the sixteen households that had been named on the land use right certificates by the district People's Committee in 2000. Eleven of these were cadres at the commune People's Committee or the heads of other villages. Four of the five certificates destined for households in Than Con used the names of anh Ba and the other three households to which anh Ba had assigned protection contracts. None of the sixteen knew, of course, that anh Ha had named them on the certificates—not even anh Ba. Anh Ha was the only person in Van Son commune who knew of the allocation.

When Phuc learned about the allocation from a district cadre and talked to anh Ha in 2004, he gave his own version of the story. Asked why he neither informed the forestland recipients nor gave out the land use right certificates to them, he explained that the land in Luoi Hai belonged to the commune. People were not entitled to individual property rights. In addition, he claimed that all of the named people would support his intentions to secure the People's Committee's rights to the land if they ever heard about the allocation. A few weeks later, after Phuc had shared his knowledge with them, two people from Than Con named on the certificates visited anh Ha in his office to inquire about the allocation. Anh Ha reacted to their questions with a straight rebuttal and told them the same story: that the land in Luoi Hai belonged to the commune.

Local state officials' actions rendered the national forestland allocation policy less effectual than intended by the central party-state, just as they did in the case of the protection contracts. Whereas villagers received certificates for a large area of barren forestland, the cadres withheld certificates for the valuable forestland containing natural forest. Moreover, the local officials' maneuvers directly contradicted the idea that the transfer of land use rights signaled a new form of exercising state power on the basis of uniform rules. The actual transfer of rights remained subject to local official's dealings, even though the policy assumed that every rural household was entitled to the same rights, independent of local officials' practices. As a result, the state continued to look "greedy" to villagers, as personified by the village head. Nonetheless, the allocation of agricultural land (see Chapter 3) and barren forestland had now also established a different image of the state in Than Con—one that related to its citizens through a set of uniform rules, even if this image revealed flaws.

Conflicts at the Frontier: The Events in Luoi Hai

The forest in Luoi Hai had come to represent another frontier in the making of property and state, similar to what we found in the Albanian village of

Bagëtia in Chapter 4. When Phuc worked in Than Con, Luoi Hai was at the frontier of property and state in three ways: first, multiple social actors asserted use rights to the forest; second, various local state entities competed with each other over control of the forest; and third, the struggles over property and control were also about the image of the party-state. We begin with the first.

Local people made multiple claims on the forest in direct competition with each other. The four households who held protection contracts in the past claimed that no one was allowed to cut any timber from the forest, and that only they were entitled to collect some minor forest products such as firewood. They based their claim not only on the protection contracts but also the time and effort they had expended on almost daily patrols since 1998. There were also the households who had been named on the forestland certificates issued by the district People's Committee in 2000, five of them living in Than Con. Once the members in two of the households found out about the allocation, they had reasonable grounds to claim that the forest should be theirs, and that they were entitled to extract forest products.

In addition, several social actors asserted claims to Luoi Hai on moral grounds. Most people from Than Con and other villages nearby demanded access to the forest to meet their own subsistence needs and make a decent living (as per our previous discussion a similar process occurred in Bagëtia and has been observed in many other places; see, for example, McElwee 2004). People said that they needed to collect firewood from the forest as a source of fuel for cooking and warmth. The fruit, tubers, mushrooms, and such like that were available in the forest provided important contributions to their diet. And the timber was a significant source of cash income for them, to buy food, pay for their children's schooling, cover medical expenses, and so on. Legitimate forest use was not about legal contracts or certificates but a matter of need. Of course, there was also the chairman of the Van Son People's Committee, anh Ha, who held up public interests in the forest as a public asset, as we have discussed above.

People did not just disagree on who was entitled to use the forest, however; they also clashed on the subject of which state agency had control over the forest. Even by 2004, eleven years after the Land Law, it remained unclear which agency possessed jurisdiction over Luoi Hai. On the one hand, anh Ba and anh Ha claimed that Tam Dai Enterprise had transferred all 321 ha to the commune People's Committee eight years before, and the sixteen forestland certificates produced in collusion with the district officials were evidence of that. Anh Ha explained to Phuc that whenever enterprise staff came to the People's Committee to discuss a return of the forest, the chairman was quick to point out that "all the forest has already been allocated to households ... There's no way the enterprise can claim back the land."

On the other hand, Tam Dai maintained that 102 ha in Luoi Hai were still under the enterprise's jurisdiction. They claimed that the forest for which they had signed protection contracts with villagers of Thanh Son in 1994 remained under their control, since the enterprise had continued to administer the forest protection contracts until 1998 (i.e., two years after the transfer of jurisdiction took place). In addition, they pointed out that Tam Dai had never formally signed any papers terminating their responsibility for the protection of the 102 ha, which is why Tam Dai had begun to assert demands for its return toward the end of the 1990s. At that time, rising wood prices once again piqued the enterprise's interest in tree plantations, and galvanized them to search for suitable land.

These arguments show how anh Ha and the enterprise used the forestland certificates and protection contracts as a means to bargain over the forest of Luoi Hai. Of course, they were interested in deriving direct benefits from the forest in the form of timber revenues and protection payments, but their primary interest was with control over land. They wanted to be the government unit in charge of issuing forestland certificates and protection contracts, and influencing the distribution of forest benefits among people. Control—and not material benefit—was at the center of their struggle. And they used the tools given to them by the central party-state to implement uniform rules as bargaining chips in their power game.

Considering these struggles over access to and control over the forest, it was surprising that protection was effective until April 2004. Its effectiveness was due to the edifice anh Ba had erected in collusion with the forest protection officers, commune chairman, and three other men from Than Con. The protection fees sent each year via the 327 and 661 programs provided sufficient incentives to keep everyone at bay. Once the Provincial Management Unit terminated the protection contracts with anh Ba and the other three villagers, the entire edifice collapsed. The protection arrangements that had been in place for an entire decade imploded in a matter of a few days, as anh Ba's protection team ceased their patrols.

Villagers from Than Con, people from nearby villages, and even anh Ba immediately rushed to the forest in Luoi Hai to cut timber and collect firewood. They did not wait for the rainy season to end, as they would usually do, to make the cutting and transportation of logs easier. They went into the forest immediately, because they did not want to miss the unprecedented opportunity. Loggers relied on simple handheld saws and used their own strength and water buffaloes to pull logs out to the road. The number of logs leaving the forest was significant, as many people participated in the rush. A villager estimated for Phuc that within six months villagers from Than Con alone had extracted about 25 m^3 of timber. He also thought that this was a relatively small volume in comparison to the total volume taken out by men descending on Luoi Hai from many other places. No one held them back; commune and district officials stood by without taking any countermeasures.

People's justification for the logging revealed a third dimension of the struggles over access to and control over forests in Luoi Hai. People now considered the forest "in the possession of nobody" (*vo chu* in Vietnamese). This was the term villagers commonly used when they spoke to Phuc about the forest of Luoi Hai in 2004. For villagers, it was the first time that no one claimed possession of the forest. They did not know that the district People's Committee had issued forestland certificates four years earlier. But the more important insight is that the villagers knew how to use the land allocation program for their own purposes, in ways not anticipated by government officials. More broadly, they exploited gaps in the discourse of the party-state to deal with its citizens through a uniform set of rules. From their perspective, the forest was not in the possession of anyone (in contrast to the barren forestland that had been allocated to them). This was the reason they felt their logging did not hurt anyone, and thus felt entitled to extract logs for their own benefit.

We suggest, then, that the image of the party-state was at stake in the struggles over access, property, and control in Luoi Hai. It was at stake not only in the sense that local officials undermined the central discourse of uniform rules; it was also at the core of villagers' access claims to forest, as villagers took advantage of apparent weaknesses in the image. The question, therefore, is how, if at all, the discrepancies between villagers' practices, local officials' dealings, and the central party-state's discourse were resolved. This is a question that lies at the core of the following story.

The Provincial Inspection Team Arrives—and Leaves

The rampant logging in Luoi Hai made provincial and national news in October 2004. That month, the newspaper of Phu Tho province ran an article with the heading "*lam tac pha rung*" (forest hijackers destroy forest). The article blamed the people of Than Con for "destroying" forest, and featured a photo of a young man from Than Con hauling a large tree out of Luoi Hai with a buffalo. The article also found the commune People's Committee and Forest Protection Unit guilty of ignoring the timber extraction, transport, and trade, and implied that local officials colluded with loggers and wood traders. Two weeks later, the national newspaper *Weekly News* carried an article of almost identical content.

The articles were part of an extensive series of newspaper articles on illegal logging practices. Newspapers commonly sent out reporters to hunt for stories of timber extraction deemed illegal by Vietnam's restrictive forest regulations. To refer to illegal loggers, the reporters coined the term *"lam tac"* (forest hijackers), conjuring up powerful images in the coverage about Luoi Hai. The implications of the term were clear in Vietnamese language: illegal loggers damage the common heritage and act against the public interest. The loggers enrich themselves by cutting national forest and acting against the national goal of forest conservation. They were not only criminals, they were also immoral.

Elsewhere, we have illuminated the processes underlying the criminalization of unwanted logging and public discourse about loggers as immoral people (Sikor and To 2011). In a nutshell, we have shown how the central government created increasingly elaborate regulations on what was not allowable in forest management. It also strengthened the Forest Protection Department's powers to enforce the regulations as reflected in the staggering 300,000 violations of forest regulations detected by the department between 2001 and 2006. The criminalization went hand in hand with public concerns about unwanted logging, which was reflected by growing numbers of press reports on the topic. Public concerns turned into outrage when it became clear that forest protection officials were colluding with loggers in many instances. Corruption was not only a key public concern in forestry but also across the entire spectrum of government functions (Gainsborough 2003). In the public imagination, the fight against corruption reached almost mythical status as being a way of reinstating the moral order that had been lost with the turn to a market economy (Luong 2007).

Once the articles appeared in the newspapers, the provincial People's Committee had to take action. The committee organized a series of meetings involving government units from the provincial, district, and commune levels within a few weeks of the articles' publication. In addition, it established an inspection team under the personal leadership of the provincial Department of Forest Development's director, including the head of the district Forest Protection Unit and anh Ha, among others. Local members of the inspection team even travelled to Than Con several times to check the situation on the ground.

The inspection team did not find any illegal practices in Than Con, nor catch any loggers, nor detect any of the timber commonly stored alongside villagers' houses. They did not notice any suspicious trading activities taking place in the village or commune center. They did not find anything illegal because, prior to each arrival of the team members, forest protection officials came to Than Con, informed villagers about the impending visit, and requested them to remove any evidence of illegal logging activities. Nor did they detect any logging activities, because they never bothered to travel the distance to Luoi Hai. They always stopped in the village and searched for timber or any other evidence of logging, but did not look at the forest itself. Thus, after several visits, the inspection team concluded that the articles were overstated, to say the least. When a team member talked to Phuc, he put it in much more drastic terms: "They [talk] nonsense!" he said, referring to the reporters. "You see, the forest here is much better than in other areas." He asserted that, without ever having set foot inside Luoi Hai.

Yet the provincial and district People's Committees could not refute the media reports as easily as the inspection team. A simple whitewash was not an option to them, because the press demanded remedial action. The People's Committees demonstrated action through public criticisms of anh Ha and forest protection officials for a lack of commitment to forest protection. In addition, they ordered the district Forest Protection Unit to conduct frequent checks of trucks leaving Than Con, effectively halting timber transports, at least until the end of 2004, when Phuc visited the village for the last time.

The events at Luoi Hai, we conclude, provide indicative insights not only into local officials' dealings but also how these served as a template to define the central party-state along the lines of Gupta's framework (Gupta 1995). Higher-level officials did not understand that the reports on illegal logging were potential evidence for inappropriate forest regulations. Instead, in line with central government policy and public discourse, they saw them as aberrations due to criminal behavior and individual greed. When local officials were unresponsive to reports or complicit with illegal logging, higher-level officials stepped in to enforce the rules made by the central party-state. The higher-level officials blamed the illegal practices on negligence by the local officials (making themselves appear untarnished) and asserted the sanctity of the central rules. Talking about logging practices in this way, they employed a particular discourse of illegal logging that connected the central party-state and higher-level officials with good statecraft, and allowed higher-level officials to assert control over local officials.

How did the local government officials react to the assertion of central rules? They erected a facade of compliance, as indicated above. In addition, they resorted to the very strategies that had proven so effective in the past. They did not raise the issue of the botched forestland allocation, which would have been in line with the rules set by the central party-state. Instead, the forest protection officers sought to resurrect the edifice that had protected the forest up to April 2004. The Forest Protection Unit hired a villager to patrol Luoi Hai—a single villager to patrol the entire forest. No one, not even the newly hired guard, believed that he would be able to keep loggers out of Luoi Hai once the forest protection officers' control of the trucks ceased. But that was only of secondary concern to the involved officials. Their primary concern was that they had proven their determination to act. If loggers descended on Luoi Hai again, they now had the unfortunate man on which to put the blame.

Thus, we find that the events in Luoi Hai brought to light underlying contestations over how the party-state ought to function in relation to citizens. Local cadres and higher-level state entities assumed different roles in the contestations, promoting different images of the party-state. Contestations between local and higher-level officials were also a key element in struggles over property regarding forest in Ba Ye, the Vietnamese village to which we turn now.

Ba Ye: Granting Forests Rights, and Taking Them Away Again

Tu Ly was the name of the State Forest Enterprise in charge of forest management around Ba Ye until the first half of the 1990s. Mirroring events in Than Con, Tu Ly Enterprise constructed a road to Ba Ye in the 1970s, brought in workers from outside, and extracted significant volumes of timber. In addition, the enterprise signed annual contracts with the Ba Ye cooperative for timber harvests. It terminated the contract with the cooperative in the late 1980s, when villagers were no longer able to find the valuable timber such as *sen* (*Fosree cochinchinensis Pierre*) and *tau* (*Vatica thorelii Pierre*) that were sought after by the enterprise. Villagers subsequently set out to "glean" the forest, just as their peers did in Than Con. They cut any timber they could sell to private traders coming into the village.

District and commune officials set out to implement forestland allocation in Ba Ye in 1995, after Tu Ly Enterprise had transferred control over the forests around Ba Ye to them. In stark contrast with Than Con, they did not try to hide the allocation or to thwart the process in favor of a few. Instead, the allocation team made sure to distribute the forestland relatively equally. They also decided to allocate all forestland located within the administrative boundaries of Ba Ye, because they considered the forest to serve productive purposes. The allocated area was formidable: it gave each household an average forestland holding of 12 ha. Two years later, all forestland holders received the corresponding land use right certificates, or Red Books, as proof of their new rights to forest.

Forestland allocation in Ba Ye showcased national policy: in particular the provision of land rights to people, and more generally the new set of uniform rules to govern the relations between party-state and citizens. Village households received long-term land use rights to forestland, as set out in the 1993 Land Law and subsequent implementation decrees issued by the central government. The Red Books they now held in their possession certified their rights to forest in accordance with the rules set by the central government, similar to the other one million households that would receive forest rights under Vietnam's forestland allocation program by 2010.[4] Unlike Than Con, they held Red Books for all of the forests that villagers considered to belong to Ba Ye.

In 1999, the People's Committee of what was now Hoa Binh province decided to reclassify all forest in Ba Ye as "protected." In that year, the chairman of the Hoa Binh People's Committee approved a new forestry master plan for Bac Minh district. The plan specified that virtually all existing forest in the district was to be conserved. The decision was partly prompted by concerns over high siltation rates of the Hoa Binh reservoir due to unsuitable land use in the Da River watershed, to which Ba Ye belonged. Because the Hoa Binh hydropower station was critical for national electricity generation, supplying at one point up to 60 percent of Vietnam's output, the central government pushed for urgent measures to protect forest in the watershed, and made significant funds available. However, the decision also reflected a broader nationwide trend to reclassify production forest for protection. In fact, protection forest eventually extended to two-thirds of Vietnam's entire forest (Forest Protection Department 2012). For Ba Ye, the new forestry master plan meant that all forest changed from "production" to "protection" status, just two years after villagers had received their Red Books. Villagers were no longer allowed to use the forest to meet their own livelihood needs, nor, in particular, to exploit any timber.

The reclassification implied that villagers lost most of the legal rights to forests that they had just gained. They kept their Red Books but were no longer allowed to make productive use of the forestland, even though that is what allocation had initially implied. Nor could they expect to receive forest protection contracts for their allocated parcels, since that was not allowed by central government regulations. In 2001, the central government reiterated that all forests in the Da and other important watersheds had important protection functions and should therefore be considered of "highly critical" significance. There was no room for agricultural cultivation, something that the villagers of Ba Ye had long practiced on the slopes surrounding their houses. The central government also prohibited further extraction of timber.

Consequently, we found that the people of Ba Ye had a similar experience with the transfer of forestland certificates as their peers in the Romanian villages (see Chapter 5), namely, they received rights, but effectively lost them again within a very short time. But villagers in both countries also feared that forestland would turn from an asset into a liability in a dynamic we have observed in other settings (Sikor 2006). The restrictions placed on the use of the forest and the obligation to protect it against encroachment threatened to turn villagers' land certificates into a liability. These restrictions and obligations also meant that the new rules set out by Vietnam's central party-state no longer delivered any tangible benefits to villagers. The appeal the certificates had held for villagers faded quickly.

Villagers Log Anyway

When Phuc visited the village of Ba Ye at the end of 2004, he did not see any men around. After searching for a few minutes, he encountered Ban Van Dong. "Where are the others?" he asked anh Dong. "In the forest," the young man replied. "Logging?" "Of course," anh Dong replied, laughing at Phuc. "Is there anything else worth doing there?"

That day, nearly every man had gone into the forest to cut timber. It was the time of year when people needed money. The lunar New Year, *Tet*, was approaching fast, enticing people to purchase new clothes and stock up on good food. Anh Dong had stayed back in the village only because he had to look after his young daughter in his wife's absence.

Over the course of his fieldwork, Phuc discovered that every adult man in Ba Ye, including the village head, anh Chan, regularly went into the forest for logging with hand-operated saws throughout most of the year. The men set out to cut *khao* trees wherever they could find them. After sawing the trees into planks, they used water buffalo to haul them back to the village. The men went into the forest because timber was the number one cash income in Ba Ye, generating 230 euros for the average household. It accounted for roughly 60 percent of total cash income in the village in 2004, thereby allowing households to purchase staple food during rice shortages, supplement their diets, and buy simple consumer goods.[5]

The obligation to protect forests, written into the forestland certificates, did not stop people from logging, because the forest protection officials did not enforce these obligations. Villagers commonly pointed out to Phuc that the officers "never come down to the village to check for logging." In any case, the legal obligation would not have prevented villagers from logging, because they considered the forest to be theirs. For them, forest was not a national treasure to be preserved for the future; rather it was a commons that they had long used for their own livelihood needs. Since the 1980s, this use had included logging for sale, initially to Tu Ly Enterprise and later to the traders offering to purchase timber.

The extent to which villagers felt entitled to log the forests is well illustrated in a story that Duong Thanh An recounted to Phuc. Just like anh An, a few villagers had tried to keep others out of the parcels allocated to them. However, none of them had met with any success, because most of the villagers rejected the rules defined in land legislation and forest regulations. Anh An told Phuc how he had tried to stop another man from Ba Ye from cutting trees on his parcel of forestland with the argument that he was the one in possession of the relevant Red Book. The other man had told An: "The trees are not yours, why are you protecting them?" He was alluding to the fact that the reclassification from "production" to "protection" had effectively taken away anh An's rights to harvest the trees. Why, then, should he care about the trees?

To emphasize his point, the other man had joked: "Will you ask the forest protection officials to do the ceremonies for you when you die?" This remark referred to the funeral customs in Ba Ye whereby, when someone dies, all villagers congregate to conduct the ceremonies for the dead. It is important that all attend, because it demonstrates their respect for the dead. In contrast, the other man was implying that villagers may not come to anh An's funeral if he were to try to stop them from entering the forest. He would risk becoming a social outcast in his own village, thus having to rely on forest protection officials to perform the ceremonies for him.

This was a stern warning to anh An; it indicated how most villagers saw the forest as village commons, similar to the ways in which they cherished their funeral rituals as collective heritage. Almost every man in the village who set out to cut timber claimed to have the customary right to do so.

Ba Ye's men set their eyes not only on their own forest but also on the forests of other villages. However, their attempts to log the latter met with mixed success. On the one hand, people from two other villages of the Tan Da commune severely fought these attempts; they would take loggers' timber by force and even seize their water buffalo temporarily. They did not want to share any of the timber left in the forests surrounding their villages with loggers from Ba Ye. On the other hand, people from Ba Ye were able to develop a favorable arrangement with villagers from the Thu Cuong commune in neighboring Phu Tho province. The villagers basically tolerated the extraction of timber in return for logging jobs. They even helped the loggers to hide from the patrols sent out by the commune People's Committee of Thu Cuong and the Forest Protection Unit there. The villagers from Thu Cuong did so in part because the forest protection officials responsible for their forests took their job very seriously. They actually enforced the ban on any transport of timber out of Thu Cuong, in stark contrast with the situation in Ba Ye, as the following section will show.

Ba Ye's people felt entitled to use the forests located around their village. They asserted property rights to the forest that other villages also considered to be theirs. They also sought access to other forests, as long as the people from other villages did not mount serious resistance. They claimed access and asserted property rights on the basis of customary understandings of entitlements to forests, similar to the dynamic we have described in Luoi Hai above and observed in the Albanian villages (see Chapter 4). They did not care that the rules set by the central government sought to restrict them from doing so.

Trips Down into the Red River Delta

The loggers of Ba Ye had a ready outlet for selling the timber. They sold the timber to Nguyen Van Nga, a trader who had built a small house near the village road to procure timber. Anh Nga was originally from the district town and had relocated to Ba Ye in the 1990s when he saw the opportunity to become involved in the timber trade. He had built a large house in the early 2000s, equipped with modern facilities. Anh Nga owned two trucks, which he used to transport logs out of Ba Ye down to the Red River Delta.

Anh Nga sold the timber to wood wholesalers in the small market town of Huu Bang, some one hundred kilometers from Ba Ye. Huu Bang had emerged as a major center of wood trade and processing in the Ha Tay province, located a mere twenty kilometers from Hanoi.[6] The town had benefited from the rapid increase in the urban demand for construction wood and furniture in the 1990s, evidenced by the large number of wood retailers, sawmills, and furniture shops. The shops and mills fed on an impressive stream of logs brought not only from various regions of Vietnam but also from Laos and Cambodia.

In order to reach Huu Bang, anh Nga's trucks had to pass a long series of inspections and checkpoints. The inspections began in the village, where the village head kept a check on his activities. They continued with the People's Committee of Tan Da commune, which had the mandate to verify the origins of the wood for transportation and trade. After leaving the commune, the trucks typically passed through four checkpoints run by different agencies of Bac Minh district: the Forest Protection Unit, public security forces, traffic police, and the tax division. Thus, within the first few kilometers of the trip, the trucks had managed to satisfy the demands of six state units.

Once they left Bac Minh district, the trucks had again to maneuver their way through a long series of fixed and mobile checkpoints. Reaching the township of Hoa Binh, they encountered the checkpoints established by the provincial People's Committee: forest protection officers and various police units concerned with economic affairs, special affairs, and traffic regulation, and others who were under the mandate of the township government such as forest protection, traffic police, and the economic affairs department. After leaving the township, the trucks still had to pass through two districts in Hoa Binh province and another two in Ha Tay province before they reached Huu Bang. In each district, the trucks had to deal with a fixed and a mobile checkpoint, run by the district public security forces and Forest Protection Units.

Talking with Phuc, anh Nga estimated that he had to "lubricate" each truck's journey by paying off an average of twenty-three officials. Every official involved expected a financial payment in return for letting the trucks pass. In fact, the trucks could not leave the village without having made the first payment. The village head had invented a fee that he collected from anh Nga for every truck leaving the village loaded with timber. Each departure incurred a fee of 5.20 euros, which the village head levied on the use of public space for uploading logs and of the village road for the transport.

The story was the same at every actual or potential inspection point that the trucks had to pass on their way to Huu Bang. Officials expected anh Nga to make a payment in return for ignoring the transport. This meant that a significant amount of the money anh Nga derived for his logs from the wholesalers in Huu Bang ended up "spread on the road," as he called it, and as we have shown elsewhere (Sikor and To 2011). Yet, if anh Nga failed to deliver the expected payment he would face the threat of hefty fines and legal prosecution. That was very clear to anh Nga, as he explained to Phuc: "It's better that I pay, even if they don't stop me, [as the payments are necessary] to maintain my business in the long run." So Anh Nga paid them off every time he transported timber. In addition, he made sure to bring them special "gifts"—usually envelopes stuffed with cash—when needed. This usually guaranteed safe passage for his trucks, and reduced the risk of detection and punishment.

Amazingly, anh Nga's timber trucks had rarely been stopped over the years, despite the fact that they traveled down the major road connecting Hoa Binh town with Hanoi. At the end of 2004, however, anh Nga ran into serious trouble on his way through Bac Minh district—the public security police compounded his two trucks loaded with timber, and detained them for a month, during which anh Nga could not continue his business. At the end, the police issued a fine of 3,120 euros and confiscated all of his logs. However, to anh Nga's great relief, they did not revoke his licenses for the timber trade or transport.[7]

The lack of legal action against anh Nga's timber transports was surprising if one considers the central party-state's heavy emphasis on forest protection. If the party-state wanted to prove its resolve against illegal logging, then anh Nga's trucks running down the major road from the northwestern mountains into the Red River Delta offered a chance to intervene. Nonetheless, in contrast with Than Con, no media ever reported about the illegal logging in Ba Ye, and no inspection team ever came to Ba Ye to investigate villagers' or local officials' dealings. The lack of state action was in part due to the payments that anh Nga always delivered to all state units involved. More importantly, it was also due to the operation of two powerful brokers in the background, to which we now turn.

The Lawmakers

The brokers anh Mot and anh Hai ensured safe passage for anh Nga's trucks. Before each run, they informed the relevant government officials over the phone. They also visited government officials at their homes or met them secretly elsewhere to cultivate personal relations. In fact, their operations were so secretive that Phuc was never able to meet them, or find out their full names. Everyone involved knew them by their first names only. But it was, by all accounts, the brokers who took care of most of the payments; they used the money they received from anh Nga and many others who asked for their services in the logging and other sectors. Anh Mot brokered deals for anh Nga and many others in Hoa Binh province, while anh Hai did so in Ha Tay. In the logging business, it was common for them to arrange safe passage for a dozen trucks driving in convoy in one night.

The operations of the two brokers reflected the significance of personal interests and patron–client relations penetrating state practice, similar to what we observed in the two Romanian villages (see Chapter 5). In Vietnam, patronage relations proliferated in many spheres and at all levels of the state, such as the privatization of state industries and the allocation of loans by state-owned banks to companies (Gainsborough 2010). Politicians and businessmen formed powerful networks, leading to personalized state practices and undermining the implementation of central rules. These personalized practices ran counter to the rule-based exercise of state power that the leadership of the Communist Party and central government sought to promote through their campaign for a "law-based state" (*nha nuoc phap quyen*).

Nonetheless, the operations of the two brokers amounted to more than personal interests and patron–client relations, for the simple reason that anh Mot and anh Hai established clear rules, and everyone else obeyed them. The significance of rules was also the reason why anh Nga and the other people involved referred to them as "lawmakers" (*lam luat*). When they called them lawmakers, they did not think of the members of Vietnam's

National Assembly, or other officials in the higher echelons of the party-state. Instead, they used the term in the same way Vietnamese people commonly described their experiences of dealing with local government officials, which typically involved extra-legal payments such as unrecorded fees and service charges, or outright bribes. The dealings also revealed significant discretionary powers that enabled local officials to engage in a range of practices at odds with the rules enacted by the central party-state, starting with ad hoc decisions about particular requests and extending to the development of systematic procedures applicable to all cases within a particular context. This was captured in the term *lam luat*, as officials "made" law in the sense of developing and enforcing binding rules.

Anh Mot and anh Hai clearly made law applicable to the transport of timber in Hoa Binh and Ha Tay provinces. They made laws such that the rules governing timber transports were clear to everyone involved. Once anh Mot and anh Hai had endorsed a timber transport, identified a night for the trucks to travel to Huu Bang, and informed all relevant officials, everyone involved stuck by the rules. The trucks drove down the roads that night and the officials let them pass. The officials, in turn, knew that they would receive a financial reward, and the amount that they could expect. Forest protection officers, having the mandate to control timber transportation, tended to receive larger bribes than their colleagues in other departments. Additionally, higher-ranking officials made more money from the timber trade than those working in lower positions, because a significant share of the bribes demanded by street-level officers eventually made its way up to their superiors. These upward transfers took the form of periodic "gifts" and payments required for appointments to lucrative inspection jobs, the latter added into the thousands of euros.

Anh Mot and anh Hai were in the position to create law because they relied on powerful networks to enforce the rules against non-compliance. These networks thrived because of the official state regulations enacted to protect forests, as well as the extra-legal powers held by officials in the higher levels of the party-state. The most critical factor for both of them was that their fathers assumed high positions in the People's Committee of each province. Being sons of provincial leaders, many doors were open to them; as a result, they came to know many influential people personally. People also understood that anh Mot and anh Hai would be able to count on powerful support in case something went wrong. In addition, both lawmakers held formal appointments in the provincial People's Committees. They could perform some of their brokering services in close connection with their government jobs. Perhaps most importantly, there was always the possibility for anh Mot and anh Hai to evoke the forest protection regulations and threaten to report involved officials.

At the same time, the lawmakers were able to offer protection to all involved state officials through their powerful networks. The officials enabling anh Nga's timber transports did not incur much risk through their involvement because the probability of detection was close to zero. In the entire Tan Minh district, officials had only once been caught accepting bribes from a wood trader. In 2004, a trader daringly recorded two forest protection officials asking for a bribe on his mobile phone. Their superiors could not avoid launching a formal investigation into the incident or finding the two officials guilty—the evidence was too strong. However, neither of the two officials lost their job, as they were merely transferred to other positions within the unit.

The fourth and final element in the lawmaking process was that the positions held by anh Mot and anh Hai allowed them to monopolize specific sectors of economic activity in the two provinces. Both had claimed the timber trade as their own territory over time. No one else was in a position to offer similar brokering services, because they were the only actors offering access to the officials involved. If anyone wanted to transport timber in Hoa Binh or Ha Tay, they had no choice but to enlist the lawmakers' services for making the transport of logs possible. This is also the reason why anh Nga visited them on a regular basis, working with anh Mot to smooth things over in Hoa Binh province, and with anh Hai to do the same in Ha Tay province. Anh Nga was very willing to pay them "service fees," as he called the payments, in return for safe passage.

As a result of the lawmaking, central forest protection regulations were not only ineffective in Ba Ye but had the perverse effect of actually sustaining the logging. The central party-state's indiscriminate criminalization of logging created the basis upon which the lawmaking unfolded in Ba Ye and beyond. The criminalization played into the hands of the lawmakers, because the access they offered to officials furnishing permits and enforcing the law would have been less valuable without it. Central forest protection regulations also provided the threat against which the lawmakers and local officials could offer protection. Thus, it was the criminalization of logging that allowed the local lawmaking to unfold, establishing rules that supported the villagers' desire to cash in on forests. The rules applicable in Ba Ye and beyond were not those made by the central party-state, but they were rules nonetheless.

Logging and Lawmaking in Than Con and Ba Ye

The villagers of Than Con and Ba Ye had similar experiences to their peers in the Romanian village regarding the transfer of forestland titles (see

Chapter 5): the transfer did not generate the benefits they expected. The problem was twofold. First, local government officials undermined the implementation of national policy for their personal gains. In Than Con, they did not allocate any of the natural forest in Luoi Hai to villagers, nor did they include them in forest protection contracts. Second, even when villagers received legal papers certifying their possession of forest, they could not make use of the certificates to the extent they expected. The people of Ba Ye received forestland certificates but subsequent regulations severely restricted legal uses of their forests.

The dynamics of forest property reflected underlying contestations over the state, and contributed to them, just as we observed in the Albanian and Romanian villages (chapters 4 and 5). In Than Con, two different state entities competed with each other for jurisdiction over the forest of Luoi Hai. They used the means afforded to them by the central government for the implementation of national policy—protection contracts and forestland certificates—as pawns in their struggle over control. Higher-level officials, alarmed by media reports about rampant logging, eventually stepped in to enforce compliance with central government regulations. In Ba Ye, local state officials colluded with traders to circumvent the regulations instituted by the central government deeming the timber trade as illegal. To do so, they actively exploited the powers accorded to them in central regulations, the very powers they held with the mandate to stamp out illegal trade.

Illegal logging was the most apparent outcome of these negotiations over property and the state.[8] Loggers did not simply set upon forests because they had found ways to circumvent central forest regulations. Of course, loggers cut a significant amount of timber from Luoi Hai and around Ba Ye. The precious ironwood was gone, and the remaining *khao* and *sang* trees were rapidly depleted. Nor would it be wrong to observe that the villagers' extraction of logs was deemed illegal by national regulations, or that their notions of what was legitimate differed from central regulations (McElwee 2004). Nevertheless, simple reference to the discrepancy between local practices and central regulations would not explain why the logging occurred, nor how it came to be considered illegal. Such an explanation requires attention to the underlying struggles over both property and state.

Struggles over the state in the Vietnamese villages took the form of conflicts between personalized and rule-based exercise of authority, very much like the situation in the Romanian villages. In Than Con, the village head and the communal officials wielded their power in a manner that was relatively unrestricted by any regulation. They managed to enlist each other and enroll others in patronage relations similar to those demonstrated by the mayor of Dragova (Chapter 5). In comparison, the exercise of state authority was much more rule-based in Ba Ye. Villagers understood what they could do: extract trees in their own forest in open daylight—and what they could not do: attempt the same thing in other villages. The trader adhered to the rules just as all the government officials did in the timber trade. Yet the rules governing the timber trade in Ba Ye were not those instituted by the central government; they were the rules made and enforced by the two lawmakers.

In Than Con, officials' everyday practices served as a template against which the central party-state was able to define the image of the state, as suggested by Gupta (1995). Central government policy set the image of the party-state apart from local officials' dealings in relation to the forest in two ways, both reliant on the rules defined by the central party-state. First, by handing out certificates for barren forestland to villagers, forestland allocation established the central party-state as the source of people's forestland rights. Central land legislation also provided the symbolic basis for villagers to question why the forest of Luoi Hai was not allocated to anyone. Second, the criminalization of unwanted logging allowed the central party-state to construct illegal logging as another critical action against which central policy and public discourse could construct the image of the good party-state. It provided the legal and symbolic grounds for higher-level officials to intervene in local affairs and reprimand local officials, even though they could not actually prove any wrongdoing, and displayed no serious interest in doing so.

The situation was very different in Ba Ye. The villagers' logging and the traders' activities did not provide a template against which higher-level officials could attribute a positive image to the central party-state. Instead, both local practices and the rules defined by the central party-state provided the grounds for local state officials to establish their own rules. On the one hand, the rules enforced by the two lawmakers were able to guarantee order for local timber harvests and the timber trade. On the other hand, they allowed villagers and other local people to benefit from valuable local resources, in defiance of the notion that forests belonged to the national treasure. They also provided protection for villagers, traders, and officials against legal prosecution or other threats. Thus, it was the very criminalization of unwanted logging by the central party-state that caused local actors to develop their own set of rules, rendering local practices invisible to central-level state officials, and thereby ruling them out as a template against which the central party-state could shine.

Contestations over the state in the two Vietnamese villages reflected two intertwined dynamics: struggles between rule-based and personalized exercises, as well as competition between local officials and the central party-state. With the latter, we arrive at a key theme in the literature on Vietnamese politics, specifically the Vietnamese party-state. The literature recognizes conflicts between local officials and the higher echelons of the party-state as a key dynamic of political change (Kerkvliet and Marr 2004). Perhaps the best example of the centrality of local–central state relations comes from the dynamics underlying the widely heralded economic reforms of the late 1980s. They did not come about as a result of a grand scheme instituted by the top leaders of government and Communist Party. Instead, the central party-state enacted a series of laws and decrees to legalize and regularize the changes that had already taken place in many localities (Fforde and de Vylder 1996; Kerkvliet 2005). Similarly, the literature interprets the decree on grassroots democracy passed by Vietnam's national parliament in 1998 as an effort by the central party-state to tighten controls on the practices of local officials (Kerkvliet 2003; Mattner 2004).

Seen in this way, the lawmaking in Ba Ye posed a much more fundamental challenge to the authority claimed by the central party-state than the lawless situation in Than Con. The central party-state looked relatively benign in comparison with local officials' dealings in Than Con. In Ba Ye, however, local actors acted together to go against the rules set by the central party-state. Thus, we see different images of the party-state emerge from the discrepancy between local practices and central rules in the two villages.

With this observation, we conclude our ethnographic inquiry into the dynamics of property and propertizing regarding forests in Vietnam, Romania, and Albania. The ethnographies provide vivid testimony to the discrepancy between the expectations and actual outcomes of postsocialist property reforms noted at the outset. In addition, they suggest a powerful explanation of changes in forestry, demonstrating how negotiations over property were closely intertwined with contestations over authority. It is now appropriate to return to the larger picture and examine the dynamics of propertizing more generally.

Notes

1. In this chapter, as in Chapter 3, we will stick to the Vietnamese custom of addressing men and women with their first names, preceded by the pronouns 'anh' and 'chi'.

2. In fact, his greed did not stop there. He required the three other men to form a protection team and made himself its leader. The other three men were required to regularly patrol the forest, a task from which anh Ba exempted himself. Yet being the leader of the team, he still claimed most of the protection fees for himself—fees which paid for the 221 ha, excluding his own 100 ha of forest, for which he did not want to share the applicable fees.

3. Unfortunately, Phuc was never able to see all certificates or a list of certificate holders, so he could not determine which households had received more than one

certificate. We suspect that anh Ha arranged for the issuance of multiple certificates to selected households to hide inequalities in the allocation—but we have no proof of this.

4. The one million is a very rough estimate on our part, in the absence of any official figures. Our estimate is based on government statistics from around 2000 reporting that roughly 10 percent of Vietnam's forestland had been allocated to some 330,000 households—or 334,446 to be exact! By 2010, an approximate quarter of all forestland had been allocated to households, leading us to put the total numbers of households in the possession of forestland certificates at approximately one million.

5. The logging also meant that villagers took a sizable volume of timber out of the surrounding forests every year. Some estimated that they removed at least 150 m^3 of timber and roundwood every year.

6. Ha Tay merged with the capital district of Hanoi in 2008.

7. Anh Nga suggested to Phuc that another timber trader competing with him at the district level had reported him to the police, who felt obliged to demonstrate action in order to cover up their collusion in the illegal timber trade. However, Phuc was unable to verify this claim from other sides.

8. Similar dynamics have been documented for other parts of the world. For example, research on "illegal" logging in Indonesia attributes a significant role to struggles between the central state and district governments. See, for instance, Casson and Obidzinski (2002); McCarthy (2002a, 2002b); Smith et al. (2003).

References

Balme, Stephanie, and Mark Sidel. 2007. "Vietnam in Comparative Communist and Postcommunist Perspectives." In *Vietnam's New Order*, ed. Stephanie Balme and Mark Sidel. New York: Palgrave Macmillan, 1–10.

Casson, Anne, and Krystof Obidzinski. 2002. "From New Order to Regional Autonomy: Shifting Dynamics of 'Illegal' Logging in Kalmantan, Indonesia." *World Development* 30(12): 2133–51.

Fforde, Adam, and Stefan de Vylder. 1996. *From Plan to Market: Economic Transition in Vietnam 1979–1994*. Boulder, CO: Westview Press.

Forest Protection Department. 2012. Annual Forestry Statistics. Hanoi, Vietnam.

Gainsborough, Martin. 2003. "Corruption and the Politics of Economic Decentralization in Vietnam." *Journal of Contemporary Asia* 33(1): 69–84.

———. 2010. *Vietnam: Rethinking the State*. London: Zed Books.

Gupta, Akhil. 1995. "Blurred Boundaries: The Discourse of Corruption, the Culture of Politics, and the Imagined State." *American Ethnologist* 22(2): 375–402.

Kerkvliet, Benedict J.T. 2003. "Grappling with Organizations and the State in Contemporary Vietnam." In *Getting Organized in Vietnam: Moving in and around the Socialist State*, ed. B.J.T. Kerkvliet, R.H.K. Heng and D. Koh. Pasir Panjang: Institute of Southeast Asian Studies, 1–24.

———. 2005. *The Power of Everyday Politics: How Vietnamese Peasants Transformed National Policy*. Ithaca, NY: Cornell University Press.

Kerkvliet, Benedict J.T., and David Marr. 2004. *Beyond Hanoi: Local Government in Vietnam*. Singapore: Institute for Southeast Asian Studies.

Luong, Hy Van. 2007. "Vietnam in 2006: Stronger Global Integration and Resolve for Better Governance." *Asian Survey* 47(1): 168–74.

Mattner, M. 2004. "Power to the People? Local Governance and Politics in Vietnam." *Environment and Urbanization* 16(1): 121–27.

McCarthy, John F. 2002a. "Power and Interest on Sumatra's Rainforest Frontier: Clientelist Coalitions, Illegial Logging and Conservation in the Alas Valley." *Journal of South East Asia Studies* 33(1): 77–106.

———. 2002b. "Turning in Circles: District Governance, Illegal Logging, and Environmental Decline in Sumatra, Indonesia." *Society and Natural Resources* 15: 867–86.

McElwee, Pamela. 2004. "You Say Illegal, I Say Legal: The Relationship between 'Illegal' Logging and Land Tenure, Poverty, and Forest Use Rights in Vietnam." *Journal of Sustainable Forestry* 19(1–2): 97–135.

———. 2001b. "The Allocation of Forestry Land in Vietnam: Did It Cause the Expansion of Forests in the Northwest?" *Forest Policy and Economics* 2(1): 1–11.

———. 2006. "Land as Asset, Land as Liability: Property Politics in Rural Central and Eastern Europe." In *Changing Properties of Property*, ed. Franz von Benda-Beckmann, Keebet von Benda-Beckmann, and Melanie G. Wiber. New York: Berghahn Books, 106–25.

Sikor, Thomas, and To Xuan Phuc. 2011. "Illegal Logging in Vietnam: *Lam Tac* (Forest Hijackers) in Practice and Talk." *Society and Natural Resources* 24(7): 688–701.

Smith, J., et al. 2003. "Illegal Logging, Collusive Corruption and Fragmented Governments in Kalimantan, Indonesia." *International Forestry Review* 5(3): 293–302.

Conclusion

Postsocialist Propertizing and the Dynamics of Property

> To clean up the shambles left by communist mismanagement,
> Eastern Europe must take a swift, dramatic leap to private ownership.
> —J. Sachs, "What Is To Be Done?"

> Creating property rights was one thing, creating effective ownership another.
> —K. Verdery, *The Vanishing Hectare*

Governments and their international advisors had high expectations for postsocialist property reforms. They considered property reforms, particularly privatization, to represent no less than the most critical step towards a market economy and democracy, as illustrated by the first quote above. In terms of the economy, the promoters of private ownership reasoned that it would facilitate growth and prosperity, mirroring the arguments made in support of privatization around the globe. Distributing property rights widely would ensure that a majority of the population would benefit from the new market economy (e.g., see Kornai 1990; Summers 1992). One of their most firmly held beliefs, according to Harvard economists Maxim Boycko, Andrei Shleifer, and Robert Vishny, was that "if only they were allowed, the … workers, managers, and the public at large would take advantage of the opportunity to become owners, and to invest their time and energy in getting rich" (Boycko, Shleifer, and Vishny 1995: 9).

Expectations about the effects of privatization on the development of democracy ran equally high. Reformers believed that private ownership would create the foundations for the rule of law. Their rationale was that privatization "creates private owners who then begin lobbying the government" for the development of rules protecting private property and ensuring an accountable state (Shleifer and Vishny 1998: 10; see also Elster, Offe, and Preuss 1998). It would help the consolidation of the new democratic regimes, since a new class of small owners would create the required political foundations.

We have shown that these expectations did not materialize for many people or in many places. Our ethnographies of Albanian, Romanian, and Vietnamese villages reveal the tremendous variation in economic and political changes characterizing postsocialist transformations. Most people in villages such as Ho So, Than Con, and Dragova were able to improve their living standards and build new houses. Yet, there was no uniform trend of economic betterment, as livelihoods deteriorated in other villages such as Dragomireşti. The rapidly widening gulf in living conditions between the countryside and cities, and between different countries, compelled many people to relocate—such as in Bagëtia, where three-quarters of the original population emigrated. Nor was there a singular transition to democracy, as illustrated by the collapse of the state in Bagëtia, the patronage politics of Dragova and Ba Ye, and the predatory practices employed by local state officials in Dragomireşti and Than Con.

The varied changes in the postsocialist countryside shed a different light on what has often been thought of as a grand transition. From a macroscopic perspective, postsocialist changes in economy, politics, and culture may look like a transition from socialism to capitalism, or a great transformation of similar scale and significance to that described by Karl Polanyi half a century earlier (Polanyi 1944).[1] Yet, the microscopic lens we have used in this book demonstrates that the changes were not as uniform as it appeared but actually arose in the form of many small transformations.[2] The great transformation came about as a result of many small transformations that occurred simultaneously, involved highly varied changes in economy, politics, and culture, and connected with each other in surprising ways. The diversity and heterogeneity of the small transformation thereby challenge any simple characterization of postsocialism.

Negotiations over property were at the core of these small transformations. Various kinds of people actively engaged with the legal reforms put in place by national governments and their international advisors, and competed with each other over land and forests. It was only through these negotiations that property reforms became effective, as indicated by the second quote above: legal reforms did not give people actual rights—they had to find ways of exercising the legal rights in practice. Legal rights only became actual rights if they involved objects of value to people, and if people could call upon politico-legal institutions to authorize their claims on resources as legitimate property rights. Negotiations over property thereby involved issues of value and authority, with direct consequences for wider changes in economy, politics, and culture. Struggles over property were about the role of the state and, more broadly, the nature of authority and the kinds of values that mattered. This is the most fundamental insight we have derived from our research for this book, highlighting the more general dynamics of property that have relevance beyond just postsocialist settings.

Negotiating Property and Value

Governments as well as citizens thought that privatization would accord people rights to land, forests, and other assets considered valuable, thereby enabling them to generate income and profits. However, many people learned that the presumable assets that they acquired under postsocialist reforms did not possess much monetary value. This observation led the economists Frydman and Rapaczynski to conclude that "privatization [was] to a large extent ... a more or less managed process of *decline and retirement* of an *ex ante* unknown, but likely substantial, portion of the assets" (Frydman and Rapaczynski 1994: 200; emphasis in original).

In fact, our ethnographies, particularly those in Part I, show how many new owners, having enthusiastically welcomed the opportunity to own land, saw the monetary value of their land decline. Some even retired their land entirely; for instance, in Bagëtia, people stopped cultivating more than four of every five hectares they had worked in 1990. In villages such as Dardha and Dragomireşti, agricultural yields and monetary returns shrank significantly, forcing people to shift from the production of commercial crops to subsistence products. Villagers' experiences resembled what happened to many new owners and shareholders of privatized state enterprises. As impressive as their physical attributes were, factories often turned out to be "worthless smokestacks" (Aslund 2007: 143–44). As the monetary value of privatized factories unraveled, so did the value of many land parcels.

Land and forest holdings came to differentiate people as part of wider processes of social differentiation.[3] As postsocialist Europe and Asia experienced a widening gap between poor and rich, some people fared well because they attained land of large size or high monetary value. Others faced problems to make ends meet because they did not acquire any land. Yet, land ownership did not always ensure that people could generate income or accumulate wealth. Whereas some landowners became rich because their land became attractive for peri-urban settlement, tourism, or other high-value uses, such as in Ho So and Dragova, others did not even generate a decent income because agriculture no longer generated significant economic returns. As a result, some villagers experienced serious declines in their income and living standards.[4] For example, deteriorating terms of agricultural trade and state de-investment caused living standards to decline drastically in remote villages, such as Bagëtia. However, most residents in Than Con, Ho So, Dragova, and Kodra prospered in the new monetary economy, as the financial value of their assets increased, and incomes rose.

Katherine Verdery provides an insightful account of this process of monetary revalorization, something to which the title of her book, *The Vanishing Hectare*, alludes (Verdery 2003). Many of the new small owners saw monetary value leave the parcels to which they held titles, diminishing or even erasing the significance of the land. Others were savvier in finding ways to attribute monetary value to their land and forests, or deriving income or profit from land and forest held by others. The practices of both winners and losers were influenced by, and in turn contributed to, larger processes of monetary revalorization, as we have highlighted in the ethnographies: (1) agriculture operated under radically different conditions than it had under socialism due to the liberalization of domestic markets, reductions in state investment, and the exposure of domestic producers to competition from abroad; (2) the opening of international borders prompted many villagers to move elsewhere in search of jobs and other sources of income; (3) the liberalization of trade and investment forced rural industries to compete with other domestic and international producers; and (4), urban residents started to arrive in larger numbers in rural areas, searching for recreation and second homes.

Nevertheless, our ethnographies demonstrate that postsocialist revalorizations of land and forests also took other forms: people gained and lost due to changes in the value regimes applicable to land and forest. Some saw the kinds of values they cherished decrease in significance in relation to other value regimes. Others benefited from the emergence and ascendance of value regimes important to them. Postsocialist contestations over value were not merely about the monetary value attached to particular parcels within the new monetary economy but also about where the primary value of land and forests lay. They involved questions about the significance of various value regimes for valorizing land and forests, causing the concurrent presence of multiple value regimes, and underlying the "multiple geographies of economic practices" noted by Adrian Smith and Alison Stenning (Smith and Stenning 2006). The primary question was about the kinds of value that mattered for people's evaluations of land and forest holdings. Only where there was a general agreement on monetary evaluation did the question about the particular monetary value in terms of Albanian lek, Romanian lei, Vietnamese dong—or US dollars or euros—assume significance.

Postsocialist contestations over the value of land and forest centered on the question of whether land was primarily a productive resource to be used for agriculture and forestry or a site providing environmental amenities to rural and urban consumers.[5] Consumptive uses made rapid ascendance in some areas, due to rural and urban residents demanding the protection of particular landscapes for tourism, recreation, or nature conservation. Struggles between productive and consumptive uses were visible in the forests of Dragova and the home gardens of Ho So, where land gained significant consumptive value. In these villages, people increasingly viewed land as a financial asset, just as in other parts of the postsocialist countryside affected by processes of urbanization or peri-urbanization. Looking beyond the villages, urban expansion often encountered strong reactions and caused deep frustrations for the original residents, which was in part due to the massive wealth made by a few well-positioned actors, but could also be attributed to the loss of land as a productive resource (Andrusz, Harloe, and Szelenyi 1996; Stanilov 2007; Hsing 2010).

When villagers continued to value land as a productive resource, they had to decide whether its value was largely one of commercial production or the production of subsistence. Many villagers increasingly put their land to commercial uses, growing crops and raising livestock for sale, as witnessed in Kodra, Dragova, and Than Con. Others grew subsistence products or raised small numbers of livestock for home consumption on their land, such as in Bagëtia, Dardha, and Dragomirești. Subsistence production became a widespread phenomenon in the postsocialist countryside, which was nothing new in Vietnam but came as a surprise in Eastern Europe. In the latter, many small producers set out to work their new land for the production of tiny amounts of grains, vegetables, or livestock—this was land that had previously served socialist collectives and state farms, and produced large quantities of crops for domestic procurement or export (Bridger and Pine 1998; Pickles 2002). Agriculture in these villages did not develop according to the expectations of agricultural economists or international institutions, with the more successful farmers consolidating small plots into large parcels for the application of modern machinery (Lerman 2001; Deininger 2003; Vranken, Noev, and Swinnen 2004). To them, subsistence production on myriads of tiny plots was a problem, one that they came to refer to as "land fragmentation," and which called for "land consolidation" as the appropriate countermeasure.[6]

From the vantage point of a productivist and modern agriculture, the situation was even worse in villages where agricultural land was "abandoned." In villages such as Bagëtia and Dragomirești, villagers stopped cultivating a significant share of the land previously worked by socialist collectives or state farms, just as in many other regions of Eastern Europe.[7]

To agricultural economists, this "abandonment," as they termed it, looked like a massive loss of productive value. However, in the eyes of villagers, the withdrawal of land from cultivation was often temporary and did not imply abandonment. Villagers still valued land as a signifier of belonging and historical justice. For example, migrants typically held on to their land even after they left their villages; and people with salaried jobs appreciated owning the land, even if they did not have time to work it.

In this book, we have shown that negotiations over property were key sites of the contestations over value, not just with regard to land but more broadly in the question of what constituted social value. As people made claims on land and forests, and recognized some claims as legitimate and rejected others, they simultaneously asserted the significance of particular kinds of value in their time. Negotiations over property involved struggles over value regimes, as claims on land and forests invoked various conceptions of what people considered proper or desirable. At the same time, the wider processes of revalorization caused people to adjust their claims on land and forests. Shifts in people's attachment to particular kinds of values affected their evaluation of which objects they considered valuable, and therefore determined which objects were worthy of their own claims or their response to others' claims.

Changes in property relations and value regimes came to influence each other in close interplay across the postsocialist countryside. The transfer of land certificates to individual households modified the conditions under which various kinds of social actors sought to valorize land and forests. As villagers claimed rights to resources and began to act upon newly acquired rights, they asserted various kinds of values in explicit and implicit ways. Thus, the individualization of land rights created the prerequisites for people to valorize agricultural land within particular value regimes. These valorizations, in turn, affected property relations in the villages as they had profound implications for the kinds of property claims recognized as legitimate. People who wanted to be commercial farmers and viewed land as a productive resource requested to rent land from their fellow villagers. Others wanting to adopt modern lifestyles evaluated their land from a financial rationale, and sold it for profit. In many places, people's dreams of becoming modern commercial farmers paved the way for land rentals and sales.

The negotiations over property and value took highly varied forms, reflecting the influence of local and historical contexts. Livelihood traditions played a key role in differentiating local struggles, as explored in Chapter 2. The practical dispositions acquired under socialism caused villagers to seek out a living in different ways, drawing on the skills, networks, and assets acquired previously. People's different traditions also became manifest in their representations of the past, particularly in rememberings about what constituted value. Such rememberings caused people to view particular products, such as locally distilled brandy and homemade cheese, as key symbols in their efforts to make sense of their changed economic and social lives. Another critical influence on negotiations over property and value originated from people's struggles over personhood and identities (Chapter 3).[8] People's efforts to valorize land and forests were closely connected to their ideas of who they wanted to be and how they wanted to be recognized. This applied to their ethnic and national identities as well as their aspirations to be commercial farmers, subsistence producers, modern citizens, and so on. A third factor was that the negotiations over property and value occurred within increasingly transnationalized settings (Chapter 1). Negotiations over property taking place in particular locations were often shaped by events abroad. In the process, property relations became as transnational as the geographies of migration, trade, investment, consumption, and lifestyles that conditioned people's land claims.

Despite the diversity of local negotiations over property and value, our ethnographies also reveal how many people increasingly viewed land and forests from the vantage point of the monetary economy. People treated land and forests as productive or financial assets that could be appropriated individually, and transferred to others on monetary terms. Central elements in the larger process of monetary valorization were people's attempts to create value inside or outside agriculture and forestry. As much as people valued the new titles to land and forests for their symbolic significance, they looked for new and in many cases monetary values to attach to the titles. This trend of monetization, as varied and heterogeneous as it was, reflected the operations of powerful forces across places and countries. The monetary economy was still far from constituting the "most gigantic, totalizing, and all encompassingly universal system of evaluation known to human history" (Graeber 2001: 89), yet people felt its powerful influence and contributed to its expansion. As people turned to monetary value, the monetary economy became progressively more dominant over other value regimes (Harms 2012).

The expansion of the monetary system of valuation affected property relations across the postsocialist countryside. As some parcels of land and forests increased in monetary value, some of the new landowners gained income and wealth. Other new owners lost because they did not see their parcels rise in monetary value, or because they sold land to urban buyers, entrepreneurial farmers, tourism investors, or others on disadvantageous terms. The move toward a monetary value regime thereby generated possession for some, but also dispossession and exclusion for others.

Possession and dispossession were closely related to the emergent move from multiple-value regimes to monetary values, or values to value.[9]

Contesting Property, Authority, and State

The economic effects of property reforms did not meet expectations, and the same was true with the political outcomes. Political scientists expected property reforms to support the consolidation of postsocialist democracy; political parties would develop, compete in popular elections, and participate in national governments (Pridham and Agh 2002; Klingemann, Fuchs, and Zielonka 2006).[10] The critical test that a country had to pass on the path to democratic consolidation was a regular (i.e., non-violent) change in government from one party to another. Accordingly, democracy was considered to be consolidated in Romania in 1996 and in Albania in 2005. Vietnam has consistently failed the test because the Communist Party of Vietnam remains firmly in power as the sole political party recognized in the constitution.

Our insights on the negotiations over property taking place across the postsocialist countryside from 1990 onward suggest a different evaluation: at stake was not merely the political regime but the very state itself. The issue was not simply about how a particular set of rules considered essential for the functioning of a liberal democracy within an existing state became consolidated, but more fundamentally how the postsocialist state could consolidate its position as the primary politico-legal institution. In what amounted to nothing less than a mad scramble for property rights to land and forests, villagers referred to the state as well as to other politico-legal institutions in the search for authorization. Moreover, the state was also at stake in the sense that struggles over property raised fundamental questions about the exercise of state authority—that is, the significance of abstract rules versus personalized power, and the relationship between local power holders and the central state.

Property was of singular importance as a field in which people contested authority in the postsocialist countryside. When people sought to legitimize the authority of various politico-legal institutions, they often referred to the particular institution's role with regard to property. For example, many people saw a role for the state because property reforms had provided the initial impetus for them to become landowners. Thus, when villagers sought "authorization" for their claims on land and forests in the general scramble for property rights, they simultaneously legitimized particular institutions and exercises of authority. Claims on land and forests influenced the exercise of state power and authority, and that very exercise tended to offer support for some claims and to withhold support for others.

The contestations over property and authority were particularly visible in forestry because the state was more directly involved in forest management than agriculture. Both agriculture and forestry experienced massive state efforts to reform property, connecting negotiations over property with contestations over authority and the state. Yet in contrast to agriculture, state authority was at stake in forestry in other significant ways. Environmental concerns continued to motivate a strong involvement of the state in forestry, even where ownership was considered "private" (Staddon 2001). In addition, the reconfiguration of state authority in the forestry sector took place against a particular historical background. Prior to nationalization, many forests were under either de facto or officially sanctioned customary authority in the form of cooperatives or village councils (Cellarius 2004; de Waal 2004). As a consequence, negotiations over property with regard to forests (chapters 4 to 6) involved contestation over authority more directly than struggles in agriculture (chapters 1 to 3), where issues of value assumed center stage.

Property relations took on highly varied dynamics as a consequence of the simultaneous negotiations over property and authority. In some villages, the key axis of negotiation was between the property rights endorsed by the state versus those sanctioned by customary arrangements. Among the sites covered in this book, this dynamic was particularly evident in the Albanian villages (Chapter 4). Even though villagers invoked various kinds of customary arrangements and different state actors in support of their property claims, "custom" in the singular emerged as an alternative to "the state." Both the idea of the state and custom emerged as an authoritative idiom that served people wishing to justify certain claims on land and forests as legitimate while denying legitimacy to other claims. As a result, local property relations centered on the state in some places and for some resources (e.g., agricultural land in Kodra), on customary arrangements in other places or for other resources (e.g., forests in Kodra), or failed to coalesce into any easily discernible constellations of authority (e.g., forests in Bagëtia).

In other villages, negotiations centered on the question of how state authority should be exercised. Struggles over property in the two Romanian villages revealed the tension between an exercise of state authority based on rules versus personalized decisions by office holders (Chapter 5). People in Dragomirești understood the transfer of forest titles as reconstituting the authority of the Romanian state over forests on the basis of the rules instituted to protect property rights. When illegal loggers encroached on their rights, villagers responded by calling for law enforcement—even though they witnessed abuses of power by the very agents of the state who were supposed to be in charge of law enforcement. In comparison, the new owners exerted little effort to rein in the mayor's practices in Dragova. Once the mayor was in office they felt helpless to act against his political manipulations and maneuvering. Many villagers in Dragova equated the mayor with the state, accepting the personalized exercise of state authority overriding compliance with applicable rules.

Property struggles in the Vietnamese villages involved conflicts between local officials and the central party-state, which overlapped with contestations over rule-based versus personalized exercises of authority (Chapter 6). In villages such as Than Con, local government officials wielded their power in a personalized manner that directly contradicted some of the rules made by the central government. They managed to enlist others in patronage relations similar to those demonstrated by the mayor of the Romanian village of Dragova. In contrast, the exercise of state authority was much more rule-based in other villages, such as Ba Ye. Villagers understood what they could do: extract trees in their own forest in open daylight—and what they could not do: attempt the same thing in other villages. Local government officials, the trader and villagers adhered to the rules. However, the rules governing forests in such villages were not those instituted by the central government; they were the rules made and enforced locally.

The differences we observed in our case studies coincide with characteristic differences in national-level politics between Albania, Romania, and Vietnam. Negotiations over property in Albania were intimately linked with contestations over authority between the state and other politico-legal institutions—contestations that took center stage in national politics during the 1990s. The crisis of state authority emerged in 1991, when the country experienced the first outbreak of violence, much of it directed against the buildings and other physical structures associated with the socialist state (Vickers and Pettifer 1997). This was followed by another crisis in 1997, when Albanians again took to the streets out of a feeling of betrayal by their political leaders (Pettifer and Vickers 2007). Many turned to custom (*kanun* in Albanian) for guidance on aspects of personal life and public matters (Voell 2003; de Waal 2004). It was the state itself, understood as a politico-legal institution, that was at stake, questioning its presumable position as the primary authorizer of claims to land and forests, as well as many other aspects of public and private life.

The state per se was not at stake in Romania, where public debate centered on the rule of law. Romania did not experience the violence or collapse of public order that accompanied Albania's immediate extrication from socialism (Gledhill 2005). Thereafter, disorganized national politics did not seriously damage the authority the state enjoyed as an institution in the eyes of the Romanian population. People instead put the blame on individual politicians, or the political leadership in power at any particular time (Pop-Eleches 2001; Tismaneanu and Kligman 2001). The primary tension in the 1990s was between the personalized politics of a few leading politicians and efforts to base their exercise of authority on rules. National politics remained highly personalized during the first half of the 1990s under the influence of the exercise of power under the Ceauşescu regime (see Weiner 1997; Hollis 1999; Pop-Eleches 1999).[11] Towards the turn of the millennium, there was the highly authoritarian leadership promoted by extremist parties, such as ultranationalist leader Corneliu Vadim Tudor. At the same time, there was an increasingly strong move towards a law-governed exercise of state authority—that is, a "law-governed state" built on a system of clear rules and procedures (Tismaneanu 1998; Pop 2006). This was particularly pronounced during the Constantinescu government between 1996 and 2000, when the government promoted Romania's accession to the European Union. The shift toward the rule of law eventually won them acceptance into the EU, even though it took somewhat longer than for other Central and East European countries.

In the 1990s, public discourse in Vietnam displayed a similar preoccupation with the rule of law after the central party-state adopted the call for a "law-based state." The central leadership introduced a series of abstract rules and procedures for the exercise of state authority (Balme and Sidel 2007). However, they neither challenged the leading position of the Communist Party nor implied that the party was subject to the rule of law. The central party-state embraced the idea of a law-based state to cement the leading position of the Communist Party, as espoused in Article 4 of Vietnam's 1990 constitution, and to strengthen the central party-state's control over local officials. The promotion of a rule-based exercise of state authority was a means by which the central party-state sought to limit the leverage that local governments held over the conduct of state affairs (Kerkvliet and Marr 2004). The relations between the central party-state and local officials have been a key element in Vietnamese politics over many decades, explaining much of the dynamism leading to the economic and political reforms of the late 1980s (Fforde and de Vylder 1996; Kerkvliet 1995, 2005). Throughout the 1990s, local governments displayed significant autonomy, using the implementation of central government programs such as land allocation to further local interests, displaying an active hand in the management of land, collecting various kinds of local taxes and fees, and so on. In reaction, the central government sought to limit local government autonomy and discipline local officials through various measures, including several anticorruption campaigns (Gainsborough 2003; Sidel 2012).

Thus, we find that postsocialist dynamics of authority did not display any shared overarching trend comparable to the move from multiple value regimes to a singular system of monetary valuation. The particularities characterizing each place and country shaped local and national struggles over authority and processes of state formation, with contestations at one level influencing those taking place at the other.[12] Larger shared trends, such as the expansion of monetary valuation witnessed at all eight study sites, were not detectable, nor was there any discernible transnational influence on authority dynamics. Clearly, there was no common turn toward a liberal democracy, no trend of democratic consolidation, nor even a shift toward a rule-based state. The emergence of the state as the primary politico-legal institution and the move toward rule-based exercise of authority was far from automatic.

Propertizing Projects and the Dynamics of Property

The insights from Albania, Romania, and Vietnam reveal the flawed premises of propertizing projects undertaken by governments: the value of land and forests was not fixed or known to people, nor were states and their rules the only route for getting claims on resources recognized as property rights. Since value remained multiple, and authority volatile, the propertizing projects generated more variable outcomes than expected by their proponents. Property changed in unexpected ways, and so did value and authority.

That propertizing projects, such as privatization and other kinds of property reforms, encounter problems is not a new insight. The literature provides abundant evidence of failed attempts to reform property due to a mismatch between the newly introduced conceptions of property and pre-existing property relations. People often attribute different meaning to property than the government officials legislating reforms with or without the advice of international organizations. This applies as much to postsocialist reforms as to other settings such as postcolonial land reforms in sub-Saharan Africa.[13] The problem of mismatch is compounded by the "embeddedness" of property in wider economic, political, and cultural relations (Shipton and Goheen 1992; Peluso 1996; Blomley 2004). Attempts to modify property tend to meet resistance because existing property relations assume important roles. Efforts to change them imply new forms of property that no longer fit the existing economy, politics, or culture. Put simply, the mismatch extends from property to wider social relations.

Our insights from postsocialist Europe and Asia reveal more general dynamics set in motion by such mismatches between propertizing projects and existing property relations. The projects modify the terrain on which negotiations over property take place, with knock-on effects on wider struggles over value and authority. As property relations are embedded in value regimes and authority constellations, their changes cause shifts in authority and value, which in turn have implications for property relations. The relationship between property, value, and authority is a dynamic and mutually constitutive one.

Negotiations over property are sites of contestation over value—with value understood in the sense of "value regimes," as well as the benefits attached to specific objects within the ranking of a particular value regime. As social actors claim rights to resources, they strengthen or weaken existing values, or add to the emergence of new ones. Wider contestations over what kinds of value matter and how objects should be ranked within each value regime, in turn, valorize, devalorize, or revalorize people's rights. Changes in value regimes and rankings tend to provoke social actors to reconsider their claims on resources, with subsequent effects on property relations. Conversely, changes in property relations motivate people to adjust the kinds of values applied in the valuation of objects and the rankings of particular objects within each regime. This leads to a mediation of value regimes and the benefits attached to particular objects.

Negotiations about property simultaneously involve contestations over authority, making property struggles an integral part of processes of state formation (see Lund 2008; Sikor and Lund 2009; Kligman and Verdery 2011). This extends to both the location of authority in particular politico-legal institutions as well as the forms by which authority is exercised. As social actors make claims on resources, they strengthen, solidify, or weaken the authority attributed to particular institutions or forms of exercise. Attributions of authority, in turn, authorize certain claims on resources as property, and deny this authorization to other claims. Claims receive authorization only if they are made to the right institutions and match the forms by which those are considered to exercise authority in legitimate ways. As a result, shifts in constellations of authority tend to cause changes in property relations, as social actors adjust their claims in reaction. In turn, changes in property relations have implications for constellations of authority due to social actors' reactions with regard to the attribution of authority.

The dynamic nature of property and its mutually constitutive relationship with value and authority explain why propertizing projects often fail to generate benefits for their intended beneficiaries, notwithstanding the good intentions by project designers and implementers. When they enact property reforms, government officials, national politicians, and international advisors often take for granted the value of the objects to be distributed. Nevertheless, in the process they and the intended beneficiaries learn that the objects' values are not fixed, or that it was impossible to know them beforehand. Value is subject to the very negotiations over property affected by reforms.[14] The value of the objects changes in the process, and as a result, presumable beneficiaries of land reforms end up empty-handed, or hold objects that prove much less valuable than expected. Experiences with land reforms, whether taking place in postsocialist, postcolonial, or other contexts, offer plenty of evidence in support of this phenomenon (see Berry 1993, 1997; Humphrey 1995; Fay and James 2009; Sikor and Müller 2009; and Lipton 2009).

Furthermore, propertizing projects do not necessarily strengthen the authority attributed to the state. Even if it is state officials who conceive of, design, and implement legislative and regulatory reforms, propertizing projects cannot take the authority of the state as a given. Authority itself is an outcome of the processes set in motion by the projects since it is contested as part of the struggles over property. Propertizing projects open up grounds for contesting the authority attributed to the state, enabling social actors to make claims on resources with reference to the state or alternative politico-legal institutions. This is a key insight from postcolonial land reforms, many of which carried an "illusion of bureaucratic or technocratic omnipotence" (Lehmann 1974: 18) but came to a halt due to competition by alternative institutions of authority.[15] Similarly, forest tenure reforms have often given rise to intense competition over authority, since they implied an expansion of state authority into terrain previously held by customary arrangements (Sikor and Tran 2007; Larson et al. 2010).

Likewise, propertizing projects cause social consequences even if they do not involve the promotion of private ownership or facilitate its spread.[16] There are significant forms of propertizing that are not about the extension of private ownership but involve temporary leasing, the expansion of public control, communal titles, new forms of public–private hybrids, and other novel forms of property (see Sikor 2008). Possession, dispossession, expansion of state authority, and changes in value regimes can result just as much from property reforms promoting community management or public ownership as from privatization policy (see, e.g., Li 2007; Sikor and Tran 2007). Similarly, many of the effects commonly attributed to privatization may not have as much to do with the creation of private ownership as they do with the general dynamics of property. Key outcomes attributed to privatization may not be due to privatization but to more general effects of propertizing.

Our insights on the dynamics of property facilitate new understanding of the nature and outcomes of propertizing projects beyond land reforms and postsocialist contexts. Contemporary propertizing ranges from the reforms of resource tenure and governance currently underway across the world, to new-style attempts of creating property rights to particular ecosystem functions, human and animal genetic codes, and intellectual content (see Introduction).[17] These initiatives tend to be based on the assumption that governments can define property rights through legislative and administrative means. There is abundant evidence by now that this is often not the case. In addition, we show that the discrepancy between property reforms and actual property relations is not only due to social actors resisting the property definitions built into propertizing projects, which has received due attention in the literature, but involved social actors may also resist the connected conceptions of social value and authority. Moreover, they may not simply resist the conceptions included in propertizing projects but may actively negotiate alternative property relations in reference to other value regimes and authority constellations (e.g., Vandergeest 2008). Propertizing projects, far from settling property relations, give rise to new struggles over property, and bring the linkages between property, value, and authority to the fore.

Our insights also demonstrate why propertizing projects are so popular with national governments and their international advisors: they promote particular conceptions of value and authority together with the new property definitions. Property has been a central element in the "high-modernist episodes" described by James Scott (1998), the Soviet-style reforms investigated by Kligman and Verdery (2011), and the improvement schemes examined by Tania Li (2007). Whether it is Tanzanian villagization, Romanian collectivization, or community-based natural resource management, changes in property relations have been a key part of the strategies designed by revolutionaries, development professionals, and other architects of social transformation. Collectivization and nationalization may have dropped out of fashion, yet their decline has not diminished the appeal of propertizing to national governments and their international advisors. Privatization has emerged as the propertizing project en vogue, particularly the model of private ownership tied to monetary valuation within a totalized global regime and the law-governed nation state.[18]

Private ownership has achieved quasi-hegemonic status within the contemporary world, as noted by Nicholas Blomley: the narrow focus on private ownership "affects legal deliberations, social discourse, and governmental interventions" (Blomley 2004: xiv).[19] Nonetheless, we have demonstrated in this book that there is nothing automatic in the emergence of private ownership, monetary value, and the nation state. Private ownership comes about as the result of specific practices within particular local and historical settings. These practices include the activities undertaken by national governments and international organizations in order to promote private ownership. They also take the form of myriads of practices employed by villagers and local government officials in their attempts to make claims to resources, or influence the making and recognition of such claims. These practices may come together in regularized patterns that resemble private ownership, converge on monetary value, and crystallize around the nation state. Still, they may also produce different combinations of property, value, and authority.

Private ownership has equally assumed a quasi-hegemonic status in some quarters of academic scholarship. It has become an important cornerstone in efforts to understand the operations and effects of a globalized capitalism on people and societies around the world, "shaping our understandings and practices relating to property" (Blomley 2004: xiv).[20] Property relations tend to be more diverse in practice than the dualism between owners and non-owners allows, and property is more dynamic than the category of ownership can explain. Struggles over property may produce dispossession from land driven by global land grabs, neoliberal conservation, or other forms of accumulation.[21] They may contribute to shifts from national sovereign territory to de-territorialized spatial relations, or from lived land relations to commodified land resources.[22] However, there is nothing automatic in the emergence of private ownership. When property relations turn into private ownership, this is due to seemingly disconnected negotiations simultaneously taking place within particular contexts (Strang and Busse 2011).[23]

The Postsocialist Moment

Having established general features of property and propertizing projects, we now turn to the question of what, if anything, has been particularly "postsocialist" about the transformations taking place across Eastern Europe and East Asia for the past two and a half decades. It is apparent that looking for similar events or shared trends would not get us far.

The open-endedness of postsocialist transformations is striking. It can be seen in the ethnographies presented in this book, as negotiations over property have overlapped with contestations over value and authority in manifold and often surprising ways. It finds reflection in the diversity of macroscopic interpretations, variously observing transitions from socialism to capitalism, from plan to market, from plan to clan (Stark 1990), or from socialism to feudalism (Verdery 1996). In the face of this open-endedness, scholars of postsocialism have learned to be modest, cautious about grand narratives of social change, and to remain open-minded about the course of history (Kligman and Verdery 1999).

Likewise, the exceptional open-endedness of these transformations challenge the scholarly distinctions commonly made between Europe and Asia, distinctions that are foundational to area studies. The open-endedness has caused more variation within each region than is compatible with simple assumptions about the distinctiveness of Europe's (or, by the same token, Asia's) economies, politics, and cultures. For example, very few would have expected in 1995 that out of two Southeast European countries, one (Romania) would join the European Union twelve years later, whereas the other (Albania) would descend into political turmoil and display many attributes of a failed state. The exceptional open-endedness also leads to surprising parallels between Asia and Europe that go beyond the often-noted similarities in postsocialist property reforms.[24] For example, customary rights and arrangements emerged as strong competitors to the property rights defined by postsocialist states in Vietnam as well as Albania—two countries considered part of very different world regions.

We surmise that the open-endedness results from three distinctive features shared by postsocialist transformations throughout Europe and Asia. First, simultaneous changes in key macro structures opened up unprecedented space for social actors' negotiations over the economy, politics, and culture, privileging small transformations over a single great transformation (Burawoy and Verdery 1999; Sturgeon and Sikor 2004). As we have shown, postsocialist transformations involved radical changes in property relations because the most fundamental pillars of economic and political life changed at once and in close interplay with property. Postsocialist transformations were not confined to isolated changes in property relations, value regimes, or authority constellations, as can be seen in the privatization programs and market liberalization reforms implemented in other parts of the world. Instead, postsocialist societies witnessed concurrent transformations of property, value, and authority, leaving people to scramble in their efforts to respond to changes in their environments.

Second, a discursive turn to the pre-socialist and socialist past offered social actors highly diverse points of reference (see Creed 1998; Bridger and Pine 1998; Hann 2003; and Kaneff 2004).[25] Pre-socialist and socialist values, moralities, and dispositions exerted strong influence on postsocialist transformations. This provided particular historical contexts with a special leverage over contemporary dynamics. With regard to property, people justified their claims to resources with discursive strategies of a return to the pre-socialist past in what Andrew Cartwright terms a "return of the peasant" (Cartwright 2001).[26] People's justifications also demonstrated the influence of socialist values and moralities as they displayed a "gut loyalty to this former everyday life" (Humphrey 1999: xii).[27] Their engagement in negotiations over property reflected the influence of socialist property notions, as well as the dispositions, material assets, and immaterial resources people had acquired under socialism (Verdery 2003).[28]

Third, postsocialist negotiations have increasingly taken place within settings characterized by uneven transnationalization (Smith 2002; Bruszt and Holzhacker 2009). Our ethnographies show how property relations on the ground came under the influence of practices beyond the reach of local residents and national governments. The influence of faraway practices was transmitted by forces operating on larger scales, such as the trend toward a system of monetary valuation integrating people and places within countries as well as across national borders. The latter became increasingly porous as postsocialist governments reduced previously tight controls on the flows of people, goods, capital, and ideas, and people looked abroad in the search for new lifestyles, employment opportunities, and ideas. Transnationalization may have been most visible in Albania, where socialist isolation gave way to a massive exodus of the country's population. It may have been most noticeable in the form of European integration and Europeanization.[29] Nonetheless, integration into transnational flows of people, goods, capital, and information was a process affecting people throughout postsocialist Asia and Europe, albeit varied in degree and form. The difference between the move toward a totalized system of monetary valuation operating on a global scale, and the continuing constitution of authority at primarily local and national levels is indicative of the heterogeneous nature of transnationalization.

The simultaneity of changes in macro structures, a discursive turn to the past, and uneven transnationalization combined to give rise to a particularly postsocialist moment characterized by exceptional open-endedness. As a result, postsocialist transformations did not proceed along the lines of a singular expansion of the monetary economy into unchartered waters, even though there is a discernible trend toward a totalizing system of monetary valuation. Instead, the transformations upended established values, gave rise to new values, and led people to articulate the relations between old and new values in novel ways. Similarly, they did not merely involve consolidation along a singular path toward liberal democracy but questioned the most fundamental parameters of political life. Postsocialist struggles were about the state itself, leading to its resurrection on new foundations in some places and countries, and nearly leading to its collapse in others.[30] The exceptional open-endedness reflected the constitutive nature of the many small transformations taking place concurrently, transformations that came about as a consequence of dynamics at local, national, and transnational levels. These small transformations were not aberrations of a great transformation. Rather, open-endedness and variation were the order of the day.

The open-endedness may be the most surprising element in our account of postsocialism, since it highlights the emergence of new possibilities for the future. It surprises because some thinkers have portrayed the demise of the socialist world as the end of a grand alternative. Frances Fukuyama's declaration of "the end of history" (Fukuyama 1992) is just one among several such statements. Putting the emphasis on new possibilities also surprises in light of views that interpret the move away from socialism as a sign of a more uniform world under the dictate of global neoliberalism (e.g., see Schwartz 2006). Our account challenges these interpretations by focusing on the tremendously colorful kaleidoscope of new possibilities that emerged from local negotiations in the postsocialist moment. Many of the possibilities may disappear again, or may have done so already, particularly with regard to matters of value and the economy, but there is nothing natural or automatic about the process. Postsocialist histories remain in the making in cities and in villages, in the centers of economic, political, and cultural life, and on the ground.

Notes

1. See Hann and Hart (2009) for an interpretation of postsocialist transformations that stresses the parallels with the great transformation described by Polanyi.
2. On the concept of small transformations, see Rona-Tas (1997) and Sikor (2001).
3. For example, the two largest societies, China and Russia, saw drastic increases in inequality during the 1990s (Hutton and Redmond 2000). This rise continued in China into the first years of the 2000s. As a result, poverty has become a regular feature of the postsocialist countryside in Asia and Europe (Kaneff and Pine 2011).
4. Meurs and Ranasinghe (2003) call this "de-development."
5. The distinction is inspired by Williams (1973) and Neumann (1998).
6. Land fragmentation and consolidation quickly rose on the agenda of national governments as well as the Food and Agriculture Organization (FAO) and World Bank in the early 2000s (FAO et al. 2002; FAO 2003; Van Dijk 2003).
7. The rate of land abandonment has been estimated as affecting around 17 percent of farmland in Lithuania (Prosterman and Rolfes 1999), 21 percent of farmland in Argues county, Romania (Kuemmerle et al. 2009), 28 percent of land in southeastern Albania (Sikor, Müller, and Stahl 2009), and more than half of the land originally cultivated in Latvia's Vidzene Uplands (Nikodemus et al. 2005).
8. See also Zhang and Ong (2008) on China.
9. For other accounts of how the change from multiple values to a single system of monetary valuation causes dispossession, see Appadurai (1986), Berry (1989), and Hall, Hirsch, and Li (2011).
10. See also Linz and Stepan (1996) for comparable analysis in Latin America.
11. Verdery (2003: 95) speaks of a "perpetual flux in political entities and affiliations."

12. See Sikor, Müller, and Stahl (2009) on linkages between local-level and national-level politics in Albania and Romania.
13. On postsocialist land reforms, see Hann et al. (2003) and Verdery (2003). On postcolonial land reforms, see Peters (1994) and Sikor and Müller (2009).
14. Economists refer to this as the "valuation problem" (Aslund 2007).
15. On competition by alternative politico-legal institutions, see Berry (2001), Lund (2008), and Sikor and Müller (2009).
16. Hall, Hirsch, and Li (2011) come to a very similar conclusion by highlighting exclusion as a feature of general property dynamics that is not restricted to the extension of private ownership.
17. See also Blomley (2004) on urban land, and Bakker (2010) on water reforms.
18. On the connections between private ownership and the state, see MacPherson (1978) and Geisler and Daneker (2000).
19. See also Strang and Busse (2011).
20. We note, in fairness to Blomley, that the reference to scholarship is ours. He does not specify who he would include among the "our."
21. On global land grabs, see White et al. (2012) and Wolford et al. (2013). On neoliberal conservation, see Heynen et al. (2007), Mansfield (2008), Fairhead, Leach, and Scoones (2012), and Corson, MacDonald, and Neimark (2013). Harvey (2005) provides a discussion of primitive accumulation as the underlying structural dynamic driving such processes.
22. See Sassen (2008) on de-territorialization, as well as Bakker (2010) and Bumpus and Liverman (2008) on commodification.
23. See also Li (2007) and Nevins and Peluso (2008), which provide insightful analyses of how larger processes result from and condition multi-sited practices.
24. Unfortunately, the two regions are rarely examined as part of the same inquiry. One of the rare exceptions is Walder (1995).
25. The differentiating effect of the discursive turn to the past is nicely illustrated by the ethnographies in Hann and the Property Relations Group (2003).
26. See also Lagerspetz (1999), Cellarius (2004), and Sikor (2004).
27. See also Kaneff (1996).
28. See also the work on "path dependency" in this regard; e.g., Smith and Pickles (1998), Smith and Swain (1998), and Stark and Bruszt (1998).
29. On Europeanization in the East European countryside, see the special issue edited by Gorton, Lowe, and Zellei (2005) and Fox (2011). See also Kaneff and Pine (2011) on the linkages between migration and rural poverty in Eastern Europe.
30. See also Verdery (1996) and Stark and Bruszt (1998) on Eastern Europe, and Zhang and Ong (2008) on China.

References

Andrusz, Gregory, Michael Harloe, and Ivan Szelenyi (eds). 1996. *Cities after Socialism: Urban and Regional Change and Conflict in Post-Socialist Societies.* Oxford: Blackwell.

Appadurai, Arjun. 1986. "Introduction: Commodities and the Politics of Value." In *The Social Life of Things: Commodities in Cultural Perspective*, ed. Arjun Appadurai. Cambridge: Cambridge University Press, 3–63.

Aslund, Anders. 2007. *How Capitalism Was Built: The Transformation of Central and Eastern Europe, Russia, and Central Asia*. Cambridge: Cambridge University Press.

Bakker, Karen. 2010. *Privatizing Water: Governance Failure and the World's Urban Water Crisis*. Ithaca, NY: Cornell University Press.

Balme, Stephanie, and Mark Sidel. 2007. "Vietnam in Comparative Communist and Postcommunist Perspectives." In *Vietnam's New Order*, ed. Stephanie Balme and Mark Sidel. New York: Palgrave Macmillan, 1–10.

Berry, Sara. 1989. "Social Institutions and Access to Resources." *Africa* 59(1): 41–55.

———. 1993. *No Condition Is Permanent: The Social Dynamics of Agrarian Change in Sub-Saharan Africa*. Madison: University of Wisconsin Press.

———. 1997. "Tomatoes, Land and Hearsay: Property and History in Asante in the Time of Structural Adjustment." *World Development* 25(8): 1225–41.

———. 2001. *Chiefs Know Their Boundaries: Essays on Property, Power, and the Past in Asante, 1896–1996*. Portsmouth, NH: Heinemann.

Blomley, Nicholas. 2004. *Unsettling the City: Urban Land and the Politics of Property*. London: Routledge.

Boycko, Maxim, Andrei Shleifer, and Robert Vishny. 1995. *Privatizing Russia*. Cambridge, MA: MIT Press.

Bridger, Sue, and Frances Pine. 1998. *Surviving Post-Socialism: Local Strategies and Regional Responses in Eastern Europe and the Former Soviet Union*. London: Routledge.

Bruszt, Laszlo, and Ronald Holzhacker (eds). 2009. *The Transnationalization of Economies, States, and Civil Societies: New Challenges for Governance in Europe*. New York: Springer.

Bumpus, Adam G., and Diana M. Liverman. 2008. "Accumulation by Decarbonization and Governance of Carbon Offests." *Economic Geography* 84(2): 127–55.

Burawoy, Michael, and Katherine Verdery. 1999. *"Uncertain Transition: Ethnographies of Change in the Postsocialist World."* Lanham, MD: Rowman & Littlefield.

Cartwright, A.L. 2001. *The Return of the Peasant: Land Reform in Post-Communist Romania*. Aldershot: Ashgate.

Cellarius, Barbara. 2004. "'Without Co-Ops There Would Be No Forests!': Historical Memory and the Restitution of Forest in Post-Socialist Bulgaria." *Conservation and Society* 2(1): 51–73.

Corson, Catherine, Kenneth Iain MacDonald, and Benjamin Neimark. 2013. "Grabbing 'Green': Markets, Environmental Governance and the Materialization of Natural Capital." *Human Geography* 6(1): 1–15.

Creed, Gerald W. 1998. *Domesticating Revolution: From Socialist Reform to Ambivalent Transition in a Bulgarian Village*. University Park: Pennsylvania State University Press.

Deininger, Klaus. 2003. "Land Policies for Growth and Poverty Reduction." World Bank Policy Research Report. Washington, D.C.: World Bank and Oxford University Press.

Elster, Jon, Claus Offe, and Ulrich K. Preuss. 1998. "Institutional Design in Post-Communist Societies." Cambridge: Cambridge University Press.

Fairhead, James, Melissa Leach, and Ian Scoones. 2012. "Green Grabbing: A New Appropriation of Nature?" *The Journal of Peasant Studies* 39(2): 237–61.

Fay, Derick, and Deborah James (eds). 2009. *The Rights and Wrongs of Land Restitution: "Restoring What Was Ours."* Abingdon: Routledge-Cavendish.

Fforde, Adam, and Stefan de Vylder. 1996. *From Plan to Market: Economic Transition in Vietnam 1979–1994.* Boulder, CO: Westview Press.

Food and Agriculture Organization (FAO). 2003. "The Design of Land Consolidation Pilot Projects in Central and Eastern Europe." *FAO Land Tenure Studies* 6: 1–55.

Food and Agriculture Organization (FAO), Gesellschaft fuer Technische Zusammenarbeit, International Federation of Surveyors, ARGE Land Development, and Technical University Munich. 2002. "The Munich Statement on Land Consolidation as a Tool for Rural Development in CEE/CIS Countries." Presented at the International FAO Symposium on "Land Fragmentation and Land Consolidation in Central and Eastern European Countries: A Gate Towards Sustainable Rural Development in the New Millennium". Munich, 25–28 February, 2002.

Fox, Katy. 2011. *Peasants into European Farmers? EU Integration in the Carpathian Mountains of Romania.* Zurich: LIT Verlag.

Frydman, Roman, and Andrzej Rapaczynski. 1994. *Privatization in Eastern Europe: Is the State Withering Away?* Budapest: Central European University Press.

Fukuyama, Francis. 1992. *The End of History and the Last Man.* New York: Free Press.

Gainsborough, Martin. 2003. "Corruption and the Politics of Economic Decentralization in Vietnam." *Journal of Contemporary Asia* 33(1): 69–84.

Geisler, Charles, and Gail Danecker. 2000. *Property and Values: Alternatives to Public and Private Ownership.* Washington, D.C.: Island Press.

Gorton, Matthew, Philip Lowe, and Annett Zellei. 2005. "Pre-Accession Europeanisation: The Strategic Realignment of the Environmental Policy Systems of Lithuania, Poland and Slovakia towards Agricultural Pollution in Preparation for EU Membership." *Sociologia Ruralis* 45(3): 202–23.

Gledhill, J. 2005. "States of Contention: State-Led Political Violence in Post-Socialist Romania." *East European Politics and Societies* 19(1): 76–104.

Graeber, David. 2001. *Toward an Anthropological Theory of Value: The False Coin of Our Own Dreams.* New York: Palgrave.

Hall, Derek, Philip Hirsch, and Tania Murray Li. 2011. *Powers of Exclusion: Land Dilemas in Southeast Asia.* Singapore: National University of Singapore Press.

Hann, Chris M. 2003. "Preface to the Series." In *The Postsocialist Agrarian Question: Property Relations and the Rural Condition*, ed. Chris M. Hann and the Property Relations Group. London and New Brunswick: LIT Verlag, vii–x.

Hann, Chris M., and Keith Hart (eds). 2009. *Market and Society: The Great Transformation Today.* Cambridge: Cambridge University Press.

Hann, Chris M., and the Property Relations Group (eds). 2003. *The Postsocialist Agrarian Question: Property Relations and the Rural Condition.* London and New Brunswick: LIT Verlag.

Harms, Erik. 2012. "Beauty as Control in the New Saigon: Eviction, New Urban Zones, and Atomized Dissent in a Southeast Asian City." *American Ethnologist* 39(4): 735–50.

Harvey, David. 2005. *A Brief History of Neoliberalism.* Oxford: Oxford University Press.

Heynen, Nik, et al. 2007. *Neoliberal Environments: False Promises and Unnatural Consequences.* London and New York: Routledge.

Hollis, W. 1999. *Democratic Consolidation in Eastern Europe: The Influence of the Communist Legacy in Hungary, the Czech Republic, and Romania.* Boulder, CO: Eastern European Monographs.

Hsing, You-tien. 2010. *The Great Urban Transformation.* Oxford: Oxford University Press.

Humphrey, Caroline. 1995. "The Politics of Privatization in Provincial Russia: Popular Opinions Amid the Dilemmas of the Early 1990s." *Cambridge Anthropology* 18(1): 40–61.

Hutton, S., and G. Redmond. 2000. *Poverty in Transition Economies.* London: Routledge.

Kaneff, Deema. 1996. "Responses to 'Democratic' Land Reforms in a Bulgarian Village." In *After Socialism: Land Reform and Social Change in Eastern Europe*, ed. Ray Abrahams. Oxford: Berghahn Books, 85–114.

———. 2004. *Who Owns the Past? The Politics of Time in a "Model" Bulgarian Village.* New York and Oxford: Berghahn Books.

Kaneff, Deema, and Frances Pine (eds). 2011. *Global Connections and Emerging Inequalities in Europe: Perspectives on Poverty and Transnational Migration.* London: Anthem Press.

Kerkvliet, Benedict J. T. 1995. "Village–State Relations in Vietnam: The Effect of Everyday Politics on Decollectivization." *The Journal of Asian Studies* 54(2): 396–418.

———. 2005. *The Power of Everyday Politics: How Vietnamese Peasants Transformed National Policy.* Ithaca, NY: Cornell University Press.

Kerkvliet, Benedict J. T., and David Marr. 2004. *Beyond Hanoi: Local Government in Vietnam.* Singapore: Institute for Southeast Asian Studies.

Kligman, Gail, and Katherine Verdery. 1999. "Reflections on the 'Revolutions' of 1989 and After." *East European Politics and Societies* 13(2): 303–12.

———. 2011. *Peasants under Siege: The Collectivization of Romanian Agriculture, 1949–1962.* Princeton, NJ: Princeton University Press.

Klingemann, Hans-Dieter, Dieter Fuchs, and Jan Zielonka (eds). 2006. *Democracy and Political Culture in Eastern Europe.* London: Routledge.

Kornai, Janos. 1990. *The Road to a Free Economy.* New York and London: W.W. Norton.

Kuemmerle, Tobias, et al. 2009. "Land Use Change in Romania after the Collapse of Socialism." *Regional Environmental Change* 9(1): 1–12.

Lagerspetz, Mikko. 1999. "Postsocialism as a Return: Notes on a Discursive Strategy." *East European Politics and Societies* 13(2): 377–90.

Larson, Anne M., et al. (eds). 2010. *Forests for People: Community Rights and Forest Tenure Reform.* London: Earthscan.

Lehmann, David. 1974. *Agrarian Reform and Agrarian Reformism: Studies of Peru, Chile, China, and India.* London: Faber and Faber Ltd.

Lerman, Zvi. 2001. "Agriculture in Transition Economies: From Common Heritage to Divergence." *Agricultural Economics* 26: 95–114.

Li, Tania Murray. 2007. *The Will to Improve: Governmentality, Development, and the Practice of Politics*. Durham, NC: Duke University Press.

Linz, Juan J., and Alfred Stepan. 1996. *Problems of Democratic Transition and Consolidation: Southern Europe, South America and Post-Communist Europe*. Baltimore, MD: Johns Hopkins University Press.

Lipton, Michael. 2009. *Land Reform in Developing Countries: Property Rights and Property Wrongs*. London: Routledge.

Lund, Christian. 2008. *Local Politics and the Dynamics of Property in Africa*. Cambridge: Cambridge University Press.

MacPherson, C. B. 1978. *Property: Mainstream and Critical Positions*. Toronto: University of Toronto Press.

Mansfield, Becky (ed.). 2008. *Privatization: Property and the Remaking of Nature–Society Relations*. Oxford: Blackwell.

Meurs, Mike, and Rasika Ranasinghe. 2003. "De-Development in Post-Socialism: Conceptual and Measurement Issues." *Politics & Society* 31(1): 31–53.

Neumann, Roderick P. 1998. *Imposing Wilderness: Struggles over Livelihood and Nature Preservation in Africa*. Berkeley: University of California Press.

Nevins, Joseph, and Nancy Peluso (eds). 2008. *Taking Southeast Asia to Market: Commodities, Nature and People in the Neoliberal Age*. Ithaca, NY: Cornell University Press.

Nikodemus, Olgerts, et al. 2005. "The Impact of Economic, Social and Political Factors on the Landscape Structure of the Vidzeme Uplands in Latvia." *Landscape and Urban Planning* 70: 57–67.

Peluso, Nancy Lee. 1996. "Fruit Trees and Family Trees in an Anthropogenic Forest: Ethics of Access, Property Zones, and Environmental Change in Indonesia." *Comparative Studies in Society and History* 28: 510–48.

Peters, Pauline E. 1994. *Dividing the Commons: Politics, Policy, and Culture in Botswana*. Charlottesville and London: University Press of Virginia.

Pettifer, James, and Miranda Vickers. 2007. *The Albanian Question: Reshaping the Balkans*. London: I.B. Tauris.

Pickles, John. 2002. "Gulag Europe? Mass Unemployment, New Firm Creation, and Right Labour Markets in the Bulgarian Apparel Industry." In *Work, Employment and Transition: Restructuring Livelihoods in Post-Communism*, ed. Al Rainnie, Adrian Smith and Adam Swain. London: Routledge, 246–72.

Polanyi, Karl. 1944. *The Great Transformation: The Political and Economic Origins of Our Time*. Boston, MA: Beacon Press.

Pop, Liliana. 2006. *Democratising Capitalism? The Political Economy of Post-Communist Transformations in Romania, 1989–2001*. Manchester and New York: Manchester University Press.

Pop-Eleches, Grigore. 1999. "Separated at Birth or Seperated by Birth? The Communist Successor Parties in Romania and Hungary." *East European Politics and Societies* 13(1): 117–46.

———. 2001. "Romania's Politics of Dejection." *Journal of Democracy* 12(3): 156–69.

Pridham, Geoffrey, and Attila Agh (eds). 2002. *Prospects for Democratic Consolidation in East-Central Europe*. Manchester: Manchester University Press.

Prosterman, Roy L., and Leonard Rolfes, Jr. 1999. "Review of the Legal Basis for Agricultural Land Markets in Lithuania, Poland, and Romania, and Implications for Accession to the EU." Report presented at the 2nd World Bank/EU Accession Workshop, "Structural Change in the Farming Sectors of Central and Eastern Europe: Lessons and Implications for EU Accession," 26–29 June, 1999.

Rona-Tas, Akos. 1997. *The Great Surprise of the Small Transformation: The Demise of Communism and the Rise of the Private Sector in Hungary*. Ann Arbor: University of Michigan Press.

Sachs, J. 1990. "What Is To Be Done?" *The Economist*, 13 January, 1–7.

Sassen, Saskia. 2008. *Territory, Authority, Rights: From Medieval to Global Assemblages*. Princeton, NJ: Princeton University Press.

Schwartz, A.H. 2006. *The Politics of Greed: How Privatization Structured Politics in Central and Eastern Europe*. Plymouth: Rowman & Littlefield.

Scott, James C. 1998. *Seeing Like a State: How Certain Schemes to Improve the Human Condition Have Failed*. New Haven, CT: Yale University Press.

Shipton, Parker, and Mitzi Goheen. 1992. "Understanding African Land-Holding: Power, Wealth, and Meaning." *Africa* 62(3): 307–25.

Shleifer, Andrei, and Robert W. Vishny. 1998. *The Grabbing Hand: Government Pathologies and Their Cures*. Cambridge, MA: Harvard University Press.

Sidel, Mark. 2012. "Property, State Corruption, and the Judiciary: The Đồ Sơn Land Case and its Implications." In *State, Society and the Market in Contemporary Vietnam: Property, Power and Values*, ed. Hue-Tam Ho Tai and Mark Sidel. London: Routledge, 123–39.

Sikor, T. 2001. "The Allocation of Forestry Land in Vietnam: Did It Cause the Expansion of Forests in the Northwest?". *Forest Policy and Economics* 2(1): 1–11.

———. 2004. "Conflicting Concepts: Contested Land Relations in North-Western Vietnam." *Conservation and Society* 2(1): 59–79.

———. 2008. "Outlook: New Publics and Property Rights." In *Public and Private in Natural Resource Governance: A False Dichotomy?*, ed. Thomas Sikor. London: Earthscan.

Sikor, Thomas, and Tran Ngoc Thanh. 2007. "Exclusive versus Inclusive Devolution in Forest Management: Insights from Forest Land Allocation in Vietnam's Central Highlands." *Land Use Policy* 24(4): 644–53.

Sikor, Thomas, and Christian Lund. 2009. "Access and Property: A Question of Power and Authority." *Development and Change* 40(1): 1–22.

Sikor, Thomas, and Daniel Müller. 2009. "The Limits of State-Led Land Reform: An Introduction." *World Development* 37(8) (*The Limits of State-Led Land Reform*): 1307–16.

Sikor, Thomas, Daniel Müller, and Johannes Stahl. 2009. "Land Fragmentation and Cropland Abandonment in Albania: Implications for the Roles of State and Community in Postsocialist Land Consolidation." *World Development* 37(8) (*The Limits of State-Led Land Reform*): 1411–23.

Smith, Adrian. 2002. "Imagining Geographies of the 'New Europe' Geo-economic Power and the New European Architecture of Integration." *Political Geography* 21: 647–70.

Smith, Adrian, and John Pickles. 1998. "Introduction: Theorising Transition and the Political Economy of Transformation." In *Theorising Transition: The Political Economy of Post-Communist Transformations*, ed. John Pickles and Adrian Smith. London and New York: Routledge, 1–22.

Smith, Adrian, and Adam Swain. 1998. "Regulating and Institutionalising Capitalism: The Micro-Foundations of Transformation in Eastern and Central Europe." In *Theorising Transition: The Political Economy of Post-communist Transformations*, ed. John Pickles and Adrian Smith. London and New York: Routledge, 25–53.

Smith, Adrian, and Alison Stenning. 2006. "Beyond Household Economies: Articulations and Spaces of Economic Practice in Postsocialism." *Progress in Human Geography* 30(2): 190–213.

Staddon, Caedmon. 2001. "Local Forest Dependence in Postcommunist Bulgaria: A Case Study." *GeoJournal* 55(2–4): 517–28.

Stanilov, Kiril (ed.). 2007. *The Post-Socialist City: Urban Form and Space Transformations in Central and Eastern Europe after Socialism*. Dordrecht: Springer.

Stark, David. 1990. "Privatization in Hungary: From Plan to Market or from Plan to Clan?". *East European Politics and Societies* 4(3): 351–92.

Stark, David, and Laszlo Bruszt. 1998. *Postsocialist Pathways: Transforming Politics and Property in East Central Europe*. Cambridge: Cambridge University Press.

Strang, Veronia, and Mark Busse (eds). 2011. *Ownership and Appropriation*. Oxford: Berg.

Sturgeon, Janet, and Thomas Sikor. 2004. "Postsocialist Property in Asia and Europe—Variations on 'Fuzziness.'" *Conservation and Society* 2(1): 1–17.

Summers, Lawrence. 1992. "The Next Decade in Central and Eastern Europe." In *The Emergence of Market Economies in Eastern Europe*, ed. Christopher Clague and Gordon Rausser. Cambridge: Cambridge University Press, 25–34.

Tismaneanu, Vladimir. 1998. *Fantasies of Salvation: Democracy, Nationalism, and Myth in Post-Communist Europe*. Princeton, NJ: Princeton University Press.

Tismaneanu, Vladimir, and Gail Kligman. 2001. "Romania's First Postcommunist Decade: From Iliescu to Iliescu." *East European Constitutional Review* 10(1): 78–85.

Vandergeest, Peter. 2008. "New Concepts, New Natures? Revisiting Commodity Production in Southern Thailand." In *Taking Southeast Asia to Market: Commodities, Nature and People in the Neoliberal Age*, ed. Joseph Nevins and Nancy Peluso. Ithaca, NY: Cornell University Press, 206–24.

Van Dijk, Terry. 2003. "Scenarios of Central European Land Fragmentation." *Land Use Policy* 20: 149–58.

Verdery, Katherine. 1996. *What Was Socialism? And What Comes Next?* Princeton, N.J.: Princeton University Press.

———. 2003. *The Vanishing Hectare: Property and Value in Postsocialist Transylvania*. Ithaca, NY: Cornell University Press.

Vickers, Miranda, and James Pettifer. 1997. *Albania: From Anarchy to a Balkan Identity*. London: C. Hurst & Co.

Voell, Stephane. 2003. "The Kanun in the City: Albanian Customary Law as a Habitus and Its Persistence in the Suburb of Tirana, Bathore." *Anthropos* 98: 85–101.

Vranken, L., N. Noev, and J.F.M. Swinnen. 2004. "Fragmentation, Abandonment, and Co-Ownership: Transition Problems of the Bulgarian Land Market." *Quarterly Journal of International Agriculture* 43(4): 391–408.

Waal, Clarissa de. 2004. "Post-Socialist Property Rights and Wrongs in Albania: An Ethnography of Agrarian Change." *Conservation and Society* 2(1): 19–50.

Walder, Andrew G. (ed.). 1995. *The Waning of the Communist State: Economic Origins of Political Decline in Hungary and China.* Berkeley: University of California Press.

Weiner, Robert. 1997. "Democratization in Romania." In *Romania in Transition*, ed. L. Stan. Aldershot: Dartmouth, 3–24.

White, Ben, et al. 2012. "The New Enclosures: Critical Perspectives on Corporate Land Deals." *The Journal of Peasant Studies* 39(3–4): 619–47.

Williams, Raymond. 1973. *The Country and the City.* London: Hogarth Press.

Wolford, Wendy, et al. 2013. "Governing Global Land Deals: The Role of the State in the Rush for Land." *Development and Change* 44(2): 189–210.

Zhang, Li, and Aihwa Ong (eds). 2008. *Privatizing China: Socialism from Afar.* Ithaca, NY: Cornell University Press.

Index

CPSIA information can be obtained
at www.ICGtesting.com
Printed in the USA
BVOW10*1612140417
481126BV00007B/221/P

9 781785 334511